PROTEST IN ARMS

THE IRISH TROUBLES 1916-1923

EDGAR HOLT

Protest In Arms

THE IRISH TROUBLES 1916-1923

COWARD-McCANN, Inc.
New York

First American Edition, 1961

Library of Congress Catalog
Card Number: 61-6832

MANUFACTURED IN THE UNITED STATES OF AMERICA

Contents

Illustrations

(between pp. 160 and 161)

Foreword

By Cathal O'Shannon

WHEN IT WAS suggested that I should contribute a brief introduction to this work by Mr. Edgar Holt on the Anglo–Irish war of 1916–21 and the civil war among Irishmen that was the tragic sequel to the Treaty signed by the British and Irish negotiators, I had grave doubts about accepting the invitation.

My doubts arose from considerations forcibly impressed upon me by comprehensive examination of what has been written on these affairs in the last forty years and by the knowledge derived from personal, but not altogether uncritical, participation in the Irish side in the events that have engaged the author's attention.

In the published history of the period the material supplied by both Irish and British participants is of the first importance and value. This material, however, is naturally and inevitably partisan and, except where it is strictly narrative, it is coloured by the positions taken by the participants in the happenings described and, consciously or unconsciously, often more expressive of opinion and feeling than of actuality, designed to drive home a viewpoint rather than to establish facts.

Too frequently the material from non-participants, Irish, English, American, French and other chroniclers, has been inadequately informed, unchecked from authoritative sources and regrettably biased. So much has this been the case that part of my own writing on the period covered by Mr. Holt has been in correction of quite a chain of errors in the printed history of what is euphemistically termed "the troubles" in Ireland. In that judgment I am confirmed by the agreement of a number of both living and dead colleagues.

In these circumstances would this *Protest in Arms* justify me in presenting a Foreword?

A careful reading has satisfied me that it would. My satisfaction is not indeed unqualified, but I am happy to be able to say that it is sincere and, within limitations, deserved. In this I will not be supported by some Irish readers or by some English. These critics are still too near the terrible and bitter experiences of 1916–23, even after the cataclysm of the Second World War, to forget or to forgive, and old memories and old prejudices die hard.

It is not for these dissidents in Great Britain or in the two constitutional jurisdictions of the Ireland of today that this book has been written. It has been produced for the benefit and the enlightenment of a new generation of more fortunate political relationship than besmirched the times of the fathers that begat them, to re-create a highly dramatic period in Anglo–Irish history and to give as accurate a portrayal as may be at this distance in time of the character and conduct of the political and military leaders, and of the rank and file who fought under their command in the years of conflict. To do that is a laudable undertaking and deserving of respect.

Taking this book as one piece, and making allowance for errors of detail that are hardly serious enough to mar the quality of the whole, Mr. Holt is to be credited with a considerable measure of success. His bold plunge into muddied waters has been less reckless than might appear on the surface and more praiseworthy than certain other predecessors in this maelstrom. He has been reasonably objective, broadminded in his conception and treatment of his subject, free from academic pedantry, untrammelled by pre-conceptions and commendably impartial in striving to understand, and to explain, provokingly complex personalities, parties, actions and conflicting interests and motives.

He has been industrious in investigating sources, as his list of books consulted will show, although I feel his reliance on some of these is misplaced. A number of the works listed are less useful than others he has omitted. In matters of opinion I find myself sometimes in agreement, sometimes in disagreement, with him, but like the rest of us he is entitled to these when made in all honesty.

DUBLIN, *June* 9, 1960

CHAPTER I

The Other Island

THE IRELAND WHICH threw off British domination by the long protest in arms that began on Easter Monday of 1916 was always imperfectly understood on the English side of the Irish Sea. This misunderstanding was neatly expressed in the title of George Bernard Shaw's play about Anglo-Irish relations. It was, indeed, as "John Bull's other island" that most Englishmen saw Ireland in the years before the First World War, and they had no reason to believe that it would ever cease to be part of the common British heritage.

It is not surprising, therefore, that English soldiers should have marched off to war in 1914 singing "It's a long way to Tipperary" or that the delectable American blonde, Shirley Kellogg, should have captivated London Hippodrome audiences with her wartime song about the Irish colleen who was waiting for her soldier sweetheart "on the road to Dublin town". Few songs were then more popular in English music-halls than those like "Mother Machree", "A little bit of heaven" and "When Irish eyes are smiling" which effusively sentimentalised over the Irish way of life (though when the news of the Easter Rising came through, an embarrassed singer at a London music-hall abruptly changed the words of the last song to "When *British* eyes are smiling"). The English soldier sang happily about Tipperary because it was part of the British Isles. He could not foresee that a few years later it would become the headquarters of a notorious brigade of rebels against the British Crown.

In political circles there were many Englishmen who held that Ireland had been cheated by the Union of 1801 and had never been given a square deal by England. This was the view of Broadbent in Shaw's play: "All I can say is that as an Englishman I blush for the Union. It is the blackest stain on our national history." Yet in general Englishmen looked on the Irish merely as rather eccentric compatriots, whose individuality showed itself in always having grievances and being ready to hail almost any event as "another injustice to Ireland". Those who went to Ireland for holidays came back full of praise for the charm of the countryside and the limpid beauty of the girls, but with little understanding of the deep-seated resentment felt against what was regarded as English oppression. "Depend on it," an Irish judge said to Augustine Birrell when he went to Dublin as Chief Secretary in 1907, "no Irishman hates another Irishman half as much as all Irishmen hate all Englishmen." That hatred was not in the least reciprocated in England, where the so-called "stage Irishman", who spoke with a thick brogue and brandished a substantial blackthorn stick, was a popular figure in theatres and music-halls and readers were delighted by the vagaries of Irish character revealed in contemporary fiction.

At that time Joyce had not yet written *Ulysses* to show Dublin as it really was, and *Dubliners* did not appear in book-form until 1914; but English readers were entertained by such amiable works as those of the two young Irishwomen, E. Œ. Somerville and Martin Ross, who turned their study of Irish courts and their knowledge of hunting to good use in *Some Experiences of an Irish R.M.* and other novels and stories, and of the Ulster clergyman who took the pseudonym of George A. Birmingham for an apparently endless series of novels describing the farcical adventures in Irish villages of the Rev. J. J. Mallon and his Anglo-Irish friend Major Kent. Such writings, though plumbing no great depths of national feeling, at least made English people familiar with the Irish scene and with the place of resident magistrates and Government Departments in Irish life.

In social contacts the personal pugnacity of the Irishman seemed amusing to the more sedate Englishman: a typical drawing in an English comic paper showed an Irishman watching a Rugby football match and asking hopefully, "Is this a private fight or can anyone join in?" But this pugnacity found a useful outlet in the British Army, which enjoyed a regular flow of Irish recruits into its ranks, except when this was temporarily checked by such Irish anti-recruiting activities as those of Maud Gonne and the Daughters of Erin. Then again the British Army had many Irish or Irish-born generals among its senior commanders—men like Lord Roberts, Lord Wolseley, Sir William Butler, Sir Hubert Gough and even Lord Kitchener, though Birrell once observed that Kitchener might just as easily have been born on the London and North-Western Railway on the way to Holyhead as in Ireland.

Much, to be sure, was missing in the conventional English estimate of Irish character, and the omissions made it easy for Englishmen to avoid taking Irish grievances too seriously. Most people knew that Ireland had made great material progress in the years since Gladstone, the English Liberal leader, had given the Irish cause a new prestige by taking it up in his old age. The misery and starvation which had led to so much crime in Irish country districts had been largely alleviated by the land-reform measures of later British Governments; and though it was true that this kind of crime had never been wholly checked, so that even in 1910 the newspapers carried many reports of incendiarism, shooting, bombing, cattle-maiming and destruction of property in Ireland, the future looked brighter now that the Liberal Party was definitely committed to the granting of Irish Home Rule. The issue was complicated by the stubborn resistance to Home Rule in one of Ireland's four provinces, which was backed by the English Conservative Party; but that problem could surely be overcome by the English genius for compromise, and in the meantime why should anyone expect trouble from those good-humoured, easy-going and talkative Irish, who appeared to live their lives on the principle that there was really no particular hurry about doing anything at all?

This comfortable feeling that Ireland would always be John Bull's other island was founded on a disregard of the warnings of history. The events of Easter Week, 1916, would have been less of a shock to the English if they had realised that the Irish have long memories and that in Ireland the past, which seems so remote in England, lives ominously on into the present. The shot which killed an unoffending policeman on point duty at Dublin Castle and began the bloodshed of the Easter Rising was to remind England that the Irish have never forgotten their history.

CHAPTER II

Irish Ireland

I

THE HISTORY WHICH Irishmen remembered in 1916 was a history of English oppression through many centuries from the Norman conquest by Strongbow to the harsh penal laws against Roman Catholics imposed in the eighteenth century and the long list of Coercion Acts with which British Governments tried to suppress Irish agrarian unrest in Victorian times. The Irish had never forgotten Cromwell, who massacred their forefathers at Drogheda and depopulated eastern Ireland by sending its native inhabitants "to Hell or Connaught"; they had bitter memories of other English rulers, soldiers and statesmen who had consolidated their hold on Ireland, had kept the Irish themselves beyond the "Pale", which was the English stronghold in eastern Leinster, and had installed Protestant settlers and landowners of their own race to become the Anglo-Irish "ascendancy"—the people who lived in the "big houses" and, though a small minority of the population, were dominant over the Roman Catholic majority. For Ireland as a whole had never accepted the Reformation. In the north-east the flow of immigrants from Scotland created a powerful enclave of Presbyterianism; elsewhere Ireland remained a Catholic country, and, as many of the great Catholic nobles went into exile after abortive revolts and risings, the priesthood of the Roman Catholic Church was left to exert a particularly strong influence on the life and thought of Ireland.

While Ireland had never accepted the Reformation, it was also her claim that she had never willingly accepted English rule. This claim is disputable, since for more than a hundred years the freely elected representatives of the people of Ireland took the Oath of Allegiance to the British Sovereign in the House of Commons; but it is not disputable that throughout her troubled history Ireland strove again and again to throw off the English yoke. Until the end of the eighteenth century Ulster, in spite of her Protestant influences, was at one with the rest of the country in seeking freedom for Ireland; and the United Irishmen who revolted in 1798 under the leadership of Wolfe Tone, himself a Protestant, were founded in Ulster. Earlier the Ulster Protestants had supported King William III—William of Orange—against the Catholic James II, deposed King of England, who was backed by his co-religionists in the rest of Ireland; yet it is only in the last 150 years or so that King William's victory in the Battle of the Boyne has become a symbol of the division between Catholic and Protestant, to be celebrated each twelfth of July with the drums and banners of Orangemen's processions throughout Ulster.

Tone's unsuccessful revolt had a profound effect on the development of Irish history, for it established a tradition of revolutionary violence which became a permanent feature of Irish life. It came at a time when Ireland had been nearer to freedom than ever before, for under the pressure of Henry Grattan, the great Irish Parliamentarian, the British Parliament in 1783 had passed the Renunciation Act, which established Ireland's right to be bound only by the laws of the King and her own legislature. But the new Irish Parliament, which sat in the splendid building on College Green, Dublin, now occupied by the Bank of Ireland, had only a short life. In 1800 it was abolished by the Act of Union, which came into force in the following year and provided for the formal union of Ireland with Great Britain, giving the Irish 103 M.P.s in the British House of Commons and representation by 40 peers in the House of Lords.

The Union, which was intended to solve the problems of Irish government, was a source of Anglo-Irish friction from its very beginning. Ireland had accepted it because Pitt, the British Prime Minister, had promised a substantial measure of Catholic emancipation, but when the time came for him to fulfil his promise he declined to do so for fear of sending the unstable King George III (then temporarily sane) into madness again. Emancipation came later, after years of agitation led and inspired by Daniel O'Connell, but Ireland entered the hard and often tragic years of the nineteenth century with the feeling that she had been cheated over the Union and that the Act should be repealed to give her back her own Parliament. It was the century of the great famine of the eighteen-forties, when the hardships caused by the failure of the potato crop were so much aggravated by British maladministration that over a million Irish men and women died of starvation and more than a million others left the country in despair. It was the century, too, of the bitter land war, in which peasants, who had been struggling to make a living on smallholdings largely owned by absentee English or Anglo-Irish landlords, resorted to violence and outrage when faced with eviction from holdings for which they could not pay the rent. Englishmen could easily forget these Irish sufferings of bygone days, but the Irish remembered them, and they helped to lay the foundations of the new revolutionary movement which finally won Ireland her freedom.

Two other factors were concerned in that movement. One was the rise of the Fenians, who inherited and elaborated the tradition of violence founded by Wolfe Tone and later expressed (though not very forcefully) in such unsuccessful risings as those of Emmet in 1803 and the Young Irelanders in 1848. The other factor—perhaps the most important of all—was the revival of interest in the old Gaelic language of Ireland. It was this revival which made patriots dream of re-creating an Irish Ireland which, as Padraic Pearse was to say, would be "not free merely, but Gaelic as well; not Gaelic merely, but free as well", and so prepared a receptive audience for the doctrine of Sinn Fein.

2

The Fenians were the spearhead of the Irish protest in the second half of the nineteenth century. There is some obscurity about the exact details of their origin, since plans for a new Irish revolutionary movement were made simultaneously in Ireland and the United States; and it was, in fact, an Irish exile in America—John O'Mahony—who gave the movement its name, which was derived from the Fianna, the army of a legendary Irish hero, Fionn mac Cumhaill. The first Fenian group in Ireland was established at a Dublin workshop in 1858. Thereafter the movement spread rapidly in both Ireland and the United States, and it was formally organised as an oath-bound secret society known as the Irish Republican Brotherhood. From its foundation the Brotherhood had one aim only—the establishment of an Irish Republic by force of arms.

It was the Fenians' boast that they were the first revolutionaries in the world to make use of dynamite. Their long series of attacks on life or property in England and Ireland began in the eighteen-sixties, but plans for a co-ordinated insurrection led only to a brief and entirely unsuccessful rising in 1867. One of the plotters seized in a raid before this rising was John Devoy, a young man from county Kildare who had served in the French Foreign Legion to learn the art of war and had since been busily engaged in winning Fenian recruits among Irish soldiers serving with the British Army in Ireland. He was sentenced to a long term of imprisonment, but was later released and deported to the United States, where he was to work for the Irish cause for half a century.

Later in 1867 three Fenians were hanged in Manchester for the unintentional shooting of a policeman and became Irish heroes as "the Manchester martyrs"; and a ferocious attack on Clerkenwell prison, London, made Gladstone give serious thought to the problem of Irish pacification. The most notorious of many subsequent Fenian outrages was the assassination of Lord Frederick Cavendish, Chief Secretary for Ireland, and T. H. Burke, his Under-Secretary, in Phoenix Park, Dublin, in 1882. This crime, which was carried out by a small group of Fenians called "The Invincibles" and not by the I.R.B. leaders, horrified England and caused a small boy named Winston Churchill to reflect how lucky it was that the Fenians had not got *him* when he had fallen off a donkey in that same park two years earlier.

Early in its career the Irish Republican Brotherhood had come into conflict with the Roman Catholic Church. Its oath of secrecy was repugnant to the Catholic Hierarchy, who formally proclaimed that Fenians should not be allowed to receive absolution. But many priests disregarded this ban, and devout Catholics still succeeded in reconciling their membership of the Brotherhood with their religious beliefs. (Eamon de Valera, for example, joined the I.R.B. in 1916 at the urgent request of Thomas MacDonagh; but he did so with great reluctance, and soon ceased to be a member.) In spite of the Catholic Church's disapproval, the I.R.B. remained in being as the chief custodian of Ireland's revolutionary traditions, though there were long periods in which it was so quiescent that it almost seemed to have been disbanded. In the twenty years before 1916 its whole membership could have met in a medium-sized concert-hall, but under the inspiration of Thomas J. Clarke, a Fenian dynamiter who had served a term of fifteen years' hard labour ending in 1898 and had later returned to Dublin to open a small tobacco shop, the Brotherhood's secret influence again became powerful. It contrived, however, to keep all its activities out of the public eye, so that even men who were closely concerned with other separatist or Irish-Ireland organisations, such as Sinn Fein and the Gaelic League, usually had no idea that the I.R.B. still existed and was still awaiting the hour when it could lead the whole Irish-Ireland movement into armed insurrection.

This movement, which was the second principal factor in creating the revolutionary situation of 1916, was fostered on its cultural side by the Gaelic League and on its political side by Sinn Fein. Over the centuries the old Gaelic language spoken by the native Irish had been gradually dying out, and by the second half of the nineteenth century it was little heard outside the Gaelic-speaking areas in Munster, Connaught and Donegal. Its decline was deplored on cultural grounds by scholars, who wanted the Irish to be able to read their own literature, and for political reasons by men such as Arthur Griffith, who declared that " We must again be an Irish-speaking people, or there can be no future of national independence before us."

The chief impetus towards the revival of Gaelic was given by two young men, Father Eugene O'Growney, a professor at Maynooth ecclesiastical college, and Eoin MacNeill, an Ulsterman who was at that time a Civil Servant. In 1891 their common interest in the Irish language drew them together, and a year later they were joined by Douglas Hyde, a Protestant graduate of Trinity College, who became president of the Gaelic League, which was founded in 1893. The League was a great success. Branches were set up all over Ireland, and Irish men and women found unexpected pleasure in being able to read books in Gaelic and to talk to each other in their own language. But its influence was not confined to culture. Padraic Pearse, who became one of its most enthusiastic members, often said that "it brought not peace but a sword", and in 1914 he wrote in *The Irish Volunteer*: "The Gaelic League will be recognised in history as the most revolutionary influence that has ever come into Ireland. The Irish Revolution really began when the seven proto-Gaelic Leaguers met in O'Connell Street. . . . The germ of all future Irish history was in that back room."

Many of the Gaelic Leaguers were also concerned in the Irish dramatic revival which began with the twentieth century. Among its leaders were W. B. Yeats, poet, dramatist and at one time a member of the I.R.B.; Lady Gregory, a wealthy patron of the arts who was also a notable writer of Irish peasant plays and a lively transcriber of Irish folklore; Edward Martyn, playwright and landowner; and J. M. Synge, the most brilliant dramatist of them all, who died before the full effects of the revival were displayed. The beautiful Maud Gonne, whom H. W. Nevinson called "the loveliest of rebels" and of whom it was said that men could thrash out on a dark night a full barn of corn by the light of one tress of her hair, was another striking figure in the dramatic renaissance. She was a gifted amateur actress, a keen propagandist against recruiting for the British Army and a friend in need of all Irish patriots who were in trouble with the police. It was she who appeared as the bare-footed old woman in the first production of Yeats's *Cathleen ni Houlihan* at St. Teresa's Hall, Dublin, in 1902.

This was the play of which Yeats asked years later:

> Did that play of mine send out
> Certain men the English shot?

The answer must surely be that it did. One of the characters in *John Bull's Other Island* cynically observes that to interest Irishmen in Ireland "you've got to call the unfortunate island Cathleen ni Houlihan and pretend she's a little old woman". That was what Yeats did in his short play, but he did it to perfection, so that it took a hard heart not to be moved by the closing lines: "Did you see an old woman going down the path?" "I did not, but I saw a young girl, and she had the walk of a queen." *Cathleen ni Houlihan* was a revolutionary parable in dramatic form, and its effect on the Gaelic Leaguers in the audience at St. Teresa's Hall was probably more profound than that of any of the later plays produced at the Abbey Theatre after the Irish National Theatre had come into being.

The Gaelic League and the dramatic revival had been preceded in 1884 by the formation of the Gaelic Athletic Association, which was designed to revive Irish sports and games and discourage English games played by the "ascendancy" and the military garrison. This was separatism applied to athletics: Dr. Croke, Archbishop of Cashel, called upon Irishmen to go back to the old pastimes of "ball-playing, hurling, football-kicking according to Irish rules, wrestling, handy-grips, top-pegging, leap-frog, rounders, tip-in-the-hat" and to abjure "such foreign and fantastic field sports as lawn tennis, polo, croquet, cricket and the like". The association soon had clubs all over the south and west of Ireland, and though it was never directly involved in the revolutionary movement, it provided many recruits for the Volunteers, since the Irish Republican Brotherhood secretly placed its own members in key positions in the G.A.A.

Side by side with these cultural, artistic and athletic developments was the great political movement of Sinn Fein, which later became the popular name for the whole struggle for Irish independence. In the years before the Easter Rising a visitor to a dusty little office in 17, Fownes Street, Dublin, would have found there a small, sturdy man with an impressive head, a heavy moustache and thick glasses made necessary by his short sight, who somehow contrived to find among a vast array of files and press cuttings the material needed for the papers he edited—first the *United Irishman* and later *Sinn Fein*. This was Arthur Griffith, who was born in Dublin in 1872, began his working career in a city newspaper office and spent some years in South Africa at the end of the century, but returned to Ireland when the Boer War broke out and soon became recognised as an outstanding journalist and a brilliant propagandist for Irish Ireland.

No one surpassed Griffith in devotion to the cause of

Irish freedom. He made no money out of his papers: Oliver Gogarty, who knew him well, said that "he was a poor man all his life, poor to the verge of starvation". Yet though, after his day's work at the office, he usually spent the evening at the National Library, he was by no means the dry, academic bookman he may seem to a later generation. He loved the open air, and found time to bathe in the sea every day except in the coldest weather; in spite of his short sight, he joined the Irish Volunteers; and it is on record that he thrashed with a South African *sjambok* the editor of a Dublin weekly for having dared to say that Maud Gonne was a spy in the pay of Dublin Castle. The central theme of Griffith's writing was that Ireland must learn to rely on herself. Though he strongly opposed the existing connexion with Britain, he would gladly have accepted a dual monarchy on the lines of the Renunciation Act of 1783, so that the British Sovereign would also have been King of Ireland, which would otherwise have governed herself. This, he thought, would have been the first step towards the complete independence that was his ultimate goal.

It was to advance this theory of Irish self-reliance that he set up *Cumann na nGaedheal* in 1900—an Irish-Ireland organisation which was amalgamated with the separatist Dungannon Clubs, established in Ulster by Bulmer Hobson and Denis McCullough, to form the Sinn Fein League in 1907. A year later the word "League" was dropped from the title, and it became known as Sinn Fein. The words mean "We ourselves", and were said to have been suggested to Griffith and his friends by a famous Irish scholar, who told them the story of a farmer's servant in Munster who was sent to a fair to sell his master's horses. It was some days before he came back, having sold the horses and enjoyed a riotous time on the proceeds, but when neighbours asked him where he had been he would answer only "*Sinn fein, sinn fein!*" He meant to convey that his exploits were entirely a family matter: he would tell his master about them, but they were nobody else's business. So, too, in

Griffith's opinion the government of Ireland was solely the concern of the Irish themselves.

Edward Martyn, the landowner and Abbey Theatre playwright, was the first president of Sinn Fein—an appointment which greatly shocked his fellow-members of the Kildare Street Club, who unsuccessfully tried to have him removed from the club for making an anti-recruiting speech. By the time that Sinn Fein was formed Griffith had published a significant book called *The Resurrection of Hungary*, in which he pointed out that Hungary had won her independence by refusing to send members to the Imperial Parliament at Vienna and suggested that Irish M.P.s should similarly refuse to take their seats at Westminster. This was a vital issue for Ireland, since the attendance of Irish M.P.s at the English House of Commons was a sign of Irish acquiescence in English rule; but Griffith's appeal made no impression on the Irish Parliamentary Party, and his faith in the example of Hungary caused the Sinn Feiners to be nicknamed "the green Hungarian band".

The inventor of this nickname was another remarkable journalist, D. P. Moran, the editor of the *Leader*, who looked at the problem of Irish self-reliance from an industrial rather than a political standpoint. Moran's special contribution to the Irish-Ireland movement was his emphasis on practical methods of encouraging Irish industries by asking always for Irish goods in shops, even if they cost more than English-made goods. He was thus the founder of the "buy Irish" campaign.

Though Moran and others poked fun at it, the publication of *The Resurrection of Hungary* in 1904 was a milestone on the road to Easter Rising. It was the foundation of the Sinn Fein policy of making Irish self-reliance so strong that the English rulers would not be able to hold out against it. Though Sinn Fein did not condemn the use of physical force, which it regarded as a legitimate means of securing national rights, it was originally a party which advocated revolution without violence. Its aims, which were actually carried out from 1919 onwards, were to make English rule impossible in Ireland by setting up Irish institutions—a Parliament, arbitration courts, a Civil Service, an Irish Bank and so on—which would take over and exercise the functions previously carried out by their English counterparts. Griffith's perseverance in urging the need for Irish self-reliance caused another indomitable and scholarly separatist, Mrs. Alice Stopford Green, to describe him as "a granite monolith".

Outside the main streams of the Irish-Ireland movement, though eventually to be associated most intimately with its revolutionary manifestation, was the redoubtable trade union organiser, James Connolly, whose genial, moustached face seemed well suited to his sturdy and unbreakable spirit. He was a wandering Ulsterman, born in 1868, the son of farm worker parents in Monaghan, where as a child he worked for long hours in the fields and then read any book or paper he could find by the light of the dying embers of the fire. When he was ten his parents had taken him to Scotland, but he had come back to Ireland in 1896 with a young wife and four small daughters and had helped to found the Irish Socialist Republican Party. Nevinson said of Connolly that he "was not merely a nationalist rebel, he was a world-wide revolutionist", and in this he differed from most of the men he commanded at the Dublin General Post Office in Easter Week. A seven years' stay in America brought him into close contact with the militant Industrial Workers of the World, and when he again returned to Ireland he was able to instil some of his own revolutionary and republican ideas into the immature Irish trade-union movement. Though he was not directly concerned with either the I.R.B. or the Gaelic League, he was one of the most formidable champions of Irish Republicanism.

3

In retrospect it seems extraordinary that such a variety of Irish separatist activities should have aroused so little interest in England; but it was easy for Englishmen to surmise that students of Gaelic and advocates of Hungarian political policies would make little headway against the stronghold of English law and order—Dublin Castle—and that Irish sentiments as a whole would continue to be guided by the Irish Parliamentary Party at Westminster, generally known as the Nationalists, who stood for a constitutional and evolutionary approach towards self-government for Ireland.

Dublin Castle, the collective name given to the congeries of buildings housing many of the Government offices for Ireland, was under the control of the Chief Secretary, an English Minister who wielded complete executive power, though the nominal head of the British administration was the official variously known as Viceroy, Lord Lieutenant or Governor-General. Chief Secretaries had to divide their time between Dublin and London, since they had to attend British Cabinet meetings and be present in the House of Commons for Irish debates and to answer questions about Irish matters; and it was hardly conducive to the good government of Ireland that some Chief Secretaries visited Dublin only from time to time to "refresh their brogue". In any case, even the best-intentioned of them were always hampered by the British Treasury officials in Whitehall, who needed much persuasion before they would agree to spend more money on Ireland.

For the actual maintenance of law and order Dublin Castle relied on the Royal Irish Constabulary, an armed police force founded, like the London Metropolitan Police, by Sir Robert Peel and also taking from him the nickname of "peelers". In the years before the Easter Rising this was a force of about 10,000 men—a large number for a population of 4,000,000—and it was responsible for the whole country except Dublin, which had its own force, the Dublin Metropolitan Police, an unarmed body partly maintained by city rates. Much of the R.I.C. was distributed in small groups of five or six men in country districts, where the unmarried constables lived in the police barracks; but although they were trained to use and carry arms, it would be wrong to imagine that they were a fully military police force. They carried arms because of the violent traditions of Irish life, but, as was pointed out by an expert witness at a public inquiry held in 1919, "at normal times an Irish Constabulary man is no more a military policeman than a London policeman is".

They were all of Irish birth and were usually on excellent terms with their village communities; the idea that they were holding down Ireland by force and intimidation is clearly dispelled by the comment of Tom Kettle, the witty young Nationalist M.P., that the R.I.C. "used to be an army of occupation; now they are an army of no occupation". If, indeed, they had really been military despots, living aloof in their barracks, there would have been no point in de Valera's proposal in 1919 that their lives should be made unbearable by social ostracism; for the policy of ostracism presupposed that the R.I.C. had previously been on friendly terms with their country neighbours. None the less, when occasion called for the use of arms the R.I.C., together with the garrisons of British troops in Ireland, provided the physical means of opposing revolutionary designs.

A further restraining influence was that of the Irish Parliamentary Party—the Nationalist M.P.s who formed the majority of Ireland's 103 representatives in the British House of Commons. The Irish Party, as it existed before the First World War, had stood since the eighteen-seventies for a form of self-government for Ireland described as Home Rule; and under the leadership of Charles Stewart Parnell, a handsome and talented Protestant landowner, it had become a powerful force in British politics. Like other Irish M.P.s of his time, Parnell became closely associated with the Land League, a militant movement for Irish agrarian reform, and he was sent to gaol for backing a "No Rent" campaign; but it was during the decade of his leadership—from 1880 to 1890—that Gladstone, as Prime Minister, pledged the English Liberal Party to support of Home Rule for Ireland and introduced the first Home Rule Bill, which was defeated in the House of Commons by 341 votes to 311.

Parnell's career ended in 1890 when a Parliamentary colleague, Captain W. H. O'Shea, brought an action for divorce against his wife Kitty, the sister of General Sir Evelyn Wood, and named Parnell as co-respondent. O'Shea's action was almost certainly prompted by Parnell's political enemies, since he had known for years that his wife was Parnell's mistress and had made no attempt to break the liaison; and it had the desired effect of driving Parnell from Westminister, when Gladstone, yielding to the moral scruples of two of his lieutenants, John Morley and William Harcourt, announced that he could no longer co-operate with a party led by a guilty co-respondent. A majority of the Nationalist M.P.s deposed Parnell from the party leadership, and in little more than a year he was dead, worn out by intense strain which had undermined his health. He will be remembered in Ireland always for the words he spoke at Cork on January 21, 1885, now engraved on his lofty monument in O'Connell Street, Dublin: "No man has the right to fix the boundary to the march of a nation. No man has the right to say to his country: 'Thus far shalt thou go and no further', and we have never attempted to fix the *ne plus ultra* of Ireland's nationhood, and we never shall."

Two years after Parnell's death Gladstone made another attempt to give Ireland Home Rule, but his second Home Rule Bill (which Queen Victoria had forbidden him to describe as a Bill "for the better government of Ireland") was rejected by the Lords after successfully passing the Commons. In another two years the Liberal Government fell, and the Conservatives, who had no intention of granting Home Rule, began their long period of rule, which was not to end until 1905.

It was during this period that the Irish Parliamentary Party, which had been disastrously split by the deposition of Parnell, was substantially reunited under the leadership of John Redmond, a member of a Catholic family which had been established in south Leinster for seven centuries, and one whose sturdy build, round head and hawk-like face clearly recalled the Norman strain in his ancestry. Though lacking the brilliance of Parnell, Redmond was an effective Parliamentary leader, and his steadfast championship of Home Rule won him well-deserved popularity in Ireland, where most people thought it safer to "trust the Old Party" than to follow the new will-o'-the-wisp of a completely Irish Ireland. Redmond's weakness was that Parliamentary business compelled him to spend so much of his time in London; he returned to Ireland mainly for rest and recreation and thus failed to understand what was really happening there. His chief lieutenants in the Commons were John Dillon, an eloquent speaker who had frequently been imprisoned in Land League days, and "Wee Joe" Devlin, M.P. for West Belfast, whose support of the rabidly Catholic organisation, the Board of Erin Hibernians, did much to keep sectarian feuds in Ulster tragically alive.

During the first years of Redmond's leadership the English Conservative Government pursued a policy of "killing Home Rule by kindness", which culminated in the extensive reform of land ownership introduced in 1903 during the Chief Secretaryship of George Wyndham. This provided for a new method of Government-guaranteed land purchase, which allowed tenants to buy their holdings on easy deferred terms, often for less than they were paying in rent. Wyndham's reform roughly coincided with the great campaign for Irish agricultural co-operation, initiated by Sir Horace Plunkett (a former Unionist M.P. and uncle of Lord Dunsany, the poet and playwright) and carried out with the help of a remarkable Ulsterman, George Russell, who wrote under the pseudonym of "AE" and at one and the same time was poet, painter, politician, editor, mystic and agricultural organiser. The co-operative creameries which sprang up all over Ireland were a proof of the growing success of Plunkett's Irish Agricultural Organisation Society.

English Conservative policy did a great deal for Ireland. But Home Rule was not to be killed by kindness. It was still the Nationalists' aim in the House of Commons, and it seemed to be appreciably nearer when the Liberals came back to power in 1905. They made no move towards Home Rule during their first term of office (apart from proposing an interesting Irish Council Bill which the Nationalists rather unwisely turned down), but a new situation arose when the House of Lords rejected the Budget of 1909 and the Liberals went to the country to ask for a mandate to curb the powers of the Lords. Two general elections in 1910 produced almost exactly the same result: the Liberals had an insignificant majority over the Conservatives and needed the votes of the Irish members to be sure of having their own way in the Commons.

This was Redmond's hour. He could now name his price for support of the Liberal Government; it seemed that the granting of Home Rule would be only a matter of time, and that Ireland, where most people were well satisfied with the social progress made in recent years and the older generation felt that Home Rule would confirm their hopes of a still brighter future for their children, would settle down to a new era of peace and contentment. This forecast, as was soon to be shown, was grossly at fault, for it failed to take account of two vital factors. One was the hidden revolutionary strength of the Irish-Ireland movement. The other was Ulster.

CHAPTER III

Orange Drums

I

DURING THE NINETEENTH century and well into the twentieth both the Home Rulers and the advocates of Irish independence expected that any new régime for Ireland would naturally apply to all four provinces—Leinster, Munster, Ulster and Connaught. No one at that time ever dreamed that one of these provinces would "contract out" of an arrangement which covered the rest of the country. Yet forces destined to bring about this very result were at work from the eighteen-eighties, and in 1885 Lord Randolph Churchill, father of Winston Churchill, privately gave his view that if Gladstone "went for Home Rule, the Orange card would be the one to play". This candid admission that Ulster was to be used to serve Conservative Party ends is in curious contrast with the lofty professions of faith in Ulster's cause made in the speeches of later Conservative statesmen; but it marks, none the less, the beginning of the long and close association between the English Conservative Party and the Ulster Unionists which was to bring Ireland to the brink of civil war in 1914.

Ulster, which was then administered from Dublin Castle like the other Irish provinces, consisted of the nine counties of Armagh, Derry, Antrim, Down, Fermanagh, Tyrone, Donegal, Cavan and Monaghan, and the province as a whole could be described as mainly Protestant and largely

Presbyterian, though it had a substantial Roman Catholic minority. The descendants of the Scottish settlers who came to Ulster in the sixteenth and seventeenth centuries gave the province a different character from that of the rest of Ireland, so that there came into being that sharp division between north and south defined in 1917 by Dr. J. P. Mahaffy, Provost of Trinity College, Dublin, as "the contrast not only of two creeds, but of two breeds, of two ways of thinking, of two ways of looking at the most vital interests of men". After the Battle of the Boyne orange became the Ulster colour, in contrast with the green favoured by the other provinces, and in 1795 the Loyal Orange Institution was founded for the defence of Ulster Protestantism. In later years the Orange Lodges became little more than convivial clubs, but the beating of Orange drums in the great processions held each twelfth of July were an annual reminder that Ulster was distinct from the rest of Ireland.

For more than a century after the Battle of the Boyne the differences between Ulster and the other provinces seemed to be of little political significance, and it was not until the Act of Union had been in operation for two or three decades that the ways of north and south began to diverge. While southern Ireland was clamouring for repeal of the Act Ulster came round to the view that Union with Britain suited her better than any form of self-government for Ireland. For one thing she saw that the Union was to her economic advantage, since she was far more industrialised than the agricultural south, and her future clearly depended on the continuance of friendly trade with Britain. Then again her Protestant majority became fearful of one day finding itself dominated by a Roman Catholic Parliament in Dublin. So religious faith combined with business acumen to arouse in Ulster a fixed opposition to Home Rule, which was later expressed in the popular slogan, "Home Rule means Rome Rule."

This was the background against which the English Conservative Party played the Orange card. Lord Randolph

Churchill himself played it with gusto. In 1886, the year of Gladstone's first Home Rule Bill, he crossed to Belfast to make an inflammatory anti-Home Rule speech in the Ulster Hall, and a little later, when expressing his views on Home Rule in a letter to a correspondent, he coined the memorable phrase, "Ulster will fight, and Ulster will be right." The words have such a declamatory ring that it is curious to find they first appeared in a written document and not in the Ulster Hall oration.

Ulster would fight. But the time for her to fight had not come in the eighteen-eighties, when even the House of Commons would not pass a Home Rule Bill. The danger-point seemed to be nearer in 1892, when Gladstone was back in office and preparing his second Home Rule Bill, and Ulster then began to get ready for action. Orange Lodges were revived by an influx of more serious-minded members and ceased to be mere drinking-clubs; and at a great convention in Belfast on June 19, 1892, the Duke of Abercorn called on the whole assembly to repeat after him the solemn vow: "We will not have Home Rule." But once again Ulster saw the danger pass away. The House of Lords threw out Gladstone's second Bill, and soon afterwards Ulster's friends, the Conservatives, began their ten years' ascendancy at Westminster. In this period, though Ulster had nothing to fear under Conservative rule, rifle clubs were started in various parts of the province, largely at the instigation of a fiery Unionist, Major F. H. Crawford.

Though the Liberals won the 1906 general election, it was not until their further victories in 1910 that the threat of Home Rule was raised again—and raised, as Ulster saw it, in a much more menacing form; for the curtailment of the House of Lords' powers by the Parliament Act meant that Home Rule could become law in spite of the Lords' opposition if a Home Rule Bill were passed by the Commons in three successive sessions. H. H. Asquith, the Prime Minister, was determined to enact Home Rule in this way, and his policy alarmed not only the Ulster

Unionists and their English Conservative friends but also the small but influential minority of Southern Unionists in the other Irish provinces. These were mainly landowners and professional men who sincerely believed that the Union was the only possible safeguard for Ireland's prosperous future. One of them was to play a leading part in the approaching drama of orange and green.

2

The huge statue of a hatchet-faced man in a lounge suit, which stands today in the grounds of the Northern Ireland Parliament House at Stormont, bears a single word of title: "Carson". It is enough. His enemies called him "King Carson", but to the north he was simply Carson, or sometimes "Sir Edward". It was a name which seemed in Ulster to be that of her Messiah, though many outside the province thought it was the name of the Devil himself.

Edward Carson, who was born at 4, Harcourt Street, Dublin, in 1854, had a Scottish grandfather who came from Dumfries, but at the time of his birth his family had been settled in Ireland for some 40 years. He spoke with a rich brogue which some thought he had carefully preserved for the benefit of his English listeners; and St. John Ervine once described him as "the last of the 'broths of a boy' " and "the final comic Irishman". But such belittlement failed to recognise Carson's passionate sincerity and his steadfast belief that union with England was for the benefit not only of Ulster but of all Ireland; even George Russell, who did not like him, admitted that he had "a kind of power and a character of his own, big in a way of *resistance*, though not of creative statesmanship".

Carson was a member of the Irish Bar who had prosecuted for the Crown in many cases of outrage and violence before his election as Unionist M.P. for Trinity College in 1892, after which he moved from the Irish to the English Bar and combined a successful legal practice with his Parliamentary duties. He was a brusque and powerful cross-examiner, and held Government office as Solicitor-General from 1899 to 1905. In the latter year he refused an invitation to become President of the Probate, Divorce and Admiralty Division of the English High Court, and when the Liberals returned to power he went back to his lucrative practice at the English Bar.

After the first general election of 1910 the Irish Unionist M.P.s at Westminster (who mainly sat for Ulster constituencies) had to look for a new leader, as their previous chairman, Walter Long, had given up his Irish seat to be returned for a London constituency. Carson was clearly their man, since he had greater political prestige than anyone else in the group; and although, as a Southern Unionist, he was little known in the north-east, he agreed to accept a post which would make him the organiser of Ulster's resistance to Home Rule. He did not take long to learn the words for his new part. Before the end of the year he was dourly proclaiming in Liverpool: "It is my wish, and the wish of those with whom I act, to be law-abiding citizens. But by Heaven I tell you this: from what I know of the men of the north of Ireland they will not yield their birthright, not one inch, without a struggle."

In Ulster Carson found a brilliant lieutenant in James Craig, youngest son of a millionaire director of a whiskey firm, who had become a Unionist M.P. in 1906 and had quickly made his mark in the House of Commons as a resolute and expert drafter of amendments to Irish Bills. His broad figure and red face might have cast him in later days as the prototype of Colonel Blimp, but in fact he was a modest, good-humoured and quick-witted man, with a personal charm that few could resist. He was 39 when he formed his alliance with Carson, who was then 56, and although it was Carson on whom the limelight played, it was the clear-thinking and determined James Craig who made the practical plans for Ulster's resistance. Carson himself said in later years: "It was James Craig who did most of the work, and I got most of the credit."

In rallying Ulster against Home Rule Carson and Craig found a fruitful field for their work both in new Unionist Clubs and in the old Orange Lodges, which were still in full swing after their reinvigoration in the eighteen-nineties. Conceivably the Lodges might have faded away again by 1910, but the Ulster Catholics helped to keep them alive by fostering a rival and aggressively Catholic organisation, the Board of Erin Hibernians. This was the northern wing, reorganised by "Wee Joe" Devlin, of the Ancient Order of Hibernians, usually known as the "Molly Maguires", whose famous slogan of "Up, the Mollies!" had helped the Nationalists to win many of their election victories; and James Connolly, the Ulster-born Irish Labour leader, was convinced that "were it not for the existence of the Board of Erin, the Orange Society would long since have ceased to exist". William O'Brien, a prominent figure in the Irish Parliamentary Party who broke away to form a splinter "All for Ireland" group, also condemned the Board of Erin Hibernians for having, from 1906 to 1916, "every demerit that could inflame sectarian passion in Ulster".

Sectarian bad feeling had been further intensified in Ulster by the Papal decree, *Ne Temere*, of 1908, which imposed stricter rules for marriages between Protestants and Catholics, and although Carson and Craig were not directly concerned with religious issues, they were greatly helped by having behind them so many devoted Protestants who were darkly suspicious of all "Papishes".

It was not until September, 1911, that Carson first appeared at one of those mammoth Ulster demonstrations which were henceforth to be a familiar feature of the anti-Home Rule movement. To an audience of 100,000 people at Craigavon, Craig's mansion on the south shore of Belfast Lough, he declared that the moment Home Rule was passed Ulster must become responsible for her own government as a Protestant province. Two days later a commission was set up, with Craig at its head, to make plans for a provisional Government for Ulster.

At this time neither Carson nor Craig had any desire to establish a separate Government for Ulster. Their object was to smash the whole idea of Home Rule for Ireland and to preserve the Union for south as well as north, and by emphasising the dire consequences of the passing of Home Rule they hoped to frighten the Liberal Government into dropping its Bill. But the Government had no intention of dropping the Bill, and in the following year Winston Churchill, who was then First Lord of the Admiralty, himself went to Belfast to campaign for Home Rule.

At 38 Churchill was already the most colourful character in British politics: he had been in the public eye ever since his escape from the Pretoria prison camp during the Boer War, and after entering Parliament as a Conservative in 1900 he had soon changed his allegiance and become a powerful figure in the Liberal Party. Early in 1912 he decided to go to Belfast and speak for Home Rule in the very Ulster Hall where his father had so fiercely denounced it; but his proposal caused so much resentment among the Ulster Unionists, who warned him that it would be hard to keep the peace if he addressed a Home Rule meeting in the centre of Protestant Belfast, that he prudently gave way, and agreed to speak instead in the grounds of the Celtic Football Club in the Catholic part of the city. Angry crowds awaited him in Royal Avenue when he came to Belfast on February 8, and at one point a number of indignant Ulstermen stepped into the roadway to seize his car and turn it over; but Mrs. Churchill had gone with her husband on his hazardous journey, and when the men saw her in the car they drew back with a cry of "Mind the wumman" and allowed Churchill to go on his way. His hosts took care that he missed Royal Avenue on his way back to the railway station after the meeting.

Churchiil's visit to Ulster was countered in April by the appearance of Bonar Law at a great anti-Home Rule demonstration at Balmoral, a suburb of Belfast. Bonar Law, whose father was an Ulsterman though he himself was born in Canada, had come back to Britain as a young man and had settled in Scotland, where he soon made his mark in both business and politics; and a few months before the Balmoral meeting he had become leader of the Conservative Party, being chosen as a compromise candidate to avoid a split between the respective followers of Walter Long and Austen Chamberlain. He sympathised profoundly with Ulster's fears of Roman Catholic rule from Dublin, though he also regarded the Irish question as a useful political device for attacking and possibly bringing down the Liberal Government; and on his first appearance in Ulster he declared to his 100,000 Unionist listeners: "You hold the pass for the Empire." Later that summer, at an English demonstration in the grounds of the Duke of Marlborough's home, Blenheim Palace, he pledged the Conservative Party to give Ulster unlimited backing if she revolted against Home Rule. "I can imagine," he said, "no length of resistance to which Ulster will go in which I shall not be ready to support them, and in which they will not be supported by the overwhelming majority of the British people." These provocative remarks, together with many other Conservative speeches urging Ulster to stand firm, were described by Asquith as providing a "complete grammar of anarchy".

3

So far the sole aim of Ulster resistance had been to force the Government to abandon Home Rule. No one had even considered the possibility of dividing Ireland, and the first proposal for partition came from a Liberal M.P., the Hon. T. G. R. Agar-Robartes, member for the Cornish constituency of St. Austell. The Home Rule Bill was introduced in April, 1912, and in June Agar-Robartes unsuccessfully moved an amendment proposing that four of the nine counties in the historic province of Ulster should be excluded from the jurisdiction of a Dublin Parliament. "Orange bitters and Irish whiskey will not mix," he observed.

Though Parliament had rejected partition, the idea now began to find favour in Government circles, and Churchill suggested to Redmond that "something should be done to afford the characteristically Protestant and Orange counties the option of a moratorium of several years before acceding to the Irish Parliament". But no one in Ireland found the suggestion palatable. Redmond thought that the "two-nation theory" was "an abomination and a blasphemy", and the Unionists felt that it was not a practicable solution, even though Ulster was ready to set up her own Government as a last resort. The Southern Unionists were particularly opposed to a partition which would make them a small Protestant minority under a Roman Catholic Government. Moreover, they believed fervently in the Union, and the idea of dividing Ireland seemed to them an outrageous betrayal of the country's best interests.

While the Home Rule Bill went on its leisurely way through the House of Commons in the summer of 1912 the Ulster Unionists prepared a big series of demonstrations, which were held in September. At each of these the audience reaffirmed the resolve of the 1892 convention, "We will not have Home Rule", a phrase soon abbreviated in popular speech to "We won't have it". A prominent speaker at the September meetings was F. E. Smith, a brilliant young barrister who had become Conservative M.P. for the Walton division of Liverpool in 1906. Handsome, aggressive, eloquent, equipped with a clear and logical mind, and looking so youthful that years later, when he was Lord High Chancellor of England, a Paddington barmaid called him "a saucy boy" for asking for a glass of beer out of licensed hours, F. E. Smith was a valuable recruit to the Ulster movement.

The climax of the demonstrations came with the signing of the Ulster Covenant in the Belfast City Hall on Saturday, September 28, which was thereafter given the name of Ulster Day. The Covenant, which was inspired by the old Scottish Covenant of 1581, declared that the signatories were convinced in their consciences that "Home Rule would be disastrous to the material well-being of Ulster as well as of the whole of Ireland, subversive of our civil and religious freedom, destructive of our citizenship and perilous to the unity of the Empire", and that they therefore pledged themselves to use "all means which may be found necessary to defeat the present conspiracy to set up a Home Rule Parliament in Ireland". It also stated that "in the event of such a Parliament being forced upon us, we further solemnly and mutually pledge ourselves to refuse to recognise its authority".

Ulstermen rallied in their thousands to sign this document, which described the lawful proceedings of the British Parliament as a "conspiracy". In all, 80,000 signed on that day, some in their own blood, and when Carson, accompanied by F. E. Smith, Lord Londonderry, Lord Charles Beresford and other leaders of the resistance movement, left for Liverpool in the evening, huge Protestant crowds went to the quayside, where a searchlight picked out Carson as he stood on the deck of the steamer, appropriately called the *Patriotic*. As the ship moved away to the strains of "Rule Britannia", "Auld Lang Syne" and "God Save the King", rockets screamed into the skies and bonfires burst into flames on the surrounding hills.

Another great demonstration was held at the Liverpool landing-stage next morning. Archibald Salvidge, who was the Conservative leader in the Liverpool City Council, always maintained that Ulster's case was better understood in Liverpool, where sectarian rivalry between Catholic and Protestant flared up every twelfth of July, than anywhere else in Great Britain; and his great hold on his native city was never shown to more telling effect than on the Sunday morning when he rallied a crowd of about 150,000 people to welcome the *Patriotic* at the early hour of 7.30. Carson went ashore to the strains of "O God our help in ages past", and as he entered the Conservative Club for breakfast an admirer seized him by the hand and shouted: "It's been marvellous, sir. Nothing like it has been seen at the Liverpool landing-stage since Crippen was brought back from America!" The comparison of Carson with Crippen, the notorious wife-murderer of a year or two earlier, might have seemed more natural in southern Ireland than among the Liverpool Orangemen; but presumably the barb in the admirer's comment was unintended, for vast crowds attended an open-air meeting in Sheil Park on the next day and loudly cheered Carson's confident assertion: "Belfast gave her answer last Saturday; Lancashire gives it today."

Two months after the signing of the Covenant the Ulster leaders moved from violent words to threats of violent action by forming the Ulster Volunteer Force, in which every man who had signed the Covenant was automatically enrolled. On the suggestion of the great soldier, Lord Roberts, the new force was commanded by a retired Indian Army officer, Lieutenant-General Sir George Richardson, and by the end of 1913 the numbers of the Ulster Volunteers had risen to 100,000. It was during a review of about 15,000 of them at Balmoral in September that F. E. Smith, who was always a keen horseman and was an officer in the Oxfordshire Hussars, made himself conspicuous by riding about the parade ground as "galloper" to the general. For years afterwards his political opponents called him "Galloper" Smith.

One problem raised by the establishment of the Ulster Volunteers was that of the legality of drilling armed men who were not part of the Crown Forces. It was ingeniously solved by the discovery that any two magistrates were empowered to authorise military drill in the areas of their jurisdiction if they thought it advisable. Orange Lodges had already been given permission to drill on the grounds that military training would "make them more efficient citizens for the purpose of maintaining the constitution of the United Kingdom", and the precedent thus established held good for the Volunteers. Moreover, what was legal in Ulster was presumably legal in the rest of Ireland, and it was thus possible for the Irish Volunteers to be formed all over the country without challenge from the authorities.

4

In 1914 the Home Rule Bill, which had already been passed twice by the House of Commons and rejected twice by the House of Lords, entered its final stage, for under the provisions of the Parliament Act it would inevitably become law when passed by the Commons for the third time. It was not a measure which gave Ireland anything approaching complete independence, but it was certainly a substantial contribution to self-government. An Irish Parliament of two Houses was to be given control of purely Irish matters, though defence, foreign policy and Customs duties were still to be administered by the British Parliament, which would also control the police for the first six years of Home Rule. Ireland was to have only a limited power over her finances, and would send 42 members to the British House of Commons. This kind of Home Rule was much more than the "gas and water" measure which the Irish separatists called it; and it would, indeed, have given Ireland a base from which her new Parliament could gradually have extended its authority. But Ulster still refused to allow Dublin to rule Belfast, and no compromise seemed possible. By this time Carson had come to consider partition as a possible solution, but no agreement could be reached with the Government either about the number of Ulster counties to be excluded from Home Rule or about the terms on which exclusion might be granted. Carson wished it to be permanent, or at least until such time as Ulster herself should decide to rejoin the rest of Ireland; Asquith would promise no more than six years' exclusion, at the end of which Ulster would come automatically into the Home Rule system. Redmond, moreover, was against exclusion altogether, though he was ready to accept "Home Rule within Home Rule"—i.e. the grant to Ulster of the widest possible local self-government under the new Irish Parliament.

While Parliament debated Ulster drilled, and the Unionist leaders threatened to encourage disobedience in the Army if the Government tried to coerce Ulster into accepting Home Rule. Bonar Law had even told King George V that in such an event he would urge Army officers to disobey the Government's orders. In March, 1914, it seemed that the testing time had come already, for in that month Churchill, then First Lord of the Admiralty, gave clear warning that force would be used against Ulster if she refused to come to terms. There were worse things, he said in a speech at Bradford, than bloodshed even on an extended scale, and he ended with a peroration that foreshadowed the style of many of his famous broadcasts in the Second World War:

"If Ulster is to become a tool in party calculations; if the civil and Parliamentary systems under which we have dwelt so long, and our fathers before us, are to be brought to the rude challenge of force; if the Government and the Parliament of this great country and greater Empire are to be exposed to menace and brutality; if all the loose, wanton and reckless chatter we have been forced to listen to, these many months, is in the end to disclose a sinister and revolutionary purpose; then I can only say to you, 'Let us go forward together and put these grave matters to the proof.'"

To assist in putting them to the proof, Churchill ordered the 3rd Battle Squadron to sail from Spanish waters to Lamlash, off the west coast of Scotland, and he is said to have told Sir John French, Chief of the Imperial General Staff, that if Belfast showed fight "his fleet would have the town in ruins in 24 hours". But before there could be any question of naval action some rather clumsily handled negotiations between the Government and General Sir Arthur Paget, Commander-in-Chief of the British forces in Ireland, had produced what was quite incorrectly described as "the mutiny at the Curragh".

It is now recognised that this was not, in fact, a mutiny at the Curragh, but rather a mutiny at the War Office, where Sir Henry Wilson, a politically-minded general and an accomplished intriguer, who was himself an Irishman, was pulling all possible strings to defeat Home Rule. The officers concerned—Brigadier Hubert Gough and 57 others of the 3rd Cavalry Brigade, then stationed at the Curragh—did not disobey orders. All they did was to declare that they would prefer to accept dismissal from the Army if they were ordered north to Ulster. But this statement, which was reported to London on the evening of Friday, March 20, was grave enough, since it appeared to threaten a disastrous split in the Army. Gough and Paget were summoned to the War Office, and on Sunday morning what was not yet known as "the establishment" began to take a hand in the crisis.

On that morning Randall Davidson, Archbishop of Canterbury, had two callers who visited him independently at Lambeth Palace. One was Bonar Law, Leader of the Opposition, the other was Geoffrey Dawson, editor of *The Times*. As a result of his conversations the Archbishop went to see the Prime Minister at 10, Downing Street, and urged him to do something to allay the nation's alarm. Next the Prime Minister went to Buckingham Palace to see the King, and after this interview Dawson was called to Downing Street, where he was given a statement for Monday's *Times* correcting prevailing rumours about the movements of troops. This five-fold alliance of Crown, Government, Opposition, Church and Press helped to reduce public disquiet, and the threat of serious trouble was removed when Gough was given a signed assurance that the cavalry would not be called upon to enforce Home Rule on Ulster. This assurance, for which Sir John French, Sir Spencer Ewart, the Adjutant-General, and Colonel J. E. B. Seely, Secretary for War, shared the responsibility, went farther, however, than the Cabinet intended—or at all events than the Cabinet *claimed* to have intended; and though Gough was satisfied, French, Ewart and Seely all resigned within a few days.

Owing to the new situation created when the First World War began, the Curragh incident had little or no effect on the events of the following years. There was greater significance in the Ulster gun-running adventure, which was successfully carried out at Larne, Bangor and Donaghadee in April.

From 1907 to 1913 there was no absolute embargo on the importation of arms into Ireland, for the Peace Preservation Act of 1881, which had imposed such an embargo, had been allowed to lapse in 1907 at Redmond's request. But the restrictions of ordinary civil law were still in operation, and most of the arms for the Ulster Volunteers had to be smuggled into the country. Both men and women helped: one woman, for instance, landed at Belfast in an apparently advanced state of pregnancy, though her bulk was really due to a large bundle of cartridges tied round her waist, and a quayside porter gleefully told a Unionist M.P., "The fun was the Custom House boys knowed rightly what it was, but they dursn't lay a hand on her nor search her, for fear they was wrong." A complete embargo was reimposed in December, 1913, but by this time Ulster was arranging to import arms on a grand scale. With the support of Carson, who declared, "I'll see you through this business, even if I should have to go to prison for it," Major Crawford, the one-time founder of rifle clubs, went to Hamburg to buy arms and ammunition. After a complicated voyage the first batch of about 35,000 German and Austrian rifles and 3,000,000 rounds of ammunition was landed from a yacht at Larne on the evening of April 24.

The enterprise had been so secret that neither the troops nor the police had been able to take measures to prevent it. But there was no secrecy when the landing actually took place. In the evening dusk all roads leading to Larne were ablaze with light, as motor-cars, motor-lorries, farm wagons and carts, packhorses and bicyclists made their way to the harbour to come back with loads of arms. Someone even took a steamroller, and there were several perambulators in this remarkable procession. Yet the authorities took no action, and the other landings at Bangor and Donaghadee were carried out no less smoothly.

The Government was indignant at this open defiance of the law. Asquith called the gun-running an "unprecedented outrage", and there was much talk of arresting Carson and his principal colleagues. But Redmond advised against the arrests, since he thought they would have little effect and would only make martyrs of the Ulster leaders, and Asquith was glad to drop a proposal which, if pressed to its logical conclusion, might have involved the arrest of Bonar Law and F. E. Smith.

On May 25, 1914, the Home Rule Bill passed the Commons for the last time, and nothing—except the virtually impossible withholding of the Royal Assent—could now prevent it from reaching the statute book. In a final effort to conciliate Ulster the Government introduced in the House of Lords an amending Bill which would have given each of the nine counties of Ulster the right to vote itself out of the Home Rule system for a limited period of six years; but Carson had already said that Ulster would not accept a "sentence of death with stay of execution for six years", and the Conservatives in the Lords therefore amended the amending Bill to provide for the permanent exclusion of all nine counties. There was no possibility of this amendment being accepted by the Commons. When Carson went to Belfast for the twelfth of July celebrations he told Ulster that he could see nothing but darkness ahead and no hope of peace.

But King George V, then in the fourth year of his reign, was not prepared to see civil war break out in the British Isles if he could possibly prevent it. Throughout the Home Rule crisis he had been in frequent touch with both Asquith and Bonar Law; he now invited the leaders of the two parties, together with those of the Irish Nationalists and the Ulster Unionists, to a conference at Buckingham Palace. When they were assembled the King opened the conference with an appeal for a peaceful settlement and then left them to their work.

It was of no avail. No agreement could be reached on

Ulster's claim to permanent exclusion from Irish Home Rule, though the conference at least helped to clarify the issue of how many Ulster counties should be embraced in this claim. Carson and Craig had asked for the exclusion of all nine counties of historic Ulster—the four with Protestant majorities (Antrim, Armagh, Derry and Down), the two more evenly balanced between Protestant and Catholic (Fermanagh and Tyrone) and the three which were unmistakably Catholic (Cavan, Monaghan and Donegal). They were now prepared to give up their claim to the last three, though they still demanded permanent exclusion of "the six counties"—a phrase which King George is said to have originated. Asquith, however, sought to reduce the six counties to little more than four by depriving Ulster of South Armagh and parts of Fermanagh and Tyrone—a proposal which the Unionists would not accept. After some desultory talk about dividing Tyrone the conference broke up with the curt announcement that it could not agree, either in principle or in detail, on the possibility of defining an area to be excluded from the Government of Ireland Bill.

One odd result of the conference was that it enhanced Redmond's respect for Carson. "As an Irishman," he said afterwards, "you could not help being proud to see how he towered above the others. They simply did not count. He took charge." Redmond also had a private talk with the King, who said that everyone in the world, himself included, regarded Home Rule for Ireland as inevitable, and he was most anxious that no one in Ireland should regard him as in any way hostile to her. But the deadlock was complete, and only the outbreak of the First World War averted the crisis for which Carson and Craig had been preparing since 1910. It was in these final days of world peace that the Irish limelight turned suddenly from Belfast to Dublin. Three months after the Ulster Volunteers had landed their guns at Larne their counterparts in southern Ireland, the Irish Volunteers, unloaded their own consignment of arms at Howth.

CHAPTER IV

Murmur of Marching

I

WHEN THE VOLUNTEERS landed their arms at Howth Ireland was not, on the whole, a discontented country. The Parliamentary progress of the Home Rule Bill, which was causing so much disquiet in Ulster, was being followed with considerable satisfaction in the other provinces, and the Irish could view both present and future with a good deal of complacency. The land troubles were over, thanks to the English Conservatives' efforts to kill Home Rule by kindness; and since the Liberals' return to power Ireland had made remarkable social progress under an enlightened and sympathetic Chief Secretary, Augustine Birrell. After the Easter Rising Birrell was generally discredited in England, but in his nine years as Chief Secretary he carried 56 Acts of Parliament through the House of Commons dealing with such vital Irish matters as agriculture, housing (though he did not cure the Dublin slums) and education. Above all, he was the founder of the National University of Ireland. It is customary to picture Birrell as an elderly dilettante looking at Ireland from the stalls of the Abbey Theatre; in fact, he knew every part of the country, and the Irish had particular cause to be grateful for his educational reforms, which had given their children the opportunity of fitting themselves for good jobs in business or the professions. In general, too, the country was becoming more prosperous, and it was not surprising that many Irishmen glibly repeated the slogan, "Trust the Old Party and the Old Leaders and Home Rule next year."

Even some of the Irish-Ireland enthusiasts gave qualified support to the Parliamentary Party. When a great Home Rule demonstration was held in O'Connell Street in 1912 three of the principal speakers were Redmond, Padraic H. Pearse and Eoin MacNeill, the former Ulster Civil Servant who had since become Professor of Early Irish History at University College, Dublin. Pearse, who spoke in Gaelic, said it was clear that Home Rule would be for the good of Ireland, but he added a word of warning. "Let the Gall (the foreigner) understand," he said, "that if we are cheated once more there will be red war in Ireland."

Pearse, who was then 32, was better known as a Gaelic Leaguer and an educational reformer than as a politician or potential rebel leader, and even when he became the commander-in-chief in the Easter Rising there were still many Irishmen who had never heard of him. His father was an Englishman, a native of Devon who had settled in Dublin as a monumental sculptor and had married a girl from county Meath; and Padraic was the eldest of four children—two boys and two girls. From boyhood he had been attracted to the study of Irish history and Gaelic. Though he read for the Bar and practised for a short time as a barrister, his heart was in education, and he founded his boys' school of St. Enda's (first at Cullenswood House, Dublin, and later at Rathfarnham) to provide elementary and secondary education for English-speaking pupils, and especially for those who wished to be educated bilingually. He had an excellent staff, which included his brother William and Tom MacDonagh, a loquacious, curly-haired young man who was equally notable as poet, essayist, critic and Greek scholar, with whose help his pupils won scholarships at the National University besides becoming proficient in Gaelic.

Pearse had a striking presence: his fresh complexion,

high forehead and blue eyes (with a slight cast in one of them) were impressively offset by the black tie and dark scholastic gown he wore at St. Enda's, and he had the habit of walking with hunched shoulders and his head down, seemingly lost in thought. His private life had all the austerity that so often goes with fanatical devotion to a cause. He was unmarried, he never smoked, he never drank, he disliked tea-parties and he rarely went to the theatre, but he read widely and had made Napoleon his particular hero in history. One of his treasures was a lock of hair that was said to be Napoleon's. When he showed it to favoured friends he would say: "Hold your breath now while I'm showing you this."

If Pearse was little known in Ireland as a whole, his influence on his own circle—and especially on his pupils at St. Enda's—was profound. His friends knew that he was much more than an educational reformer, a Gaelic student and a sensitive poet; his brother William remembered the pledge Padraic had made to him as a very young man: "I swear before God and before you that I will free Ireland or die fighting the English." Only a year after the O'Connell Street demonstration he was to speak publicly of "the high and sorrowful destiny of heroes: to turn their backs to the pleasant paths and their faces to the hard paths, to blind their eyes to the fair things in life, to stifle all sweet music in the heart, the low voices of women and the laughter of little children, and to follow only the faint, far call that leads them into battle or to the harder death at the foot of a gibbet". The theory of the blood sacrifice, which he was to carry into action in 1916, is clearly implicit in these words.

This was the man who in 1912 gave his qualified blessing to Home Rule as a step on the way towards Irish independence. But before many months were out Dublin had another problem on its hands which temporarily overshadowed Home Rule. Workers challenged employers in the great transport strike of 1913–14.

The strike arose from the transport employers' refusal to allow their workers to belong to a union of their own choice, but it became in essence a struggle for power between James Larkin, the trade-union leader, and Martin Murphy, director of the Dublin Tramway Corporation. They were worthy champions of their respective causes. Handsome, fiery and possessing a deep, husky voice that had a rousing effect on Dublin crowds, Larkin did much to inspire the Irish working-classes to stand up for their rights, though Griffith derided him because of his links with English trade unionism; Murphy, the employers' leader, with his calm manner, quiet voice and trim white beard, was described by G. K. Chesterton as being quite different from the conventional business chief and "more like some morbid prince of the fifteenth century, full of cold anger, but not without perverted piety". For six months the struggle went on: the Dublin workers, who had lived so long in their festering slums and had suffered so much economic hardship, gallantly responded to Larkin's lead, and some 20,000 of them held out grimly in spite of the misery and starvation caused by the strike. One of the few alleviations of their distress was a free food kitchen at Liberty Hall, the Transport Union's headquarters in Beresford Place, where Countess Markievicz (of whom much more was soon to be heard) was seen daily in spotless apron and with an enormous ladle in her hand as she distributed soup to strikers and their families.

All through the winter the workers held out, but the strike ended at last in a stalemate, with the men going back to work on the best terms they could get. The Irish Transport Workers' Union was depleted in both members and money, and it seemed that the workers had gained nothing from all their sacrifices. Yet the strike was not a failure: it had revealed the resolute spirit of the Dublin workers and it had created the Irish Citizen Army—the first of the two armed bodies which were to fight for Ireland in the Easter Rising.

2

The decision to enrol trade unionists in an Irish Citizen Army was the result of a police baton charge on a strikers' meeting in Dublin in August, 1913, when two men were killed by the police and a young woman was shot dead by a "free labourer" hired by the transport employers. Two months later Larkin presided over another meeting, at which one of the speakers was Captain J. R. White, a Protestant Ulsterman and son of an English field-marshal, whose belief in freedom for Ireland had taken him from Belfast to Dublin. White and others pointed out that if workers were drilled and disciplined they would be better able to withstand the bludgeoning tactics of the police, and it was decided at once to set up a Citizen Army. White trained it for six months, and then resigned because his naturally rebellious temperament made it impossible for him to co-operate with the Army's advisory committee. By that time the strike was over, and enthusiasm for the Citizen Army waned rapidly. It was not, indeed, until October, 1914, when Larkin went to America and James Connolly took over the Transport Workers' Union's affairs, that the Army became a significant military body. In the meantime a much larger voluntary armed force had also been established in the south of Ireland.

The Irish Republican Brotherhood had acted at last. It had never believed that Ireland could achieve freedom by Parliamentary discussions, and it had resolved to put arms into Irishmen's hands at the first opportunity. It feared, however, that any military movement sponsored by known separatists would be immediately suppressed by the British authorities. What was needed, therefore, was some thoroughly respectable national figure who would take the nominal lead of an armed force while the I.R.B. pressed on with its undercover activities.

This opportunity came in October, 1913—the month when the Citizen Army was founded. Eoin MacNeill, who was just the kind of respectable man the I.R.B. had been waiting for, published an article in the Gaelic League's journal entitled "The North Began", which urged southern Ireland to follow Ulster's example and set up her own volunteer force. The I.R.B. seized its chance. While keeping very much in the background, so that MacNeill was unaware of its intervention, it arranged for the establishment of an influential committee under MacNeill's chairmanship. This committee, whose members included Pearse, Sean MacDermott, Eamonn Ceannt and The O'Rahilly, organised a big public meeting which was held in November at the Rotunda, Dublin, where the audience overflowed from the rink and the concert room into the grounds outside. The moment for arming Ireland had come.

Though the I.R.B. had secretly decided that Sean MacDermott was to run the volunteer movement, MacNeill was the principal speaker at the meeting. He made it clear that no one in southern Ireland wanted to fight the Ulster Volunteers, but the south, he insisted, should have its own armed volunteers because it was "the right and duty of a freeman to defend his freedom with all his resources and with his life itself". A motto, "Defence, not defiance", was chosen for the new force established that evening, and the name of Irish Volunteers was given to it. A manifesto declared that the Volunteers' duties "will be defensive and protective, and they will not contemplate either aggression or domination". Before the meeting dispersed 4,000 people (among whom was Eamon de Valera, a professor of mathematics and keen Gaelic Leaguer) signed the enrolment form, which bore the innocuous words: "I, the undersigned, desire to be enrolled in the Irish Volunteers founded to secure and maintain the rights and liberties common to all the people of Ireland without distinction of creed, class or politics." So the Irish Volunteers were launched, and the I.R.B. (with which the Volunteers had no formal connexion, either then or later) was soon moving secretly to place its own members in key positions in the new organisation.

By the end of the year there were 10,000 Volunteers, and as yet there was nothing to indicate that they could ever become a revolutionary army. It was a proof, indeed, of their eminent respectability that Colonel Maurice Moore, brother of George Moore, the novelist, and formerly an officer in the British Army, became their Inspector-General and took a prominent part in their training; and the appointment of Sir Roger Casement, who had just ended a distinguished career in the British consular service, as the Volunteers' treasurer seemed another guarantee of their good faith. There was no alarm at Dublin Castle as the Volunteers marched through the city streets in their green uniforms. In any case, though they were theoretically an armed body, they actually had few arms and little likelihood of getting more, since the total embargo on arms importation was now in force again.

But the formation of the Irish Volunteers had aroused a new spirit in Ireland. When Pearse went to the United States in the spring of 1914 to raise money for St. Enda's he was able to tell a Brooklyn audience: "Today Ireland is once more arming, once more learning the noble trade of arms. There is again in Ireland the murmur of a marching, a talk of guns and tactics." This was a memorable visit for Pearse: in the previous November he had joined the I.R.B., and in New York he met the Brotherhood's chief Irish-American liaison officer, the old Fenian, John Devoy, who was then 71. The "little deaf man", as Pearse called him, had long been editor of the *Gaelic American* and a leading member of the powerful Irish-American society, the Clan na Gael. Pearse was deeply impressed by his burning faith in Irish freedom and later acclaimed him as "the greatest of all Fenians".

3

More and more recruits joined the Irish Volunteers in that spring of 1914, and their growing success made Redmond and his Parliamentary Party wonder what attitude they should adopt towards this rival claimant for national leadership in Ireland. The Volunteers played into Redmond's hands. They, too, thought there should be some liaison between the military and Parliamentary wings of Irish nationalism, and in May MacNeill suggested to Joe Devlin that Redmond's brother Willie (also an M.P.) should join the new governing body it was proposed to set up for the Volunteers in place of the original provisional committee. Redmond was not satisfied with this suggestion, and insisted that he should be allowed to nominate 25 representatives to join the existing 25 members of the provisional committee. This was more than the committee had bargained for, but after much discussion it reluctantly accepted Redmond's proposal. This summer the Volunteers reached a total of 129,000, of whom 41,000 were in the nine counties of Ulster. But though Redmond's representatives had nominally a half-share in running the Volunteers, they were not concerned in the event which brought the new force still more prominently into the public eye—the Howth gun-running in July.

Many interesting people had a hand in this exploit. One was an enterprising young woman, Mary Spring-Rice, daughter of a Southern Unionist peer, Lord Monteagle, and cousin of Sir Cecil Spring-Rice, British Ambassador in Washington and author of the hymn, "I vow to thee, my country". Mary Spring-Rice had enthusiastically taken up the cause of Irish nationalism. She was a keen Gaelic student, and Sean O'Casey recalls that a letter she wrote in Irish "converted important persons by showing them that the Gaelic movement had the support of elegant and respectable people". She was also a friend of Erskine Childers, the son of an English father and an Irish mother, who had fought for Britain in the Boer War and had been for some years a clerk in the House of Commons, but had resigned in 1910 to devote himself to writing and speaking, largely on Home Rule.

Some time in the spring of 1914 Mary Spring-Rice

burst into the London sitting-room of Childers and his American wife, threw down her gloves with what was apparently a characteristic gesture, and cried: "Isn't it about time the South ran in some guns for its own use?" Her suggestion was passed on to the Volunteers' leaders in Dublin, and with their approval gun-running plans were worked out in London at the home of Mrs. Alice Stopford Green, widow of J. R. Green, the historian, and herself a distinguished writer on Irish nationalism. Besides Miss Spring-Rice and Mr. and Mrs. Childers, Sir Roger Casement was present at some of these meetings at Mrs. Green's house. So, too, was Darrell Figgis, a handsome, red-bearded author and journalist, who played a considerable part both at Howth and in later Sinn Fein developments, though always retaining a certain air of dilettantism among his more single-minded colleagues.

None of them knew anything about the similar plans being made by the Ulster Volunteers until the Larne gun-running actually took place; but the upshot of the London meetings was an arrangement that arms should be bought on the Continent and shipped to Ireland in three yachts. One of these was Erskine Childers's *Asgard*; the others —the *Kelpie* and the *Chotah*—belonged respectively to two other sympathisers with the Volunteer movement, Conor O'Brien and Sir Thomas Myles. Figgis and Childers went to the Continent and bought 1,500 secondhand Mauser rifles and 49,000 rounds of ammunition. Most of these were to be taken by tug to the North Sea and there transferred to the *Asgard*; the rest were to be shipped by O'Brien in the *Kelpie* and passed on to the *Chotah* for the final stage of the journey to Ireland.

The smaller consignment was duly, if rather belatedly, landed at Kilcoole, in county Wicklow, and there handed over to a Volunteer contingent under the command of Sean T. O'Kelly and Sean Fitzgibbon; but it was the voyage of the *Asgard* which led up to the main drama of the gun-running. Childers was a keen and experienced yachtsman;

with him in the *Asgard* were his wife, Mary Spring-Rice, Gordon Shephard (a young English officer) and two fishermen from Connaught. Miss Spring-Rice was new to ocean sailing, but Shephard thought her "a wonder" and wrote in a letter that "she was hardly ill at all, and looks and is most useful". Mrs. Childers had an unusual role: as the *Asgard* approached Howth, the chosen landing-place, she was to sit at the helm wearing a red jersey as a sign that all was well. Then, when an answering signal had been received from the shore, the *Asgard* was to enter the harbour to land her cargo.

The day of the landing was Sunday, July 26. In the morning about 1,000 members of the Dublin contingent of the Irish Volunteers marched the nine miles from Dublin to the little port of Howth. Figgis was there to supervise the unloading, and MacDonagh and Bulmer Hobson were in command of the Volunteers. Among them were Griffith, Eamon de Valera and a little man with grey eyes and a flowing moustache who was the founder and director of a firm of ecclesiastical candlemakers. This was Cathal Brugha, who was the son (like Pearse and Childers) of an English father, and was soon to be famous for his courage and martial spirit.

Few of the rank and file knew that they were engaged on anything but an ordinary route-march, and the Dublin police, who by then were used to the spectacle of Volunteers marching and drilling, also had no idea that anything unusual was afoot. In any case they would never have expected the Volunteers to have the effrontery to land arms in broad daylight. But that was the Volunteers' plan, and it was perfectly carried out. The *Asgard* duly approached the harbour with Mrs. Childers wearing her red jersey; there was some slight confusion about the signal from the shore, but the yacht was soon at her berth, the arms were unloaded in less than half an hour, and a little later the 1,000 Volunteers were marching back to Dublin with rifles on their shoulders.

By this time news of the landing had been telephoned to Dublin Castle, where William V. Harrel, Assistant Commissioner of the Dublin Metropolitan Police, decided that he must take action. Since his own men were unarmed, he called for military assistance, and was soon on the road to Howth with a few policemen and about 100 men of the King's Own Scottish Borderers. At Clontarf they halted and blocked the roads to Dublin while they awaited the approach of the Volunteers. As the Volunteers arrived Harrel ordered them to give up their rifles, but Figgis began a discussion on the legality of his order and kept the conversation going so long that most of the Volunteers were able to slip quietly and unobtrusively away, taking their rifles with them. At last Harrel ordered the troops to seize the arms, but by then there were few Volunteers left, and only 19 rifles were seized. The others were taken to sympathisers' houses in Dublin or hidden in places where they could be recovered later.

That seemed to be the end of the affair, and police and military returned to Dublin, the 100 Scottish Borderers being joined at Fairview by 60 more. But the Dublin crowds had heard the story of Howth, and as the troops marched along the quays they were greeted with jeers and eventually with stones. By the time that they reached Bachelor's Walk many of the soldiers were injured, and the commanding officer, fearing fatal accidents, ordered a number of his men to halt and be ready to fire if he gave the word. It was never established that he actually gave the order to fire, but some of his men thought that he had, and 21 of them fired, killing two men and a woman and wounding 32 others. The crowds then dispersed.

The Bachelor's Walk incident caused understandable anger in Ireland. The K.O.S.B. became known as the King's Own Scottish Murderers; the three fatalities were magnified into a "massacre"; in a great funeral procession the victims' coffins were followed by a company of Volunteers, marching with arms reversed, and thousands of mourners, while thousands of others lined the streets; memorial services were held in churches all over Ireland on the following Sunday; and "Remember Bachelor's Walk" became an Irish rallying-cry. The shooting was certainly a tragic blunder, but it was not the act of callous brutality which the Irish chose to call it; and when a Royal Commission inquired into the affair in August it was content to put the blame on Harrel, who was censured for having exceeded his powers in calling for military aid. He was therefore dismissed from his post. The moral of his departure was not lost on the R.I.C. and the Dublin Metropolitan Police, who saw, and not for the first time, that a policeman who took resolute action was likely to be disowned by the Government. This growing feeling of insecurity in the Irish police forces was one reason why there was no official interference with the Volunteers' military training.

Bachelor's Walk was soon overshadowed by world events. Nine days after the Howth gun-running Britain was at war with Germany. The men of the K.O.S.B. were loudly cheered in Dublin as they left for the front.

CHAPTER V

Hour of Decision

I

DUBLIN'S CHEERS FOR British soldiers in 1914 were not so illogical as they may seem today. At that time only the separatists looked upon British troops in Ireland as the garrison of a foreign Power. To most Irish people these troops were worthy representatives of an Army which usually attracted large numbers of Irish recruits. It was only natural to cheer soldiers who were going to fight by the side of Irish regiments in the British Army.

It remained, however, for southern Ireland's representatives at Westminster to define her attitude towards the European War. They could hardly delay, for the Ulster Unionist leaders had at once called off their plans for revolt against Home Rule, and a pledge of loyal support had been given to the Government on their behalf by Bonar Law. It was because of this pledge that Sir Edward Grey, the Foreign Secretary, said in the House of Commons on August 4: "The one bright spot in the very dreadful situation is Ireland. The position in Ireland—and this is a thing I should like to be clearly understood abroad—is not a consideration among the things we have to take into account now." (The point of this reference to foreign opinion was that Germany had been following the Irish dispute with close attention, and some of her diplomats felt sure that civil war in Ulster would make it impossible for

England to fight in Europe. They were quickly shown to be wrong.)

Redmond could not allow Grey's remark to pass in silence. He had no time to consult his whole Party, and he made up his own mind about Ireland's attitude. He invited the Government to withdraw all troops from Ireland, as her own Armed Forces would be able to defend her against any threat of invasion. "For that purpose," he said, "the armed Catholics of the South will be only too glad to join arms with the armed Protestant Ulstermen."

This offer was wildly cheered in the Commons by members of all parties, who wrongly interpreted it as a pledge of complete support in the war; but what Redmond had really proposed was that the Irish Volunteers should be given arms by the Government for home defence. This idea made no headway either then or later. For one thing, it was not at all to the liking of Lord Kitchener, the distinguished soldier whom Asquith had appointed Secretary for War. Though actually born in Ireland, Kitchener had been brought up to despise the Irish people, and he had no more sympathy with Ulster than he had with the South. It was about this time that he said brusquely to Carson: "If I had been on a platform with you and Redmond I should have knocked your heads together"; and though Redmond found him superficially friendly, it was soon clear that he had no thought of arming the Volunteers and was interested only in getting more recruits from Ireland for the British Army. "Get me 5,000 men and I will say 'Thank you'," he said to Redmond. "Get me 10,000 and I will take off my hat to you."

First of all, however, the Government had to decide what to do about the Home Rule Act, which became law in September, and it very reasonably considered that such a vast and controversial political change could not be introduced in wartime. The amending Bill proposed in the Lords was therefore dropped; instead another Act was hurried through Parliament postponing the introduction of Home Rule for 12 months or until the end of the war (whichever was the longer period), and the Government also promised a new amending Bill dealing with Ulster before Home Rule came into operation. It was said in Ireland afterwards that Redmond should have bargained with Asquith and offered Irish support in the war only in return for immediate Home Rule; but such bargaining could hardly have been successful, since Asquith would have been unlikely to change his opinion that the beginning of a world war was no time for political experiment in Ireland. Irishmen who claimed that England had cheated Ireland by not giving her the Home Rule authorised by Parliament were overlooking the genuine political difficulties of the situation. There is no evidence that the Government's promise to bring in Home Rule after the war was in any way insincere.

In that first autumn of the European War Redmond was deep in negotiations over Irish recruitment for the British Army. In the opinion of Lloyd George, who was then Chancellor of the Exchequer, the behaviour of the War Office towards southern Ireland amounted to "stupidities which almost look like malignancy"; for although Kitchener allowed the Ulster Volunteers to be enrolled in the Army as an Ulster Division and authorised them to use the Red Hand of Ulster as their divisional emblem, he refused to embody the Irish Volunteers as a separate Division and would not permit the Irish harp to be used as an emblem by southern Irish troops. In the end two southern Irish Divisions—the 10th and the 16th—took part in the war as well as the Ulster Division. The 16th was part of Kitchener's New Army, and it was typical of the War Office attitude that no Roman Catholic commanded a battalion in it and only about half a dozen Catholics were field officers.

2

To Redmond it seemed only right and proper that Ireland should fight at England's side in a war against German tyranny. This was the view of many other fervent Home

Rulers, and it was expounded with particular force by Tom Kettle, a brilliant young barrister who had given up his seat in the House of Commons to become Professor of National Economics in the National University. Kettle was a lively character, and various stories were told of his turning up drunk at important meetings; but neither his intellectual power nor his loyalty to Ireland was ever in doubt. At the outbreak of war he was buying arms in Belgium for the Irish Volunteers, but he hurried home to join the British Army. He did so because he considered that England was as right in the European War as she had been wrong in the Boer War, and that Ireland could not stand aside when Germany was attacking Western civilisation and the rights of small nationalities.

> "In such a conflict [he wrote] to counsel Ireland to stand neutral in judgment is as if one were to counsel a Christian to stand neutral in judgment between Nero and St. Peter. To counsel her to stand neutral in action would have been to abandon all her old valour and decision, and to establish in their places the new cardinal virtues of comfort and cowardice."

But while Kettle and Redmond were urging Irishmen to join the British Army the hour of decision for Ireland had already come. The Supreme Council of the Irish Republican Brotherhood had not forgotten the saying of a famous Irish revolutionary, John Mitchel: "England's difficulty is Ireland's opportunity." On September 5 it summoned a meeting at Sean T. O'Kelly's office in the Gaelic League building in Parnell Square, Dublin. Among the eight or nine people present were Tom Clarke, the veteran Fenian, Arthur Griffith, Padraic Pearse, Sean MacDermott, manager of the I.R.B. journal, *Irish Freedom*, and chief I.R.B. representative in the Volunteers, Eamonn Ceannt, a member of the governing body of the Gaelic League, and O'Kelly himself, who was a Volunteer officer, a Gaelic Leaguer and a member of the I.R.B. Most, but not all, of those who attended the meeting were members of the I.R.B.

The decision to make a protest in arms against British rule in Ireland was taken at this meeting. The date for a rising was not fixed, but it was agreed that it should take place if either the Germans invaded Ireland or England tried to enforce conscription on Ireland, or the war were seen to be coming to an end and there had been no rising hitherto. The rising was to be accompanied by a declaration of war on England, and in virtue of this declaration it was also decided that Ireland should claim to be represented as a belligerent nation at the peace conference after the European War. Ireland's destiny was now determined. All that remained was for the I.R.B. to fix the date and to organise forces for armed revolt.

A split in the Irish Volunteers soon indicated the strength of the forces on which the I.R.B. would be able to call. The Volunteers had risen to 180,000 since they had become formally associated with the Irish Parliamentary Party, but MacNeill and the members of the original provisional committee strongly objected to Redmond's recruiting speeches. In September they issued a manifesto dismissing his nominees from the Volunteers' governing body, and the Volunteers were then asked to decide by vote whether they would support Redmond or remain with their old leaders. It is a significant indication of Irish opinion at that time that only about 12,000 out of the 180,000 chose to follow MacNeill. Though Home Rule was suspended, Ireland as a whole was still ready to trust "the Old Party".

The minority, which included all those whose names were to become famous in 1916, kept the name of the Irish Volunteers; Redmond's followers became known as the National Volunteers, but their numbers gradually dwindled, since they supplied the bulk of the southern Irish recruits for the British Army. At a convention held in the Abbey Theatre on October 25 the Irish Volunteers pledged themselves to resist any attempt to impose conscription on Ireland and asserted their resolve to replace the Dublin Castle administration by an Irish Government. As yet, however, there was no talk among the Irish Volunteers of armed revolt. Only those officers who were deeply involved in the I.R.B. knew what had been decided at the fateful meeting on September 5. MacNeill was not one of them.

At the time of the Volunteers' split the Irish Citizen Army was also entering a new life. Connolly was now Commandant of the I.C.A., and he quickly showed that he would not tolerate the slipshod methods of training which had been followed since the end of the strike. He insisted on punctual parading and keen drilling, and he both lectured and wrote on the tactics of street-fighting. He had a valuable assistant in Michael Mallin, the Chief of Staff, a pale young man with a brown moustache and an attractive smile. Like Connolly, Mallin was a trade-union organiser, but he had served in the British Army and had profited from his experience. Connolly was much impressed by his quiet efficiency, and he told his daughter Nora that he had "discovered a great military man".

The I.C.A. had women as well as men among its members, and there was one woman, in particular, who drew the attention of both police and public whenever the Army marched through the city streets. This was Countess Markievicz, who had run the soup kitchen during the strike and had become so enthusiastic about the Citizen Army that she had produced her own version of its uniform. The men in the I.C.A. who wore uniform (and Connolly himself did not acquire one till much later) had tunics and slacks of dark-green cloth and slouch hats; the Countess wore a dark-green woollen blouse, dark-green breeches, black stockings (or sometimes puttees) and a black velour hat with a large plume. Nora Connolly gaily told her she looked like a field-marshal, but her Dublin critics (of whom she had many) sourly called her "a Rosalind in green tights".

Constance Markievicz was then in her late forties. In spite of her foreign name (which most people skated round by calling her simply "Madame"), she was an Irishwoman, the daughter of Sir Henry Gore-Booth, fifth baronet, of

Lissadell, Sligo. This was the house recalled by Yeats in his poem in memory of Constance and her sister, Eva Gore-Booth, the poetess:

> The light of evening, Lissadell,
> Great windows open to the south,
> Two girls in silk kimonos, both
> Beautiful, one a gazelle . . .

As the typical "wild Irish girl", and a very lovely one at that, Constance Gore-Booth had been a great rider to hounds; but she had soon grown tired of social life in London and Sligo and had decided to take up art, overcoming her parents' objections by saying that if they would not pay for her studies she would make her own living by posing in the nude. The pursuit of art took her first to London and then to Paris, and it was there that she met and married the gay and handsome Casimir Markievicz, a Polish Count, who was himself a skilful amateur artist. They made their home in Dublin, but Constance again grew weary of the social round, and after a brief flirtation with the women's suffrage campaign (during which she drove a four-in-hand through the streets of Manchester to demonstrate women's right to serve in public-house bars) she threw herself whole-heartedly into the Irish-Ireland movement—first as a member of Sinn Fein, then as founder of the Irish Boy Scouts and later as a close colleague of James Connolly in the revolutionary labour movement.

Those who disliked Constance Markievicz had good grounds for calling her an eccentric and an exhibitionist, but her work as organiser of the Fianna Eireann, the Irish Boy Scouts, would alone be enough to ensure her place in Irish history. It was Bulmer Hobson, then a leading member of the I.R.B., who encouraged her to start the Fianna Eireann in 1909, and she trained her young charges with great enthusiasm. The boys of the Fianna were given shooting practice as well as drill, and the revolutionary purpose behind the movement was shown in the oath they took on joining: "I promise to work for the independence of Ireland, never to join England's Armed Forces and to obey my superior officers." The I.R.B. had its eye on the future when it encouraged Constance Markievicz to start the Fianna; for the boys' training was invaluable when the Irish Volunteers were founded, and some of the younger Volunteer officers (such as Liam Mellows, Con Colbert and Sean Heuston) had been closely associated with the Fianna as assistants to the Chief Scout. So the Fianna Eireann fitted into the general revolutionary pattern, while their irrepressible Chief Scout looked happily forward to the day of armed rebellion. The police made careful note of her various activities, and some time in 1914 they raided her house for arms but found nothing. After they had gone Constance pulled a few cartridges out of her pocket and said gleefully: "Won't it be a grand day for Ahland when we put all these through her enemies?"

Such martial ardour was very welcome in the Citizen Army, which went its own way without contact with the Irish Volunteers. At times, indeed, the Citizen Army showed active opposition to the Volunteers—an opposition which Tom Clarke thought to be "largely inspired by a disgruntled fellow named O'Casey". This was Sean O'Casey, then a Dublin labourer; but Constance Markievicz, for one, did not share his hostility to the Volunteers. She was ready to support any movement that would stand up and fight on the "grand day for Ahland".

3

That first winter of the European War found Ireland sharply divided in both action and opinion. In the north-east, Ulster had moved from threatened rebellion to unquestioning loyalty to the British Crown, and the Ulster Volunteer Force had provided a complete Division for the British Army; but in the rest of Ireland recruiting was making only moderate progress, in spite of Redmond's insistence that the way to make Home Rule certain after the war was to join the Army. His efforts were largely offset by the unsympathetic attitude of the War Office, the anti-recruiting campaign conducted openly by Sinn Fein and secretly by the I.R.B., and the purely personal reluctance of some Irishmen to enter a war that was not of their making. ("Enlist? Is ut me enlist? An' a war going on!" was the reported answer of one young Irishman to a girl recruiter who called at his house.) Moreover, while Irishmen in the British Regular Army and the many others who had joined up for the war were fighting with the pluck and endurance for which Irish regiments have always been famous, in Ireland both the Citizen Army and the dissident Volunteers —those who had stayed with MacNeill—were arming and drilling for an eventual trial of strength with the British Government. Irish soldiers of the King coming home to Dublin on leave must have looked with some astonishment at the big banner Connolly displayed on the front of the Transport Workers' Union headquarters at Liberty Hall— "We serve neither King nor Kaiser, but Ireland." It was only one of many signs that a clash of some kind could not be far away.

All over the south and west of Ireland speakers and organisers sent from Dublin were stirring up disaffection towards Britain. For the most part the police seemed content to watch what was going on and send reports to Dublin Castle, but they pounced from time to time on leading Sinn Feiners. So in May, 1915, after Liam Mellows and Sean MacDermott had addressed a meeting at Tuam, in Galway, MacDermott was arrested and sentenced to four months' imprisonment for "a most seditious speech". Another organiser who went to gaol at this time was Ernest Blythe, who had been active in Clare and Kerry and was imprisoned for refusing to obey a deportation order.

But public meetings were not the only outlets for anti-British propaganda. There was also a powerful separatist Press, led by *Sinn Fein* (the paper founded by Griffith it 1905, in succession to his original *United Irishman*), *Irish*

Freedom (the mouthpiece of the I.R.B., for whom it was edited by Bulmer Hobson and managed by Sean MacDermott), the *Irish Worker* (Connolly's journal for the Labour movement and the Citizen Army) and *The Irish Volunteer* (the organ of MacNeill's followers, who had kept the old name of their movement). Their constant theme was that Ireland had no quarrel with Germany and should keep out of the war. Three of the four were suppressed before Christmas, 1914.

Yet they still went on in different forms. After the suppression of the *Irish Worker* Connolly brought out a new paper, the *Workers' Republic*, which was printed in Liberty Hall to avoid the risk of raids on printing offices; and it was in this journal that Connolly wrote his articles on street-fighting, based on a careful study of what had happened in various European revolutions. Griffith, too, could not be kept quiet. When *Sinn Fein* was banned he produced *Scissors and Paste*, consisting of nothing but extracts from English, Irish, American and Empire newspapers, which had already passed the Dublin Castle censors, and passages from Irish books, all ingeniously arranged as Sinn Fein propaganda. It was a clever idea, but the censors stopped it after a month. The I.R.B. then found a Belfast printer who was not afraid of raids on his office, and with his help Griffith brought out yet another paper, *Nationality*, a penny weekly which ran until the Easter Rising.

Apart from the Press there was also a steady output of pamphlets giving the views both of the Sinn Fein Party and of the I.R.B. Some of the most famous were written by Pearse.

The I.R.B. still held its hand, waiting for the appropriate time to stage a rising; and in May, 1915, southern Ireland was given further cause for complaint against Britain by the reconstruction of the Government. In that month Asquith formed a coalition Ministry to carry on the war more vigorously and took into it a number of Unionists who had been prominent in organising Ulster's resistance to Home

Rule. Bonar Law became Secretary for the Colonies, Carson Attorney-General and F. E. Smith Solicitor-General. Redmond was also invited to join the Government, but he refused on the grounds that the Nationalists could never accept posts in any British Ministry. With Carson and "Galloper" Smith in the Government, and no Nationalists to counterbalance them, many Irishmen felt that the prospect of Home Rule after the war had become more remote, but in fact Asquith's choice of men for the coalition had nothing to do with the Home Rule question. He could hardly have left able men out of the Government simply because they disagreed with him on a subject which was being held in abeyance until the end of the war.

For the Irish separatists the great event of 1915 was the funeral of O'Donovan Rossa, an old Fenian, whose body had been brought back from America, where he died, for burial in Ireland. After lying in state for four days in the City Hall, Dublin, where it was guarded by armed men of the Irish Volunteers and the Irish Citizen Army, the coffin was taken in procession to Glasnevin cemetery on August 1. Special trains had brought mourners from all over the country, parties had come from England and Scotland, a thousand members of the Cumann na mBan (the Irish women's organisation) followed the hearse, and units of the Citizen Army and of the Irish Volunteers—some in green uniforms, some in civilian clothes except for Volunteers' caps and bandoliers, and some wearing ordinary clothes with green ties—marched in the procession, which took an hour and a half to pass any one point.

Among the mourners were the chief officers of the Irish Volunteers, all wearing full military dress except Pearse, whose plain commandant's uniform was unadorned with any badge of rank. But it was Pearse who delivered in his deep resonant voice the panegyric at Rossa's graveside which will always remain a classic statement of Ireland's protest against British rule.

He was speaking, he said, "on behalf of a new generation

that has been re-baptised in the Fenian faith and that has accepted responsibility for carrying out the Fenian programme". He acclaimed Rossa for having, "almost alone in his day, visioned Ireland as we of today would surely have her: not free merely, but Gaelic as well, not Gaelic merely, but free as well". The seeds sown by young men in earlier days were now coming, he declared, to their miraculous ripening.

> "Rulers and Defenders of Realms had need to be wary if they would guard against such processes. Life springs from death, and from the graves of patriot men and women spring living nations. The defenders of this realm have worked well in secret and in the open. They think that they have pacified Ireland. They think that they have purchased half of us and intimidated the other half. They think that they have foreseen everything, provided against everything; but the fools, the fools, the fools!—they have left us our Fenian dead, and while Ireland holds these graves Ireland unfree shall never be at peace."

After Pearse's speech the Volunteers fired a volley over Rossa's grave, the mourners dispersed and most of the Volunteer officers drove back to the city. But Pearse was not with them. He had inspired his hearers with new faith in the fight for Irish freedom. His message given, he walked slowly back to St. Enda's, head down and shoulders hunched, alone.

CHAPTER VI

Knight Errant

I

WHILE IRELAND WAS gradually moving towards the crisis of 1916 Sir Roger Casement, who had been the first Treasurer of the Irish Volunteers and had helped to draw up the plans for the Howth gun-running, had begun the adventures which were to lead to his death on the scaffold. By any standard Casement was a remarkable man. He was an Ulsterman by origin, and he had been in the British consular service until he took his Government pension and returned to his own country in 1913. As a consul he had exposed the iniquities of rubber planters in the Belgian Congo and the Putumayo area of Peru, and he had done so with a personal courage and a reformist zeal that had won him wide respect and a knighthood from King George V.

Casement was 48 when he came back to Ireland—a tall, handsome, swarthy, bearded man looking more like a Spanish adventurer than a retired British Civil Servant. In spite of his Ulster origin and his Protestant religion ("All the Casements," it was said, "were black Protestants"), he had become a keen separatist during an Irish holiday in 1905–6, though his interest in Sinn Fein had at first been literary and academic. It was not until 1912, shortly before he left the British Government's service, that he became actively engaged in separatist propaganda as a contributor first to the *Irish Review*, successively edited by Padraic Colum and by Tom MacDonagh and Joseph Plunkett, and later to *Irish Freedom*. The main theme of his writings was that a European war was clearly coming and that Ireland must seize the opportunity to free herself from England.

These articles were written under a pseudonym, and their author was little known in Ireland in 1913. He was soon in the thick of the Volunteer movement, though an incident at Cork in December of that year showed that he was curiously ignorant of the feelings of his fellow-countrymen. He and Eoin MacNeill went to Cork to start a branch of the Volunteers there, and at a public meeting they declared that all Ireland should feel grateful to Carson for having established the principle that Irishmen should carry arms. This praise of Carson was too much for Cork, and particularly for the "Mollies"—the Ancient Order of Hibernians—who had attended the meeting in force because they were deeply suspicious of the Volunteer movement. There was an immediate uproar, indignant patriots climbed on to thc platform and the meeting ended as a free fight, in which MacNeill and Casement were lucky to escape injury.

Casement was not deterred by this unhappy experience. He continued his work for the Volunteers, and in the summer of 1914 he decided to go to America to try to raise funds for arming them. It was there that he became involved in the plans to gain German support for a rising in Ireland.

The Irish-Americans were following Irish developments with close interest. Connolly, who had got to know them well during his years in America, used to say that the snakes which were driven out of Ireland by St. Patrick had crossed the Atlantic and become Irish-Americans, but that was an unfair criticism of men who, in spite of their frequent wrangles and jockeyings for power, were genuinely concerned about the fate of their old country. A sharp cleavage in their ranks was evident at the time when Casement arrived in New York. The members of the United Irish League of America, the transatlantic branch of a world-wide organisation founded in 1900, were still supporting

Redmond and the Parliamentary Party; but the delay over Home Rule was undermining the League's influence and increasing the membership of the Clan na Gael, the separatist society linked with the I.R.B. and led by John Devoy and Judge Cohalan, of the U.S. Supreme Court.

The Clan na Gael had adopted the Sinn Fein policy in 1906, when Devoy saw no hope of Ireland's ever being able to overcome England on the battlefield, but its leaders had never completely lost faith in the I.R.B. policy of physical force and armed rebellion. The outbreak of the European War, which occurred a few days after Casement's arrival, gave them the idea of bringing in Germany to help Ireland to win her freedom. Devoy at once made contact with Count Bernstorff, the German Ambassador in Washington, and Bernstorff was sufficiently attracted by the suggestion of intervention in Ireland to authorise Devoy to draw on German secret-service funds for Irish revolutionary purposes—the apparent origin of the statement, stoutly maintained and as stoutly denied, that the Easter Rising was financed by German gold. Since Devoy could draw funds from Germany and was also sending money to the Irish revolutionaries, it could be argued that German money was indirectly behind the Rising, but there seems to be nothing to indicate that such money played any substantial part in the preparations for rebellion.

Casement had come to America with high hopes of success in raising funds for the Volunteers. Before leaving Ireland he had written to a friend: "The Irish in America will not desert us in this crisis. I believe I can get you help from them the English little dream of today." But the coming of war changed his plans. He saw Devoy, he saw Bernstorff, and he made up his mind to go to Germany instead of staying in America. Before leaving New York he wrote an "open letter to Irishmen", which was published in the American Press and later in the *Irish Independent*. In this he declared that "our duty as Irishmen is to give our lives for Ireland" and that "no Irishman fit to bear arms in the cause of his country's freedom can join the Allied millions now attacking Germany in a war that at best concerns Ireland not at all".

The publication of such a letter, signed with his own name, by a man who was still using the title of knighthood conferred on him by King George V was a clear indication that Casement had burnt his boats. He could never go back as a free man to the country he had so openly spurned; there could be no more tea-parties in London with Mrs. Green or Miss Spring-Rice or Erskine Childers (least of all, perhaps, with Childers, who had responded at once to the British call to arms and was doing reconnaissance work at sea for the Admiralty before joining the Royal Flying Corps as observer and intelligence officer). Casement's devotion to Ireland had thrown him into Germany's arms for the rest of his life. With Devoy's encouragement he left for Berlin, there to begin his futile attempt to gain German support for Ireland's fight for independence.

2

Casement left New York in October, 1914. He sailed in a Norwegian ship and took with him as friend and bodyguard a tough young Norwegian sailor called Adler Christensen whom he had met on Broadway on his first night in America. As a simple disguise Casement had shaved off his beard, and he was lucky enough to escape notice when the ship was intercepted and boarded by a British naval vessel. He landed safely in Norway, where the British Minister, who soon discovered his identity, made a rather bungling attempt to have him kidnapped or otherwise put out of the way; and he arrived in Berlin in November. He stayed in Germany until early in April, 1916. The sum total of his 17 months' visit was an unconvincing promise by the German Government to give Ireland freedom after the war, the enrolment of a handful of Irish prisoners of war in a so-called Irish Brigade and an arrangement (for which he was only partly responsible) for a small consignment of almost obsolete weapons to be sent to Ireland. He had virtually no influence either on the course of the European War or on the preparations for the Easter Rising.

The high hopes with which Casement had left America were soon dissipated in long months of frustration, during which he was glad to find solace from time to time in the company of Count Blucher and his beautiful English wife. By the end of the year he persuaded the German Government to give him a signed agreement providing for the formation of an Irish Brigade (which would fight only for Ireland, not for Germany) from Irish prisoners of war and pledging German support and goodwill if the Irish people succeeded in setting up an independent Government. But neither the Germans nor the Irish regarded him as a very important envoy. The Germans preferred to negotiate on Irish matters with Devoy in New York—a practice greatly appreciated by the British Admiralty, which was able to tap and decode all transatlantic messages; and the I.R.B. leaders in Dublin were so dubious about Casement's abilities that they sent Joseph Plunkett, the editor of the *Irish Review*, who was also a keen Volunteer and a member of the I.R.B.'s military committee, to report on his progress and negotiate directly with the German Government. Plunkett reached Berlin in the spring of 1915. He saw Casement and after some delay had an interview with Bethmann-Hollweg, the German Chancellor, who agreed to supply arms and ammunition for an Irish rising, but not the artillery and officers for which the I.R.B. had also asked.

In the meantime Casement had begun his vain attempt to form an Irish Brigade from Irish prisoners of war in Germany. Only a dreamer could have imagined that Irishmen who had voluntarily joined the British Army and had fought in France at the side of Englishmen, Scotsmen and Welshmen would accept freedom at the price of deserting their comrades in arms; but the German Government, hoping that some good might come for Germany out of Casement's activities, collected all the Irish prisoners in one camp at Limburg and allowed Casement to visit them. The prisoners were not unnaturally surprised by the arrival of a tall Irish civilian, wearing a long coat and a soft hat and carrying an umbrella and a parcel of newspapers, who told them that they had all been misled about the war and that really Germany was fighting in self-defence against the wicked aggression of England, France and Russia. He gave them copies of the *Gaelic American* to read and asked them to think over what he said; and on his next visit he openly urged them to leave the British Army and join an Irish Brigade to fight against England. Casement did not know his men. Boos and hisses greeted his speech, a Munster Fusilier seized his umbrella and aimed a blow at him, and Casement went gloomily back to his hotel to brood over his failure. In the following months he returned to the camp again and again, but in the end only about 50 prisoners joined the Irish Brigade. It was not much return for his labours.

Early in 1916 Casement had a nervous breakdown and spent some weeks in a Munich sanatorium. By the time he was well again the German General Staff had been told in a cable from New York that an Irish rising was planned for the Easter week-end and that the I.R.B. was asking for German arms to be landed at Fenit, in Tralee Bay, between Good Friday and Easter Sunday. Another I.R.B. agent, Robert Monteith, was now conducting the negotiations in Germany, and Casement was not informed of them until the plans were well in hand. He was shocked to realise that the Germans were sending only ammunition and 20,000 old Russian rifles, since he believed that the rising could not be successful without German artillery and machine-guns and at least a small expeditionary force.

Throughout March he had a series of tempestuous interviews with the German Admiralty and Foreign Office. At the end of them he felt that all he could do was to try to call off the Easter Rising. But he could find no one to take a message to Dublin, and though it had been arranged that he was to go to Ireland himself, he felt there was little hope of his arriving in time to stop the revolt. The final plans were that the arms should be sent in the *Aud*, a 1,200-ton vessel which would carry a Norwegian flag, and that Casement himself, together with Monteith and Daniel Bailey, one of the recruits to the Irish Brigade, should go in a submarine which would put them ashore by dinghy in Tralee Bay. In preparation for his journey Casement again shaved off his beard.

The Germans had arranged with Devoy to send him the code message "Oats" to indicate that the submarine had sailed with Casement aboard, with the alternative "Hay" if there had been any hitch. On April 12 the message "Oats" was duly sent across the Atlantic and gratefully intercepted by the British Admiralty. Casement had sailed for Ireland.

CHAPTER VII

"Do You want Us to be Wise?"

I

THE WRITINGS OF Padraic Pearse in the year before the Easter Rising showed clearly enough that an insurrection was coming. His pamphlets called on the youth of Ireland to fight for their country's freedom; in his plays and poems he foresaw the suffering and sacrifices of the Rising itself. In one play, *The Singer*, which was written in the late autumn of 1915, though it was not acted till after his death, he described how the young MacDara comes home after years of wandering to lead his people against the Gall (the foreigner), and finds that his resolve to fight is challenged by less sanguine spirits. "We thought it a foolish thing for fourscore to go into battle against four thousand, or maybe forty thousand," says Diarmaid in the play. And MacDara proudly replies: "And so it is a foolish thing. Do you want us to be wise?" In another passage Pearse foretold the first reactions of Ireland to the bloodshed of Easter Week: "I seemed," says MacDara, "to see myself brought to die before a great crowd that stood cold and silent; and there were some that cursed me in their hearts for having brought death into their houses. Sad dead faces seemed to reproach me. Oh, the wise, sad faces of the dead—and the keening of women rang in my ears." Less symbolically Pearse envisaged the Rising in his little prayer for Christmas, 1915:

O King that was born
To set bondsmen free,
In the coming battle
Help the Gael!

And about the same time his own spirit of self-dedication was beautifully expressed in his "Renunciation", which ended:

I have turned my face
To this road before me,
To the deed that I see
And the death I shall die.

Others, too, were using the printed word to call Ireland to arms. Connolly was preparing the Citizen Army for battle in the *Workers' Republic*, and Griffith, was gradually abandoning the old non-violent policies of Sinn Fein. The Fenians, said a leading article in his new paper, *Nationality* (actually written by Cathal O'Shannon, of the Irish Labour Party), "can only be commemorated by men of another fighting and revolutionary generation. That generation we have with us today. For we have the material, the men and stuff of war, the faith and purpose and cause for revolution".

All that winter of 1915–16 great events were stirring beneath the surface of a country where the majority of the people were quite content to stand at England's side in the European War, and where, moreover, the farming community was enjoying unprecedented prosperity through having a ready and profitable market for all the food and cattle they could send across the Irish Sea. (A *Punch* joke of the period depicted one Irishman telling another that the war was coming to an end, to be answered with an exasperated: "Och, it's always you that has the bad news.") But one significant change in Irish life was that emigration to America had stopped after a rowdy scene at Liverpool docks. English crowds there had jeered at a party of Galway emigrants and called them shirkers from military service, and the crew of the emigrant ship had eventually refused to take them on board.

The stoppage of emigration left Ireland with far more young men of military age than she had had for many years. This had a twofold effect on the Irish situation. It increased the ranks of potential fighters against British rule, and Lord French, indeed, was to say as Viceroy in 1920 that all the Irish disorders were the result of "having 100,000 surplus young men". At the same time it made the Irish even more anxious about the possible introduction of conscription for the British Army. The threat of conscription was soon to be one of the major factors working against all hope of a settlement in Ireland.

In the meantime voluntary recruiting for the British Army and Navy continued, in spite of Sinn Fein efforts to break up recruiting meetings, and by January, 1916, all Ireland had sent about 100,000 more men (including 30,000 from the Ulster Volunteer Force) to join the many Irishmen already serving in the Regular Army. The number of recruitments varied greatly according to the strength of Sinn Fein influence in each locality. For example, in two west Irish towns which were only 40 miles apart—Ballina and Westport—the British recruiting officers found a splendid response in the former and no recruits at all in the latter. The reason was that Westport was dominated by Major John MacBride, who had led the Irish Brigade on the Boer side in the South African War and had married Maud Gonne (who later secured a judicial separation). Such varying results did not satisfy the British Government, and the Unionists were constantly urging that compulsory service should be introduced in Ireland.

While the British recruiting officers were hopefully beating their drums and holding their torchlight processions the Supreme Council of the I.R.B. was perfecting its plans for revolt. There was now, in effect, a dual control of the Irish Volunteers. The nominal heads were MacNeill, Chief of Staff, Hobson, Secretary, and Pearse, Director of Organisation; but through Pearse the real control was being exercised by a secret military council appointed by the I.R.B. The council, which was first called the military committee, consisted of Pearse, Joseph Plunkett, Eamonn Ceannt, Sean MacDermott, Tom MacDonagh and Tom Clarke, and the Supreme Council had already chosen Pearse to be Commander-in-Chief in the coming insurrection. MacNeill knew nothing of these plans.

By this time the Sinn Fein movement and the Irish Volunteers had become linked in the public mind, and members of both organisations were loosely described as "Sinn Feiners". They were all regarded with suspicion by the R.I.C., and between November, 1914, and April, 1916, nearly 500 prosecutions were conducted under the wartime Defence of the Realm Act for seditious speeches or the possession of arms and explosives. Yet the Dublin police took no action (beyond noting the names of the leaders) when the Volunteers or the Citizen Army or the girls of the Cumann na mBan marched in uniform through the streets of the city, and even a Volunteer exercise in the neighbourhood of Dublin Castle itself was carried out without interference. Birrell held his hand because he thought that any attempt to suppress the Volunteers would "promote disloyalty to a prodigious extent". The police, remembering Harrel's fate after the Howth gun-running, were unwilling to act without orders from the Castle.

As the months went by Connolly, whose Citizen Army still had no connexion either with the Volunteers or with the I.R.B., began a separate campaign for an armed rising. His attitude was very different from the fatalism which was already apparent in Pearse's writings. When Pearse declared that the last 16 months had been the most glorious in the history of Europe, for "the old heart of the earth needed to be warmed with the red wine of the battlefields", Connolly angrily retorted in the *Workers' Republic*: "No, we do not think that the old heart of the earth needs to be warmed with the red wine of millions of lives. We think anyone who does is a blithering idiot." Connolly really thought that a rising could be an immediate success, and not merely a first sacrificial step towards the freeing of Ireland. It was with this thought in his mind that he wrote a leader in his paper in January, 1916, provocatively asking, "Are we not waiting too long?"

This open call to arms was not at all to the liking of the I.R.B. In that very month the Supreme Council had fixed Easter Sunday, April 23, as the date for the rising, and it feared that all its plans would be upset if Connolly recklessly marched out with his miniature army, numbering only about 200 men and a few women, while the Volunteers were still waiting for the appointed day. In one way or another Connolly had to be stopped, and on January 19 he was summoned to a meeting with Pearse, Plunkett and MacDonagh, who was Commandant of the Dublin Brigade of the Volunteers. It has often been said that the I.R.B. military council "kidnapped" Connolly, but it now seems certain that he went voluntarily, though his two days' absence from home made his Citizen Army colleagues fear that he had been forcibly abducted, and Mallin and Constance Markievicz made ready to march on Dublin Castle with their 200 men if he were not returned to them. But Connolly came back in time to prevent this reckless move. He had been told of the I.R.B.'s plans and co-opted as a member of the military council. From then onwards he had no thought of acting independently of the Volunteers. The two armed forces of the revolutionaries were thus coordinated for the Easter Rising.

2

The coming of spring brought greater activity by both the Volunteers and the Citizen Army. Hitherto their city manoeuvres had been carried out at night, but on St. Patrick's Day some 2,000 men of the Volunteers' Dublin battalions, mostly armed with rifles and bayonets, paraded on College Green, and held up trams and other traffic while they drilled and marched past Eoin MacNeill. The police watched, but again took no action.

Three weeks later, on Sunday, April 9, the Volunteers marched through the city again, this time in protest against the deportation to England of Liam Mellows and Ernest Blythe; and on Palm Sunday the Citizen Army paraded outside Liberty Hall, where one of the Army girls—Mollie O'Reilly—was seen climbing to the parapet to fasten the Irish flag of green with a gold harp to the flagstaff. It was only a symbolic gesture, but it was greeted with wild applause by the crowd which had gathered to watch the ceremony.

In Holy Week the I.R.B. military council made its final preparations for the Rising. Pearse, as the Volunteers' Director of Organisation, had already arranged for mobilisation by publishing an apparently innocuous order in the *Irish Volunteer* on April 8. It simply said:

> "Following the lines of last year, every unit of the Irish Volunteers will hold manoeuvres during the Easter holidays. The object of the manoeuvres is to test mobilisation with equipment. Each brigade, battalion or company commander, as the case may be, will, on or before May 1 next, send to the Director of Organisation a detailed report of the manoeuvres carried out by his unit."

The disarming request for reports by May 1 was an ingenious touch in an order which, if fully carried out, would have put 10,000 Volunteers in the field for Easter Week.

The council was still expecting the cargo of arms from Germany to arrive in Fenit Bay before the week-end, but its immediate task was to get the Volunteers in the mood for action without revealing its secret plans. It was Plunkett who found the solution for this problem. He had had private information that Dublin Castle was considering the arrest of the leading Sinn Feiners. With the help of Rory O'Connor, who was an engineer employed by Dublin Corporation and a member of the I.R.B., he prepared a document which was ostensibly a Dublin Castle order for such arrests and for raids on the premises of the Volunteers, the Citizen Army, Sinn Fein, the Gaelic League, *Nationality*, and other buildings and private houses. The document was probably an accurate forecast of a projected British round-up, though Major-General L. B. Friend, then commander of the British troops in Ireland, said afterwards that the list of places to be raided included several that the military could never have thought of; but in the form presented by Plunkett it was certainly a forgery.

The bogus order was shown to the full Volunteers' Executive on the Monday of Holy Week and made an immediate impression. Copies were printed and widely distributed; the document was read at a meeting of Dublin Corporation on Wednesday, when the councillors were duly indignant at Dublin Castle's iniquity; and MacNeill, who may also have believed that the document was genuine, issued an order to the Volunteers warning them to be ready to resist suppression. Plunkett's device for getting the Volunteers "on their toes" was thus a complete success.

At a secret meeting the I.R.B. named the members of a provisional revolutionary Government, and appointed Pearse to be President of the Irish Republic; and it seemed that nothing remained but to wait for the arrival of the German cargo of arms and the mobilisation of 10,000 Volunteers and the Citizen Army for the Easter week-end. But the 10,000 Volunteers were not, after all, to be mobilised. MacNeill, who still regarded them as solely a defensive body, and Bulmer Hobson, his closest colleague, had been kept in the dark about the military council's plans; but a conversation overheard by Hobson at a Volunteers' Executive meeting made him suspect that a rising was being prepared. He at once told MacNeill what he had heard, and between them they drafted the first of the countermanding orders which were to change the course of the revolution. This order put Commandant J. J. O'Connell in command in Cork and told the Munster Volunteers that "all orders issued by Commandant Pearse, or by any other person heretofore, are hereby cancelled or recalled".

On the next day—the Thursday of Holy Week—MacNeill and Hobson went out to St. Enda's to ask Pearse bluntly whether a rising was being planned. When Pearse told them the truth MacNeill said he would do everything in his power to stop it, short of informing the British Government; and accordingly on Good Friday morning he issued a further order cancelling Pearse's instructions for the Dublin area and putting Hobson in command there.

In spite of the growing confusion, the I.R.B. military council was still determined to call out the Volunteers at the week-end. Later on Good Friday morning Pearse, MacDonagh and MacDermott went to see MacNeill and told him for the first time that a cargo of German arms was expected at any moment. The news took MacNeill by surprise: he now realised both how far the plans had gone and how much better the chance of success would be when the German arms were distributed among the Volunteers. He felt, therefore, that he must let Pearse and his friends go ahead, and he told them that he would resign his post as Chief of Staff and allow them to take over command. The military council was thus left, as it seemed, in complete control of the situation. MacDermott sent messengers to various parts of the country to assure the local leaders that the Rising was to proceed according to plan; and to be on the safe side in Dublin the council arrested Hobson and kept him in custody over the week-end.

Elsewhere in Ireland, however, events were happening on that Good Friday which were to make MacNeill again change his mind about the Rising. Early that morning Casement, Monteith and Bailey were put ashore in a dinghy from the German submarine which had brought them to Ireland, and found themselves at Banna Strand in county Galway. Casement had apparently given up his idea of trying to stop the Rising, for during the voyage he had written a letter to be taken back to the German General Staff, asking them to send a further supply of arms; but in any case he could have done nothing, for in a few hours he was captured by the R.I.C., who soon guessed that their clean-shaven prisoner was Sir Roger Casement. It seems curious that the local Volunteers did not try to rescue Casement while he was locked up for the night in the R.I.C. barracks in Tralee; but their leader, Austin Stack, was arrested on the same day, and since Pearse had given them strict orders that no shot should be fired before the Rising began in Dublin, they may have felt that they dared not take the risk of making an armed attempt at rescue. Casement was kept at Tralee until the next day and then taken to London; Bailey was also caught by the police, but Monteith escaped and later went to America.

The fate of the *Aud* and her cargo of obsolete rifles was also settled on Good Friday. There had been a misunderstanding about the day fixed for her arrival off Ireland, and no Volunteers were waiting for her when she reached Tralee Bay on the Thursday evening. On the next day, while she still awaited a signal from shore, she was noticed by British warships, who ordered her into Queenstown harbour, where the German captain disposed of his contraband cargo by blowing up his ship. So the efforts of Devoy, Plunkett and Casement had all been in vain. There were no foreign arms to distribute to Volunteers in the south and west.

When the news of Casement's capture and the sinking of the *Aud* reached Dublin on Saturday, MacNeill came back to his earlier view that the Rising could not succeed and must therefore be stopped. He decided to act as though he had not resigned his position of Chief of Staff, and soon another batch of messengers was speeding all over the country bearing MacNeill's instructions to local Volunteer leaders that "all orders for special action are hereby cancelled and on no account will action be taken". To ensure that there would be no disturbances in Dublin he sent a notice to the *Sunday Independent*, stating emphatically:

> "Owing to the very critical position all orders given to Irish Volunteers for tomorrow, Easter Sunday, are hereby rescinded, and no parades, marches or other movements of Irish Volunteers will take place. Each individual Volunteer will obey this order strictly in every particular."

To make doubly sure he ordered MacDonagh, as Commandant of the Dublin Brigade, to inform the men in his command of the cancellation, and a Brigade order to this effect was sent out over the signatures of MacDonagh and his adjutant, Eamon de Valera.

By Easter Sunday, therefore, MacNeill had performed what he considered to be his duty in the best interests of Ireland: he had done everything he could to stop the Rising short of informing the British Government. Once again the military council had to reconsider its position, and at a meeting at Liberty Hall on the Sunday morning it decided to go ahead with its plans as best it could, on the grounds that an armed rising was vitally necessary for Ireland's sake. To avert the risk of further intervention by MacNeill, the council took no open action until Easter Monday morning, though it knew that delay would make it virtually impossible to assemble the full force of Volunteers; but belated messages saying "We start at noon today" were sent to provincial centres.

Early on Monday morning MacDonagh issued yet another Dublin Brigade order, stating: "The four city battalions will parade for inspection and route march at 10 a.m. today. Commandants will arrange centres. Full arms and equipment and one day's rations." Copies were hastily sent round the city and suburbs to Volunteer officers, who were told to get in touch with their men as quickly as possible; but only about 1,000 insurgents were mobilised instead of the 2,000 needed to carry out the full Dublin plans. Connolly had a splendid response from the Citizen Army: the 219 members—192 men and 27 women—who responded to his mobilisation order were nearly the Army's full strength. MacNeill was not informed of the final order, and though the council had promised to keep Griffith in touch with its movements, he, too, was sent no word of what was being done. As it happened, his wife had gone to Cork for a holiday on Easter Sunday, and he was staying quietly at home, looking after his two young children, while other men were preparing to put his Sinn Fein doctrines into desperate action.

Dublin Castle had no suspicion of what was going on. Other Irish rebellions had been wrecked in advance by spies and informers, but before the Easter Rising no Irishman gave or sold secret information to the British authorities. The messages intercepted by the Admiralty had suggested that trouble might be expected at Easter, but MacNeill's order in the *Sunday Independent* seemed to indicate that all plans had been called off, and there appeared to be no need to recall either the Chief Secretary or General Friend, who were both spending Easter in England. The public, too, had no suspicion of anything unusual as they strolled through the sunny streets in holiday mood and watched car-loads of British officers setting off for the Fairyhouse races. But in Liberty Hall that morning seven men sat round a table waiting for the hour of mobilisation—Pearse, Commandant-in-Chief of the Republican Army, who saw the Rising as a blood sacrifice that had to be made so that Ireland might be reborn; Connolly, who had been appointed Commandant-General for the Dublin district and still retained his old faith that the Rising would be successful; Joseph Plunkett, Director of Military Operations, who had left his sick-bed in a nursing home, where he was a tuberculosis patient, to be with his comrades on this great day; MacDonagh, Commandant of the Dublin Brigade; Eamonn Ceannt, commander of the 4th Battalion of that Brigade; and two men who held no military authority but without whose brains and inspiration the Rising could hardly have taken place—Tom Clarke, the old Fenian, and Sean MacDermott.

At this meeting the Volunteer officers were in their familiar green uniforms, Connolly in the darker green of the Citizen Army. They had come to the point of no return. When they rose from the table to go to their posts they were beginning the long struggle that was to end English rule in the 26 counties of the south and west.

CHAPTER VIII

Easter Monday

I

AT ELEVEN O'CLOCK on that Easter Monday morning of 1916 Constable James O'Brien, of the Dublin Metropolitan Police, was on duty at Dublin Castle, directing traffic at the Cork Hill entrance to Upper Castle Yard. Like all the D.M.P., he was unarmed. A party of about 20 Volunteers approached the Castle, and when O'Brien refused to let them enter they shot him dead. This was the first shot fired in the Easter Rising.

The only British troops in the Castle at that moment were some half-dozen men of a corporal's guard, armed with blank ammunition; and the small party of Volunteers could have captured the whole place, even before Pearse and Connolly had left Liberty Hall. But when the sound of the shot brought out the guard they imagined there must be many other troops behind them, and they hastily withdrew to neighbouring newspaper offices and to the City Hall, where they posted snipers to cover the Castle entrance.

Because of the conflicting orders of the week-end, none of the Volunteer units had been mobilised at full strength, and the Castle raiding party was much smaller than had been intended in the original plan for the Rising. So its proposed attack on the Castle had been abandoned, and it had been given the minor objective of trying to prevent troops from leaving the precincts. The possibility of the

Castle being virtually unguarded had presumably never occurred to the insurgent leaders.

The Volunteers' battle plan, which was largely the work of Joseph Plunkett, was to set up a defence ring round the centre of the city and hold it against all attacks while, as they hoped, their comrades rose in other parts of the country and set the whole of Ireland ablaze. It was Connolly's theory that they would have nothing to face except rifle and machine-gun fire, for he had the strange idea that the English would not shell public buildings or valuable private property, even if occupied by insurgent forces. The choice of headquarters had been between the Bank of Ireland on College Green and the G.P.O. in O'Connell Street: Connolly had favoured the Bank, but had been overruled, though the G.P.O., hemmed in as it was and is by other buildings, was quite unsuitable for prolonged defence. In the end the insurgents did not even try to occupy the Bank, and their lack of a strong point on College Green left a wide and important area exposed to fire from the soldiers and Officers' Training Corps cadets in Trinity College.

Since no Volunteers could be spared for an additional outer ring of defences, little could be done to check the transport of British reinforcements to Dublin, and the weakness of the battle plan was that it could be only a matter of a day or two before the Volunteers were heavily outnumbered. Even on Monday there were about 2,000 British troops in the various Dublin barracks, and against these there were only the 1,000 Volunteers and members of the Citizen Army who were effectively mobilised. In the next day or two the Volunteers' strength grew substantially, as units were reinforced by men who had been on holiday or had held back because of the confusion of orders. According to the Roll of Honour compiled in 1936, the total of all insurgent forces in Dublin amounted to 1,528; allowing for possible omissions, there were perhaps 1,600 Volunteers and men and women of the Citizen Army in action during the week, while on the other side the British

Army brought in thousands of men as reinforcements to its original 2,000 troops.

The G.P.O. was the central point of the Rising, but the Bank Holiday crowds in O'Connell Street were only mildly interested when a column of about 150 Volunteers, commanded by James Connolly, came round the corner from Lower Abbey Street. A British officer who was going into the G.P.O. to buy stamps saw them coming, and said to a friend: "Just look at that awful crowd; they must be on a route march." The Dubliners thought the same, but they were soon to learn differently. When the column reached the Imperial Hotel, just opposite the G.P.O., Connolly gave the order, "Left wheel—the G.P.O.—charge," and in a few moments a large party of Volunteers had rushed through the main doors while others hurried round to Henry Street to secure the side entrance.

There was no difficulty in occupying the G.P.O. The single unarmed policeman and the clerks could only put up their hands when confronted with the Volunteers' revolvers. Staff and public were turned out of the building; windows were shattered, and mail bags and furniture put in the window-frames as barricades; and a large banner bearing the words, "The Irish Republic", was put up outside. A little later the Republican tricolour of green, orange and white was hoisted on the flagstaff. "O Lord save us," cried an old woman as she hastened away to safety, "it's the Citizen Army, and they've taken the Post Office!"

But onlookers quickly learnt that the occupation of the G.P.O. was not a mere escapade of the Citizen Army. As Commandant-General of the Irish Republican Army, Padraic Pearse stepped out into the portico and read in his deep voice a proclamation which had been drawn up earlier in the week, though to ensure secrecy it had not been printed until Easter Sunday. All the members of the military council had shared in its preparation, but the style leaves little doubt that Pearse himself was mainly responsible for the phrasing.

This was the proclamation:

POBLACHT NA H EIREANN

The Provisional Government of the Irish Republic to the People of Ireland

IRISHMEN AND IRISHWOMEN: In the name of God and of the dead generations from which she receives her old traditions of nationhood, Ireland, through us, summons her children to her flag and strikes for her freedom.

Having organised and trained her manhood through her secret revolutionary organisation, the Irish Republican Brotherhood, and through her open military organisations, the Irish Volunteers and the Irish Citizen Army, having patiently perfected her discipline, having waited for the right moment to reveal itself, she now seizes that moment, and supported by her exiled children in America and by gallant Allies in Europe, but relying in the first on her own strength, she strikes in full confidence of victory.

We declare the right of the people of Ireland to the ownership of Ireland, and to the unfettered control of Irish destinies, to be sovereign and indefeasible. The long usurpation of that right by a foreign people and Government has not extinguished the right, nor can it ever be extinguished except by the destruction of the Irish people. In every generation the Irish people have asserted their right to national freedom and sovereignty; six times during the last 300 years they have asserted it in arms. Standing on that fundamental right and again asserting it in arms in the face of the world, we hereby proclaim the Irish Republic as a Sovereign Independent State, and we pledge our lives and the lives of our comrades-in-arms to the cause of its freedom, of its welfare, and of its exaltation among the nations.

The Irish Republic is entitled to, and hereby claims, the allegiance of every Irishman and Irishwoman. The Republic guarantees religious and civil liberty, equal rights and equal opportunities to all its citizens, and declares its resolve to pursue the happiness and prosperity of the whole nation and of all its parts, cherishing all the children of the nation equally, and oblivious of the differences carefully fostered by an alien government, which have divided a minority from the majority in the past.

Until our arms have brought the opportune moment for the establishment of a permanent National Government, representative of the whole people of Ireland and elected by the suffrage of all her men and women, the Provisional Government, hereby constituted, will administer the civil and military affairs of the Republic in trust for the people.

We place the cause of the Irish Republic under the protection of the Most High God, Whose blessing we invoke on our arms, and we pray that no one who serves that cause will dishonour it by cowardice, inhumanity or rapine. In this supreme hour the Irish nation must, by its valour and discipline and by the readiness of its children to sacrifice themselves for the common good, prove itself worthy of the august destiny to which it is called.

Signed on behalf of the Provisional Government

THOMAS J. CLARKE
SEAN MAC DIARMADA THOMAS MACDONAGH
P. H. PEARSE EAMONN CEANNT
JAMES CONNOLLY JOSEPH PLUNKETT

This was the great moment for which all seven signatories had lived and worked. But it was not enough to read the proclamation in O'Connell Street, where it was heard by some 300 to 400 people; it had also to be put up in prominent places all over the city, and before Pearse had read it Connolly called on Captain Sean T. O'Kelly to look after the distribution. The military council had thought of many things, but it had not thought of paste for sticking up proclamations. O'Kelly had to commandeer flour from a grocer's shop to make paste with, and then, with 20 men and a small handcart, he went round posting up the notice in O'Connell Street, Dame Street, Westmoreland Street, Henry Street, Mary Street, Abbey Street and elsewhere. That, said O'Kelly in later years, when he had himself succeeded to the presidency, was how he became billposter to the Republic.

Yet in spite of the brave words of the proclamation, it had no effect on the general public. Apart from a dozen Redmondite National Volunteers, no Irishman seems to have joined the Rising unless he was already a member of one of the revolutionary organisations. Later in the week de

Valera said wistfully: "If only the people had come out with knives and forks!" But the people preferred to stand aside and wait on events.

2

While the insurgents' headquarters were being established at the G.P.O. other detachments were taking up their appointed positions in other parts of the city. St. Stephen's Green was allotted to the Citizen Army under the command of Michael Mallin, who rather strangely (though presumably in accordance with Plunkett's master-plan) set his men to dig trenches in the Green instead of occupying the buildings overlooking it. There were about 20 girls in the St. Stephen's Green contingent, and Constance Markievicz was Mallin's second-in-command. One of the stories told in Dublin after the Rising was of two unsuspecting English officers walking near the Green on Easter Monday morning and saying in surprise, "Why, there's Madame Markievicz holding a rifle! By Jove, she's pointing it over here!"—and then scurrying for safety as a couple of bullets whizzed past their heads; but it may be doubted whether "Madame" would really have been taking pot-shots at stray men in uniform in the first hour of the insurrection.

Another insurgent centre was Jacob's biscuit factory in Bishop Street, where MacDonagh was in command: one of his senior officers was John MacBride, who had known nothing of the plans for a rising and happened to have come into Dublin that day to attend a wedding, but had cheerfully joined the rebellion so that he could fight the English again as he had fought them in the Boer War. Edward Daly and Piaras Beaslai led a party which occupied the Four Courts; Eamonn Ceannt and Cathal Brugha held the South Dublin Union in James's Street; and Boland's Mills, the big grey building on the canal bank in the Ringsend district, was the headquarters of a battalion commanded by Eamon de Valera, adjutant of the Dublin Brigade, who had the responsible task of covering the south-eastern approaches to the city, including the roads from Dun Laoghaire, as well as holding Westland Row station and Mount Street bridge.

Up to that day the name of Eamon de Valera was little known to the Irish public. He was 33 at the time of the Rising, and had been born in New York, the son of a Spanish father and an Irish mother. After his father's early death his mother had sent him back to Ireland at the age of three, to live with an uncle at Bruree in county Limerick. Even as a boy he had a strongly scholastic bent; as a young man he became a teacher of mathematics and physics, and narrowly failed to be selected as Professor of Mathematics at Cork University in 1913. He was greatly attracted to Gaelic, so much so, indeed, that at one time he said, "Were I to get my choice, freedom without the language or the language without freedom, I would far rather have the language without freedom"; and it was through his Gaelic studies that he met a pretty blonde teacher, Janie O'Flanagan, whom he married in 1910.

For de Valera, as for so many others, the Gaelic League was a stepping-stone to other Irish-Ireland activities: he was one of the first to join the Irish Volunteers, and when the split came in 1914 he unhesitatingly followed MacNeill. As Adjutant of the Dublin Brigade he showed an unexpected gift for military leadership, and at MacDonagh's request he joined the I.R.B., though he did so with many qualms because of the Catholic Church's ban on I.R.B. membership. Before the Rising few people would have recognised him in a Dublin street, but soon all Ireland was to acclaim the tall, dark and slightly foreign-looking Volunteer who commanded about 100 men at Boland's Mills.

It was not long before the insurgents in the G.P.O. had their first engagement with the British Army. Part of a troop of Lancers who had been escorting munition wagons to the magazine in Phoenix Park came back to the city by way of the north end of O'Connell Street, apparently without knowing what was going on. As they approached the Nelson Pillar in the middle of O'Connell Street the insurgents fired at them from the roof and front windows of the G.P.O. Four Lancers and one of their horses was killed; the rest of the party withdrew to the Parnell monument, and later returned to their barracks. During the afternoon the G.P.O. garrison sent out detachments to guard some of the principal approaches to O'Connell Street. At the O'Connell Bridge end the corner shops of Kelly's, the gunsmiths, and Hopkins and Hopkins, the jewellers, were occupied; and other outposts were placed in Henry Street houses and in Reis's fancy goods warehouse at the corner of Lower Abbey Street, where they barricaded the street with newspaper rolls taken from the *Irish Times* reserve printing offices, and with furniture and bicycles.

Minor engagements took place in other areas on that first afternoon of the Rising, and the insurgents holding the South Dublin Union were attacked and driven into a single part of the premises, where they stayed for the rest of the week. But the heaviest British casualties were those inflicted by men from de Valera's command on a company of the Dublin Veterans' Corps—a volunteer body consisting largely of elderly dons from Trinity College who were known as the "Gorgeous Wrecks" because of their armbands bearing the letters "G.R." (Georgius Rex). This unfortunate company, whose members were carrying rifles but had no ammunition, had set out on a route-march to Ticknock before the Rising began; and as it marched home along Haddington Road it was ambushed and fired on by one of de Valera's outposts, evidently on the principle that anyone wearing a British uniform was a fair target, whether combatant or not. Five of the Veterans were killed and 46 wounded; the wounded and those who were unhurt found refuge later at Beggar's Bush barracks.

By evening the Republican headquarters were firmly established in the G.P.O. Pearse, Connolly, Clarke, MacDermott and Plunkett were all there, and among the officers were Sean T. O'Kelly, The O'Rahilly (one of the founders of the Volunteers, who had gallantly joined the

Rising though he thought it was all a tragic mistake) and a young man called Michael Collins who had recently returned to Ireland after several years in England. The garrison had been modestly reinforced by the members of a small volunteer organisation, the Hibernian Rifles, and women of the Cumann na mBan had arrived to do nursing and kitchen duties. British officers who were held prisoner in the G.P.O. were impressed by the appearance of the girls who served in the dining-room; they admired the smart dresses and green, white and orange sashes, though they also noted the knives and revolvers that some of the girls had in their belts. Bedding for the garrison had been commandeered from the Metropole Hotel, and as night fell the men in the G.P.O. settled down to await attack, while Pearse and Connolly carefully studied reports from the other insurgent posts.

2

The British authorities had been quite unprepared for the Rising, and Birrell and General Friend were still in England on Easter Monday; but Lord Wimborne, the Viceroy, was in Dublin, and he at once acted to summon reinforcements. By seizing the telegraph office in the G.P.O. the insurgents hoped to have cut off Dublin from contact with England; but the post office superintending engineer had hurriedly driven round the suburbs with some of his staff and had linked up cables with lines leading to the Amiens Street telegraph office, which remained in British hands all the week. Lord Wimborne was thus able to telegraph to England and to maintain touch with the rest of Ireland by telephone; for although the insurgents had meant to occupy the Dublin telephone exchange in Crown Alley, they had not, in the end, had enough men to spare for it. So the 20 girl operators went on with their duties throughout the week, and Civil servants who were outside Dublin on Easter Monday had no difficulty in ringing up the Castle to ask for news and instructions.

The first hint of the Rising reached the Irish Office in London on Monday morning. It was a telegram in code, and since it was Bank Holiday and Birrell's secretary was away, there was no one in the Irish Office who knew how to decode it. Birrell sent the message across to the Foreign Office, where a young official called Duff Cooper succeeded in having it deciphered. It said that Bailey, who had landed with Casement and had been arrested later, had disclosed that a rising was planned for Easter Sunday. Since Easter Sunday had passed and there was no rising, there seemed to be nothing very disturbing in this message; but later in the day Lord Wimborne's telegrams brought news that the insurrection had begun and that he had already called for reinforcements from the Curragh and Belfast. In its first alarm the British Government suppressed the publication of all news from Ireland, and it was not until Tuesday that anyone in England except those in the highest Government circles knew what had happened. Even then the news was "played down", and it was later still before the gravity of the situation became generally understood in England.

Lord Wimborne understood it from the first. He knew that the moment of crisis had come, and because of Casement's landing and the sinking of the *Aud* he imagined that Germany had inspired the Rising. On Easter Monday afternoon he issued his own proclamation to the citizens of Dublin. It said:

"Whereas an attempt, instigated and designed by the foreign enemies of our King and Country to incite rebellion in Ireland, and thus endanger the safety of the United Kingdom, has been made by a reckless though small body of men, who have been guilty of insurrectionary acts in the City of Dublin:

"Now we, Ivor Churchill, Baron Wimborne, Lord Lieutenant-General and Governor-General of Ireland, do hereby warn all His Majesty's subjects that the sternest measures are being and will be taken for the prompt suppression of the existing disturbances and the restoration of order;

"And we do hereby enjoin all loyal and law-abiding citizens to abstain from acts or conduct which might interfere with the action of the Executive Government, and, in particular, we warn all citizens of the danger of unnecessarily frequenting the streets or public places, or of assembling in crowds:

"Given under our Seal on the 24th day of April, 1916.

"WIMBORNE."

The Viceroy's appeal to the public to keep off the streets had little effect. That evening people still moved freely in the city centre, where only a few barricades and the occasional crackle of rifle-fire showed that a revolution was in progress. But the crowds soon realised that there was something unusual about the streets: there were no policemen on duty. Dublin was not safe for men in uniform, whether armed or not, and the Commissioner of the Dublin Metropolitan Police had withdrawn the whole of his unarmed force after several of his men had been shot or shot at by insurgents.

It was a night for looting. With no policemen to stop them, men, women and children poured out of the city slums and were soon breaking the windows of shops in O'Connell Street and helping themselves to the goods displayed. A shoe shop was the first to be entered, and other shoe shops, drapery establishments, tobacconists, sweet shops, jewellers and toy shops were the looters' principal targets on that first evening and the two which followed. (On Thursday, when they turned their attention to Grafton Street, they were dispersed by rifle-fire from the roof of Trinity College.)

Earl Street and Henry Street suffered as well as O'Connell Street, as slatternly children burst into sweet shops and came out loaded with boxes of chocolates, big bottles of sweets and bars of rock, while their elders sat on the pavement trying on looted boots and shoes. Gold watches were taken from a jeweller's shop and offered for sale at a shilling each, girls put gold bangles on their ankles, and at a big store men delved eagerly in boxes of shirts and pyjamas. Clothing shops were the biggest attraction for women looters: slum girls proudly paraded in smart tweed skirts and luxurious fur coats with silk vests and knickers crammed in the pockets, some pulled new clothes over their old ones, and one girl stripped naked in the street to try on expensive underwear, throwing garment after garment away until she found those she liked best. The bars were crowded with looters of both sexes. Landlords were powerless against the surging mobs; men and women seized whole bottles of whiskey and drank so deeply that many were soon reeling along the streets, caring nothing for snipers' bullets, while others lay unconscious in the roadway in drunken stupor. From time to time the sound of breaking glass showed that another shop had been entered.

From their sniping posts the Volunteers watched these scenes with disgust, and occasionally fired a shot or two over the looters' heads to frighten them away. But nobody cared, except that someone in the crowd might angrily growl, "You dirty bowsies, wait till the Tommies bate your bloody heads off." The day that had brought Pearse's heroic proclamation of Ireland's destiny ended with Irishmen reeling drunkenly home through the Dublin streets and unkempt women staggering back to the slums with heavy loads of stolen finery.

CHAPTER IX

Collapse and Surrender

I

MONDAY HAD BEEN fine and sunny, but the Tuesday of Easter Week was a sultry, lowering day, and for a time there was rain in Dublin. Though the fine weather was soon to return, that change in the weather was almost symbolic, for the insurgents' high hopes of Easter Monday were already doomed to disappointment. British reinforcements were beginning to reach the outskirts of Dublin, and there was no effective backing for the Rising in other parts of the country.

Outside the city the only important fighting was in county Dublin; in most districts the conflicting orders of the preceding week had held back Volunteers who might otherwise have been in the field. There was no rising in Cork: a thousand men were mobilised on Easter Sunday, but after reading MacNeill's final order in the *Sunday Independent* the local commanders, Tomas MacCurtain and Terence MacSwiney, sent the Volunteers home. Both MacCurtain and MacSwiney were out of Cork on Easter Sunday, when the military council's message, "We start at noon today," reached the city, and by the time that they read the message it was too late to take action; they could only man their headquarters and await further developments. In Wexford the Volunteers occupied and held Enniscorthy, but their action had no military significance; and the same could be said of the more elaborate rising in Galway, where the Volunteers (gallantly led by Liam Mellows, who had escaped from an English gaol with Nora Connolly's help) captured Athenry and had several minor engagements with troops and police before their rising collapsed in encirclement and surrender. The I.R.B. military council had hoped that the full strength of 10,000 Volunteers would be mobilised in the provinces; the 2,000 or so who actually came out had no influence on the course of the Rising.

It was soon clear that the Sinn Feiners (as the British troops and most of the Irish public called the insurgents) had little or no popular support. The Rising was merely a spectacle, and one in which Dubliners' sympathies were mostly with the British. Old women sat in chairs in side-streets to watch the shooting, and when the body of a dead insurgent was being removed from the pavement near St. Stephen's Green one of them shouted: "Let the carrion rot, bringing disgrace on the fair name of Ireland." So, too, when people stood on high ground outside the city to see the fires later in the week, someone would grumble: "They're as bad as the Germans, so they are . . . destroying the people . . . murdering everyone." Such feelings were exacerbated by the incidents, of which there were many, in which civilians going peacefully about their business were shot and killed by Volunteer snipers who mistook even the opening of a door or a window for some kind of hostile demonstration.

In the G.P.O. the garrison still awaited attack by the strengthened British forces. The insurgents' numbers were slowly increasing, as Volunteers who had been away on Easter Monday rejoined their units; and a few others came from outside the city—some from Kildare and Kilkenny, and a Maynooth contingent led by Donal Buckley. Father John Flanagan, a priest at the Roman Catholic pro-Cathedral in Marlborough Street, came regularly to the G.P.O., where he ministered to the wounded and dying; and Arthur Griffith had come to join the garrison, but had been sent home by MacDermott, who said that his work for Sinn Fein was too important to be placed at the mercy of a random English bullet.

The *Irish War News*, a small paper which had been largely prepared beforehand, made its only appearance on Tuesday, and later Pearse issued a communiqué calling for help in building barricades, which were going up in various central streets. The insurgents also began to make safe passages from one street to another by boring holes in the walls of shops and houses. One such passage went along Henry Street to the Coliseum (where Diarmuid Lynch reported back to headquarters, "We captured three British generals—in the waxworks"); others went along O'Connell Street from Eden Quay to Abbey Street and from the Imperial Hotel to Noblett's sweet shop at No. 34.

By this time Mallin had realised the absurdity of entrenching the Citizen Army on St. Stephen's Green, and on Tuesday he moved his men and girls into the Royal College of Surgeons, overlooking the Green. The girls took their full share of duty: some went out in the street with revolvers and held up bread vans, and all were quite unmoved by thoughts of death. "What is there to be afraid of?" said one. "Won't I go straight to Heaven if I die for Ireland?" In fact, none of the girls was killed, though one was badly wounded in a raid on a house where a British machine-gun was posted.

This Tuesday of Easter Week was a lull before the storm, but the British made a strong attack on the Volunteers in the City Hall and the *Daily Express* office, and began to move artillery into the grounds of Trinity College, which was held by a mixed force of soldiers and the undergraduates' Officers' Training Corps. Gradually, too, the British were occupying a complete line of posts running from Trinity College to Kingsbridge, thus cutting off the insurgents north of the Liffey from those in the south of the city. That evening the Viceroy proclaimed martial law, but looting still went on, and people were still able to move about the streets if they were prepared to face the risk of chance bullets from snipers. It was, indeed, this freedom of movement which led to the tragic shooting of Francis Sheehy-Skeffington and two Dublin journalists.

Sheehy-Skeffington was a great Dublin character. As pacifist, humanitarian and social reformer he was the friend of every good cause and an untiring speaker and writer on behalf of the oppressed. One of his special enthusiasms was women's suffrage, and when Asquith addressed a Home Rule meeting in Dublin shortly before the war it was Skeffington who slipped into the theatre disguised as a clergyman and disrupted the proceedings with sharp cries of "Votes for women!" He and Tom Kettle had married sisters, and though many people regarded "Skeffy" as a crank, he was at all events a very endearing one. Since he was a pacifist, he had no part in the Rising, but when once it had started he was anxious to minimise its harmful effects. On Tuesday evening he addressed a meeting (which he had summoned himself) on the need for co-operative public action to stop looting. As he walked back from the centre of the city to Rathmines a small group of people followed him, and the British officer in charge of a picket on Portobello Bridge, fearing some sort of riot might develop, decided to take Skeffington temporarily to Portobello barracks. This was common practice during the Rising, and in the ordinary way he would have been released in a short time.

Unfortunately for Skeffington one of the officers at the barracks was an Irishman, Captain J. C. Bowen-Colthurst, of the Royal Irish Rifles, a member of an old Southern Unionist family. One look at "Skeffy", with his beard, glasses, cloak, knickerbocker suit, untidy umbrella and a little "Votes for Women" badge in his buttonhole, should have told anyone that he was harmless, but Bowen-Colthurst affected to believe that he was a dangerous rebel. Later that evening, with no authorisation from a senior officer, Bowen-Colthurst raided a house near by and arrested two equally innocent journalists, Thomas Dickson, editor of the *Eye-Opener*, and Patrick McIntyre, editor of *Searchlight*. In Bowen-Colthurst's imagination all three of them were rebel leaders, and on the following morning, again acting entirely without his seniors' authorisation, he had them taken out to the barracks yard and shot dead by a firing-party. It was a shocking affair, and one for which no defence could ever be offered, since no one accepted Bowen-Colthurst's story that he had the three men shot because otherwise they might have escaped. He was court-martialled after the Rising, was found guilty of the murder of Skeffington, Dickson and McIntyre and was ordered to be detained in a criminal lunatic asylum "during his Majesty's pleasure". In August the circumstances of the shootings were further examined by a Royal Commission, who reported that, apart from the defence of insanity, there could be no excuse or palliation for Bowen-Colthurst's conduct from first to last.

Some Irish writers have created a myth that Bowen-Colthurst was soon released from Broadmoor criminal lunatic asylum and was commanding British troops in northern Ireland a year after the Rising. This is quite untrue. Bowen-Colthurst held no further command in the British Army, and though he was eventually released from Broadmoor, he was certainly there as late as October, 1917—eighteen months after the Rising. In that month a doctor wrote to *The Times* complaining of the authorities' harshness in keeping Bowen-Colthurst in Broadmoor, when he would, in the doctor's opinion, have been more properly placed in a hospital for shell-shock cases.

2

On Wednesday morning the British guns were brought out of Trinity College and stationed on Butt Bridge, at the end of Tara Street. At the same time an Admiralty vessel, the *Helga*, was brought up the Liffey to bombard Liberty Hall —a somewhat unnecessary action, since the hall had been evacuated by the Citizen Army on Monday and was no longer an insurgent stronghold. As British shells began to fall in the city the inequality of the contest was glaringly revealed. The insurgents had no artillery at all, and there could be only one end to a battle between rifles and guns.

By now Dublin was settling down to its new life. The rain had gone, the sun was shining brilliantly and people went about the streets with smiling faces, confident that their inconveniences would soon be brought to an end. Public hostility to "the Sinn Feiners" was unabated. Women, in particular, thought that no punishment could be too harsh for them, and as random bullets took their toll of domestic pets a girl commented sadly: "There's not a cat or dog left alive in Camden Street. There's lots of women will be sorry for this war, and their pets killed on them." Yet here and there the Volunteers had their admirers. In a laneway near Kelly's, the gunsmith's shop at the corner of O'Connell Street and Bachelor's Quay, James Stephens, the poet, saw a pretty 19-year-old girl in shawl and apron, watching with a little group of men while British machine-gun fire rained down on a handful of Volunteers who were holding the shop. The girl was white-hot with fury. She was cursing the men at her side in the most obscene language, daring them to go out into the roadway and face the bullets, and calling down horrible diseases on everyone in the world except the gallant Volunteers in Kelly's shop.

In England the seriousness of the Rising was still not understood. The first statement on it had been given to the Press by Birrell on Tuesday evening: it was mild and reassuring. After listing the casualties as "three military officers, two loyal volunteers, four or five soldiers and two policemen" killed, and "four or five military officers, seven or eight soldiers and six loyal volunteers" wounded, Birrell added that the situation was well in hand. The whole thing, in fact, sounded rather like a glorified street riot, and it is hardly surprising that even a week later *Punch* began its Charivaria page with the flippant comment: "Sir Roger Casement, it appears, landed in Ireland from a collapsible boat. And by a strange coincidence his arrival synchronised with the outbreak of a collapsible rising."

But the Rising had not collapsed by Wednesday, and on this day the British Army suffered its worst defeat of the week in the battle of Mount Street bridge, now commemorated by a monument with a Gaelic inscription. The victims were the 7th and 8th Battalions of the Sherwood Foresters, part of the 178th Infantry Brigade, which had arrived at Dun Laoghaire on the previous night. Half the brigade marched safely to the Royal Hospital, Kilmainham, by way of Stillorgan, Donnybrook and the South Circular Road; the Sherwood Foresters were ordered to make for Trinity College by the main tram route through Blackrock and Ballsbridge. These were the men who walked into the trap which de Valera had set on Monday.

On that first afternoon he had detached a dozen Volunteers from his Boland's Mills headquarters to take up positions around Mount Street bridge, covering Northumberland Road. Commanded by Lieutenant Michael Malone, two of the party were in 25, Northumberland Road, three in the schools to the east of the bridge and seven in Clanwilliam House on its west side. Early on Wednesday afternoon the advance guard of the British troops marched up Northumberland Road, with the 7th Battalion of the Sherwood Foresters close behind. The Volunteers, who had rifles and revolvers, held their fire until the advance guard had almost reached Mount Street bridge; then the outposts in the schools and Clanwilliam House opened fire on the leaders, while the two men in the Northumberland Road house—one was Malone himself—raked the main body with shots from the flank.

Well placed as they were, these few resolute men were able to hold up the British column until well into the evening. The schools position was soon captured, but Malone and his comrade held out for five hours in Northumberland Road. They shot down successive waves of attack until at last the British stormed the house and shot Malone dead as he coolly came down the stairs to meet them, his pipe in his mouth. The Clanwilliam outpost held the bridge even longer. Firing carefully from concealed positions, they drove off half-hourly charges, and it was not until eight o'clock, when the British had brought up a small naval gun and were dropping incendiary shells on the house, that the four survivors gave up the struggle and escaped from the burning building. Then the Sherwood Foresters crossed the bridge.

The casualties that these few Volunteers, supported by snipers on high buildings round Boland's Mills, inflicted on the British troops in this engagement were given in the official dispatch on the Rising as four officers killed, 16 wounded and 216 other ranks killed or wounded—nearly half the total casualties suffered by the British forces in the whole week. It was not surprising that the scene of the battle became famous after the Rising and was proudly shown to visitors as the Dublin Dardanelles. Britain, too, paid tribute to heroism shown on her own side during the battle. When military honours for services in the Rising were awarded some months later a Dublin girl, Louisa Nolan, was given the Military Medal for her bravery in tending wounded soldiers in Northumberland Road, where she had risked being hit by Volunteers' bullets while looking after the men and bringing them water. She was also presented with a gold wrist-watch by the trustees of the Carnegie Hero Fund, and—a more curious reward—was given a part in the *Three Cheers* revue at the Shaftesbury Theatre, London.

But the Mount Street battle was only an isolated success for the insurgents. While it was being fought the first surrender had been made—by the little garrison in the Mendicity Institution on Usher's Island. This was an outpost of the main Four Courts garrison and was commanded by Sean Heuston, who had been one of Constance Markievicz's principal assistants in running the Fianna Eireann. Though he had little more than 20 men and was under continuous attack from British troops, who cut him off from the Four Courts, he held out from Monday till Wednesday evening, when the Institution was completely surrounded and there was no alternative but to surrender.

By this time the steady increase in British fire-power had warned the insurgent leaders that the end could not be far away. On Thursday Ceannt's garrison was strongly attacked in the part of the South Dublin Union it still occupied, but it was able to hold out after a seven hours' battle, in which Cathal Brugha, though severely wounded, led the main defence with great courage. The British field guns were now directing their fire at Bachelor's Walk, Eden Quay and the insurgents' posts on the east side of O'Connell Street, and it was not long before incendiary shells began the great fires which raged in Dublin till the end of the week. The main outbreak began shortly after noon on Thursday in the *Irish Times* reserve printing office in Lower Abbey Street, where it spread rapidly because of the inflammable barrier of furniture and rolls of newsprint the insurgents had placed across the street. There was too much shooting for the fire brigade to be brought out, and that afternoon the blaze spread along both sides of Lower Abbey Street until it reached O'Connell Street, where it turned south to the Dublin Bread Company's building and north to Clery's drapery store. Before morning all the O'Connell Street shops from Lower Abbey Street to Eden Quay were destroyed, and in the north the fire had demolished Clery's and gone behind it into Earl Street, where it swept over Sir Joseph Downes's new bakery and restaurant. As O'Connell Street went up in flames the insurgent outposts tunnelled their way through house and shop walls to safety, emerging at last in what was then Gloucester Street and is now Cathal Brugha Street.

In spite of the great width of O'Connell Street, the heat from the eastern side began to spread across the roadway, and soon the G.P.O. began to smoulder. That Thursday afternoon Connolly was wounded twice by British snipers when he daringly left the G.P.O. to inspect insurgent posts in the neighbourhood. He was carried back on a stretcher and continued to direct operations from a bed on the G.P.O. floor. Plunkett was also lying seriously ill in the G.P.O.; this was the penalty for his impetuous departure from his nursing home.

As the flames lit up O'Connell Street on Thursday evening Pearse sat down to compose his valedictory message to the people of Ireland. When he wrote it he knew that the Rising was doomed and his own life almost certainly forfeit, but his spirit was unsubdued as he bade his countrymen farewell.

"I desire now, [he wrote] lest I may not have an opportunity later, to pay homage to the gallantry of the soldiers of Irish freedom who have during the past four days been writing with fire and steel the most glorious chapter in the later history of Ireland. Justice can never be done to their heroism, to their discipline, to their gay and unconquerable spirit in the midst of peril and death. . . . For four days they have fought and toiled, almost without cessation, almost without sleep, and in the intervals of fighting they have sung songs of the freedom of Ireland. . . . If they do not win this fight they will at least deserve to win it. . . . They have redeemed Dublin from many shames and made her name splendid among the names of cities."

He paid special tribute to Connolly, who "lies wounded, but is still the guiding brain of our resistance", and ended movingly:

"If we accomplish no more than we have accomplished, I am satisfied. I am satisfied that we have saved Ireland's honour. I am satisfied that we should have accomplished more, that we should have accomplished the task of enthroning as well as proclaiming the Irish Republic as a Sovereign State, had our arrangements for a simultaneous rising of the whole country, with a combined plan as sound as the Dublin plan has proved to be, been allowed to go through on Easter Sunday. Of the fatal countermanding order which prevented those plans being carried out, I shall not speak further. Both Eoin MacNeill and we have acted in the best interests of Ireland. For my part, as to anything I have done in this I am not afraid to face the judgment of God, or the judgment of posterity."

Fanatical and egoistic though Pearse may have been, the nobility and integrity of his character are impressively shown in his reference to MacNeill. Later Irish history might have been very different if other leaders had recognised as generously that those who disagreed with them might still be acting in the best interests of Ireland.

3

The Rising was nearly over, and the people of Dublin were beginning to feel that they had had enough of it. A food shortage, which had hardly been noticed at the beginning of the week, was becoming acute, since no supplies (except milk for hospitals) had been reaching the city, and the shelves of grocers' shops were virtually empty. Even tinned foods which had lain untouched for months had found ready purchasers. Moreover, even where food was available, people were surprised to realise that they had no means of getting money to pay for it. Banks and post offices were closed; old-age pensioners could not draw their pensions; and in some districts the city authorities had to give out relief tickets to save the destitute from starvation. Cooking was difficult, for the gas supply had been cut off to prevent the risk of explosion, and on the Friday and Saturday there were no papers of any kind to be bought in Dublin. The *Daily Express*, the *Irish Independent* and *Freeman's Journal* had ceased publication early in the week, but the *Irish Times*, which had an independent gas-suction plant, continued to appear except on two days when continuous firing in Westmoreland Street made it impossible for any of the staff to venture outside the office.

The British operations had become too big to be entrusted to a major-general. On Friday morning Lieutenant-General Sir John Maxwell arrived in Dublin to take over the command from Major-General Friend, and he at once issued a proclamation saying he would take most rigorous measures "to stop the loss of life and damage to property which certain misguided persons are causing by their armed resistance to the law". He would not hesitate, he said, "to destroy all buildings within any area occupied by the rebels".

While Maxwell was reviewing the situation the insurgents outside Dublin fought their only major battle of the week. A substantial Volunteer force had been mobilised at Swords, in county Dublin, under the command of Thomas Ashe, a handsome, fair-haired giant with a shy and unassuming manner, with Richard Mulcahy as his chief lieutenant. On Wednesday they had set out in force to capture the wireless station at Skerries, but had hastily withdrawn when a patrol boat carrying two companies of British troops, escorted by two gunboats, had put into the harbour. They had more success on Friday, when they first attacked the R.I.C. barracks at Ashbourne and then ambushed a body of about 50 police sent to the rescue from Navan. The police were heavily outnumbered, and after a five hours' encounter in which both sides fired at each other from cover the police exhausted their ammunition and had to surrender. Eight R.I.C. men, including a county and a district inspector, were killed, and 15 were wounded, but the Volunteers' casualties were believed to be even heavier. The Ashbourne fighting had no effect on the course of the Rising, but it set the pattern for many other ambushes in later years.

In Dublin the Rising had turned into a series of separate sieges. De Valera's garrison was confined to Boland's Mills; Ceannt and Brugha were trapped in the South Dublin Union; the Citizen Army could no longer move from the College of Surgeons; and MacDonagh was closely besieged in Jacob's factory, as he had been for most of the week. As the G.P.O. headquarters withdrew their outposts from burning O'Connell Street, the only area in which there was still open fighting was that of the Four Courts, where Daly had outposts at various points between Church Street bridge and North King Street.

The Four Courts garrison had built many barricades and occupied many houses in adjoining streets, so that they were well placed to resist the concentrated advance on their position which began on Friday morning. The British troops engaged were men of the 2nd/6th South Staffordshire Regiment, and they were hampered because non-combatants, including women and children, were still living in the area. Moreover, since not all the Volunteers wore uniform, the British often could not distinguish their enemies, and it was not surprising that some civilians were killed in the house-to-house fighting, which lasted until a virtual stalemate was reached on Friday afternoon. The Irish made many allegations later of deliberate acts of murder and brutality by British soldiers in this area, and General Maxwell admitted that "possibly unfortunate incidents, which we should regret now, may have occurred"; but British courts of inquiry found it impossible to attribute any responsibility for civilians' deaths either to individuals or groups of individuals in the British Forces. By the intervention of one of the Capuchin Friars from Church Street a local truce was arranged for the Four Courts area on Saturday afternoon, but it was overtaken by the general collapse of the rebellion.

By Friday the G.P.O. had become untenable. In the morning British shells began to fall on the roof; in the afternoon the upper floors were ablaze, and fire was sweeping into the front of the building from the roof of the portico. All the Volunteers were ordered into the general sorting room at the back of the building, and the wounded men, together with most of the Cumann na mBan women, were sent out under a Red Cross flag. Pearse shook hands with all the women before they left. When they had gone he gave the order for general evacuation.

The first to leave the G.P.O. were a party commanded by The O'Rahilly, who went out by the Henry Street door and tried to make their way up Moore Street to Parnell Street; but their advance was stopped by heavy fire from a barricade farther up Moore Street, and The O'Rahilly fell mortally wounded in a lane on the right-hand side, where a plaque on the wall now recalls his gallantry. The main body of the garrison left at dusk—Clarke, MacDermott and Plunkett with the leading party, followed by Connolly on his stretcher and Pearse with the rearguard. They made no attempt to reach Parnell Street, but set up a new headquarters in a number of Moore Street houses which, as had been so often done in the Rising, they linked together by boring holes in the walls. There they stayed all night; there on Saturday morning, as brilliant sunshine poured in through gaps in the barricaded windows, the members of the Republican Provisional Government (with the exception of Ceannt and MacDonagh, who were still at their separate commands) decided there was nothing to do but surrender.

Three Cumann na mBan Red Cross nurses had stayed behind with the headquarters garrison. At one o'clock on Saturday afternoon MacDermott came out of the Government's conference room and told the girls to make a white flag. A message was drawn up, saying briefly that the Commandant-General of the Irish Republican Army wished to negotiate with the Commandant-General of the British forces in Ireland, and one of the nurses, Elizabeth O'Farrell, was asked to take it to the British post in Parnell Street. She set out with the flag high over her head, while Connolly gently comforted her friend, Julia Grenan, who feared she had gone to her death.

But the British troops did not fire on a Red Cross nurse. She passed through the barricade, and after a British colonel had curtly commented on her message, "The Irish Republican Army? You mean the Sinn Feiners", she was taken to Tom Clarke's shop, which the British were using as local headquarters. There she was interviewed most courteously by Brigadier-General W. H. M. Lowe, who was in charge of the military operations in Dublin city. The general would hear nothing of negotiation and demanded unconditional surrender. Miss O'Farrell went backwards and forwards with other messages, and soon after three o'clock the insurgent leaders agreed to surrender unconditionally. Pearse himself then went with her to General Lowe, gave up his sword and agreed to send orders to the other commandants telling them to cease fire. In these he said:

> "In order to prevent the further slaughter of Dublin citizens, and in the hope of saving the lives of our followers, now surrounded and hopelessly outnumbered, the members of the Provisional Government present at headquarters have agreed to an unconditional surrender, and the commandants of the various districts in the city and the country will order their commands to lay down their arms."

A separate message for the Citizen Army was signed by Connolly.

The Rising was over. That evening and the next morning Elizabeth O'Farrell, escorted by a British officer, went round the insurgent positions and delivered Pearse's message. Sadly the commandants agreed to surrender, though MacDonagh would not do so until he had been allowed to speak to Pearse and Ceannt. At the College of Surgeons the British military party which came to accept the surrender early on Sunday afternoon was received by Constance Markievicz. In her Citizen Army uniform, with the feather waving on her hat, she shook hands with her fellow-officers and kissed her revolver before handing it over to the British.

Pearse's order was also sent to the few Volunteer detachments still in arms in the provinces. By Monday, May 1, all the insurgents had surrendered unconditionally.

The British military and police casualty list issued on May 11 stated that 103 military officers and other ranks were killed in the Rising, 357 were wounded and nine were missing, and 14 officers and other ranks of the R.I.C. were killed and 23 wounded. In addition, three members of the Dublin Metropolitan Police were killed and three wounded. The number of Irish Volunteers reported to be killed in action was 52, and the complete Irish casualty list, including civilians, was given later as 450 dead and 2,614 wounded. The first part of Pearse's vision was fulfilled. The blood sacrifice had been made.

CHAPTER X

The Terrible Beauty

I

As a party of captured Volunteers was being marched to prison under its British escort a girl's clear voice pierced the otherwise hostile silence of the onlookers. "Long live the Republic!" she cried. There were not many like her in Dublin in those early days after the Rising. Sometimes the crowds were silent, sometimes they jeered and hissed as the prisoners passed, whether on foot with an armed escort or in prison vans with cavalry riding in front and behind with drawn swords. The fighting was over, but half O'Connell Street was in ruins, the G.P.O. was a burnt-out shell and the city had suffered £2,500,000 worth of damage; in North King Street and elsewhere corpses were still being brought out of shattered houses. Dublin was glad to see the last of a revolt for which John Redmond, as Ireland's spokesman in the House of Commons, had expressed "a feeling of detestation and horror", which he believed was shared by "the overwhelming mass of the people of Ireland".

Yet his colleague John Dillon, who had been in Dublin throughout the week, was not sure that this feeling would last. "A reaction," he wrote to Redmond, "might very easily be created", and he added that "if there were shooting of prisoners on a large scale the effect on public opinion might be disastrous in the extreme".

In London Birrell had resigned the Chief Secretaryship.

He did so with much regret, and a few months later, when Asquith had been forced out of office and someone suggested he might welcome a rest after ten years as Prime Minister, Birrell retorted: "Nonsense, of course it hurt him. I know how much it hurt me when I fell off my donkey, so I can imagine what he felt when he fell off his elephant." Redmond and Asquith talked over the appointment of a new Chief Secretary, and the Prime Minister's first choice was Edwin Montagu, a young Liberal politician who was later distinguished for his share in Indian reforms and might have been a happy choice for Ireland. But Montagu was passed over. The post was offered to Lloyd George, who at first accepted it and then decided that he could not "pin himself" to such an office in the middle of the war; and in the end it was left temporarily vacant, since General Maxwell had been given full powers for dealing both with the insurrection and with its aftermath.

Maxwell—soon to be known in Ireland as "Bloody" Maxwell—was a professional soldier who had served without unusual distinction in the Sudan and South Africa, where he had won the approval of Kitchener; and he seems to have had no particular qualifications for dealing with the difficult and largely political problems which faced him. The procedure he followed was to hold a series of courts-martial, beginning on May 3, and to have the insurgent leaders executed whenever sentences of death were passed and confirmed.

It has often been suggested that this procedure was entirely wrong, and that the British Government would have done better if it had ridiculed the whole Rising and had the ringleaders tried by a magistrate. But the Rising could not be ridiculed because it was not ridiculous. It had not only caused the deaths of British soldiers and substantial damage to the city of Dublin, but it seemed all the more sinister because of its direct association with Germany—an association openly admitted by the insurgent leaders in the reference to their proclamation to "gallant Allies in Europe".

The importance of the link was certainly exaggerated at the time. Redmond, who knew something of the three-way traffic between Devoy in America, the I.R.B. in Dublin and the German Government, went so far as to say of the Rising that "Germany plotted it, Germany organised it, Germany paid for it". Though this was a wild over-statement, it was still true that I.R.B. funds were swollen by contributions from German–American sources, and that the leaders of the Rising were, through Casement and Devoy, in direct contact with Britain's enemies. Moreover, all of them, except de Valera, were British subjects. It is hard to believe that men who had organised such a revolt would have escaped the death penalty in any other country in the world.

Maxwell's blunder lay not so much in his authorisation of the executions as in his dilatory handling of the courts-martial. Ireland was gravely disturbed. In addition to those who were known to have taken part in the Rising, hundreds of other Sinn Feiners were being rounded up for deportation to detention centres in England. It would have been wise to get the executions over as quickly as possible and allow the country to settle down again. But Maxwell kept up the tension by trying two or three leaders at a time and then issuing brief announcements of the sentences and the shooting of those whose death sentences had been confirmed.

The first shootings were on May 3, the last on May 12: it is not surprising that Dublin began to wonder if they would ever stop, and that the change of feeling foretold by Dillon came even earlier than might have been expected. "Pearse and his colleagues," as G. K. Chesterton observed three years later, "desired to be in the Greek and literal sense martyrs; they wished not so much to win as to witness. They thought that nothing but their dead bodies could really prove that Ireland was not dead." By his long-drawn-out handling of the executions Maxwell made certain that the men of Easter Week would achieve the martyrdom they desired.

In all, 14 men were shot for their part in the Easter Rising in Dublin, and one—Thomas Kent—for killing an R.I.C. head constable in resisting arrest at Fermoy, county Cork, on Easter Tuesday. All the signatories of the proclamation were executed—Pearse, MacDonagh and Clarke on May 3, Plunkett on May 4, Ceannt on May 8 and Connolly and MacDermott on May 12. Connolly's execution seemed particularly gruesome, because one of his wounds had gangrened and he had to be carefully nursed until he was well enough to be put into a chair to face the firing-party. The other seven who were shot were Edward Daly, commandant at the Four Courts, Sean Heuston, who had held the Mendicity Institution, John MacBride and Michael O'Hanrahan, MacDonagh's chief lieutenants at Jacob's factory, Michael Mallin, commandant at St. Stephen's Green, Con Colbert, one of Ceannt's senior officers, and William Pearse, who was not in the insurgents' inner councils and was apparently executed for the crime of being Padraic's brother. Many other death sentences were passed, but were commuted to terms of penal servitude either for life or for ten years. Among those whose sentences were commuted to life imprisonment were William T. Cosgrave, Constance Markievicz, Eamon de Valera, Thomas Ashe and Robert Brennan. The courts-martial went on after the executions had ceased, and the last, which began on May 22, was on Eoin MacNeill, who, though he had taken no part in the Rising, had to face eight charges of attempting to cause disaffection among the civil population of Ireland and four of acting in a way likely to prejudice recruiting. He too was sentenced to penal servitude for life.

Of the Dublin commandants only de Valera escaped execution. This was largely due to the curious point of his nationality. He was not a British subject, for his father was Spanish, and British nationality could not descend to him through his Irish mother; yet he was not legally an American. To acquire permanent American citizenship he would have had to register with a U.S. consulate at 18 and take the Oath of Allegiance at 21, and he had done neither of these things. Technically he was a stateless person, yet the fact of his American birth remained, and appeals for mercy were made on his behalf both by Redmond and by the U.S. consulate in Dublin. The appeals were readily heard by Asquith, who was equally anxious not to affront American feelings and to call a halt to the apparently endless stream of executions; and on May 11, the day before the last executions took place, it was announced that the sentence of death passed on de Valera had been commuted to life imprisonment.

An additional complaint against Maxwell's policy was that the courts-martial were held privately, and no record of their proceedings was ever published, apart from the bare statement of their findings; but in spite of this secrecy, some of the dead men's last words became known later. At their last meeting Connolly gave his daughter Nora a statement in which he had written: "Believing that the British Government has no right in Ireland, never had any right in Ireland and never can have any right in Ireland, the presence in any one generation of Irishmen of even a respectable minority ready to die to affirm that truth makes that Government for ever a usurpation and a crime against human progress." Tom MacDonagh's "last and inspiring speech" was soon to be sold as a broadsheet in the streets of Dublin: it had the gallant ring to be expected in the words of a lively poet and critic unexpectedly turned into a man of action. "It will be said," MacDonagh proudly told his judges, "that our movement was doomed to failure. It has proved so. Yet it might have been otherwise. There is always a chance of success for brave men who challenge fortune." Of Pearse's speech there is no record, but in his last hours in prison he wrote one of the loveliest of all his poems, "The Wayfarer", in which he poignantly recalled the beauty of the world to which he was soon to say good-bye. Plunkett, too, used his last moments of life to write a poem, which began touchingly:

Life that's sweet, so sweet,
Crumbles at my feet.
I would not retreat
From a course so meet.

It was written to his bride of a few hours, Grace Gifford, whose sister was the wife of Tom MacDonagh, though their family was strongly Unionist. Plunkett and Grace Gifford would have been married on Easter Sunday if there had not been a hitch over the church arrangements. Their wedding took place in the prison chapel at 11.30 on the night before Plunkett's execution.

In the weeks which followed the Rising 3,149 men and 77 women were arrested in Ireland by the British authorities, though some were soon released. The majority were sent to England, where, in addition to some 160 who had been convicted by courts-martial, 1,862 men and five women were interned without trial. Prisoners who had been sentenced to penal servitude were sent to English prisons, and a few of the internees who were thought to be particularly influential, such as Arthur Griffith, were also detained in gaol; but most of the internees were eventually collected in a big camp at Frongoch, in Wales.

It was as these prisoners and internees were marched to the quays that the change in Dublin's feelings began to make itself evident. Pearse's belief that Ireland needed a blood sacrifice to arouse her national spirit was proved correct; the great architects of the insurrection did more for Ireland by their deaths than they had been able to do by their lives. The Irish had not, indeed, become Sinn Feiners. Those who believed in Redmond and Home Rule before the Rising had not lost their faith; the wives of the many Irish soldiers serving in the British Army still formed a solid anti-revolutionary block. But many Irishmen and Irishwomen had now shed the hostility to the insurgents they had felt during Easter Week. Internees were no longer hissed or jeered at; instead friends rushed out to shake hands with them and half-bottles of whiskey were thrust into their pockets. "God save you," cried the watching crowds. "God have pity on you! Keep your hearts up!" The Sinn Feiners were "dirty bowsies" no longer; the Rising had become a saga, an heroic story to be told with pity and pride in the years to come. It was the moment immortalised in the poem that Yeats wrote within a few weeks of the executions, though it was not published till 1920:

All changed, changed utterly;
A terrible beauty is born.

2

The echoes of the marching feet died away, and with them the first phase in Ireland's new struggle for freedom was abruptly closed. Old names had gone, new ones were soon to take their places, though de Valera, O'Kelly, Brugha, Cosgrave, Mellows and the irrepressible Constance Markievicz were among those who remained to provide a link between Easter Week and the later years of terror and counter-terror. Soon, too, the whole character of the leadership was to change. Instead of professors, poets, schoolmasters and trade-union organisers, the leaders of Ireland's protest were to be young men who made revolution their whole and only career. Few would have time to engage in ordinary civil occupation, though Brugha kept his candle-making business going even when he became a Minister in the first Dail Eireann.

On the English side a famous name disappeared from the Anglo-Irish story in June, when Kitchener was drowned in the *Hampshire* on his way to Moscow. Though the *Hampshire* was actually sunk by a German mine, there were rumours in later years of an Irish Republican plot to destroy Kitchener on this voyage; but since neither the I.R.B. nor the Volunteer Executive was in any shape to arrange plots so soon after the Rising, it is difficult to put much faith in these rumours. Asquith, too, was to be moved from the helm in a few months, when he was jockeyed out of office to make room for Lloyd George; but in May, 1916, Ireland was still his responsibility, and when the executions were over he went to Dublin to study the situation for himself.

To learn more of the motives for the Rising he saw some of the Volunteers who were in Dublin prisons, and he asked one of them, who was not much more than a boy, what he thought of the rebellion now. The youth said he thought it was a great success, and when Asquith asked, "How do you make that out?" he gaily retorted, "Well, if not, what are you here for?" It was a pertinent question. Asquith's visit was a clear proof that the British Government was considering some new means of conciliation as an answer to the insurgents' show of violence. He went back from Dublin to tell the House of Commons that the existing machinery for the government of Ireland had broken down and that an Irish Government responsible to the Irish people must be created at the earliest possible moment. He was therefore, he said, taking steps to bring the Home Rule Act into immediate operation, and he had asked Lloyd George to open negotiations at once with the Nationalist and Ulster Unionist leaders.

So the first result of the Easter Rising was to make the British Government reverse its previous decision that Home Rule could not be introduced during the war. Asquith's move completely refuted the opinion held by many Irishmen that Britain never seriously intended to give Ireland Home Rule. For a brief period, at all events, Asquith clearly hoped that the Irish problem could be peacefully solved at last.

The Government had a further reason for anxiety over Ireland. The United States was still neutral in the European War, and it was feared that the hope of her joining the Allies would be gravely prejudiced by continued unrest in Ireland, which would swing the Irish–American vote over to the German side. This fear was shared by Lord Northcliffe, who at that time was chief proprietor of *The Times* besides controlling the *Daily Mail* and other papers and periodicals; and in an expansive moment he summoned

Martin Murphy, the Dublin tramcar owner and proprietor of the *Irish Independent*, urgently to London and told him he could have a dukedom if he could settle the Irish question. Presumably Northcliffe had been impressed by Murphy's tenacity during the Dublin strike, but nothing came of his visit to London. Murphy said drily that he was not a magician and that in any case he did not want to be a duke. The immediate responsibility for working out an Irish settlement remained with Lloyd George.

In many ways Lloyd George seemed an excellent choice as negotiator. He was a distinguished and widely experienced politician; as a Celt himself he could be expected to feel sympathetically towards Ireland; he had a great admiration for the Parliamentary skill of the Irish Nationalists; and his support for Home Rule went as far back as 1890, when he had pledged himself to give "justice for Ireland" in his first election address for Caernarvon Boroughs. One of Lloyd George's failings, however, was an unfortunate fondness for ambiguity, which could leave rival parties in negotiations with completely different impressions of what he really meant; and Redmond, who was a shrewd judge of character, was well aware that he was not a man to be trusted implicitly. In their first talks over a new Irish settlement Redmond bluntly asked: "What guarantee have we that even if Carson and I agree the Cabinet will carry out the settlement?" Lloyd George replied impressively: "You have the best of all guarantees. I am staking my political existence on this matter. If the Cabinet does not carry out an agreed settlement I shall resign."

The upshot of Lloyd George's talks with Redmond and Carson was a paper called Headings of Agreement which they were asked to take to Ireland to discuss with their respective followers. In this paper the division of Ireland into the six and the 26 counties was formally proposed, thus demanding a sacrifice on each side. Redmond was asked to surrender southern Ireland's claim to Fermanagh and Tyrone with their Catholic and Nationalist majorities;

Carson was called upon to repudiate the Ulster Covenant (which had applied to all nine counties of historic Ulster) and to place the Unionist minorities of Cavan, Monaghan and Donegal under Home Rule government from Dublin. Neither side liked these proposals, but after much debate they were approved in both Belfast and Dublin. When they were discussed in Dublin at a United Irish League meeting Tom Kettle, home on leave from France, put up a strong argument for acceptance. "If," he said, "a very needy and somewhat dishonest individual owed you £32, and when you proceeded to sue him you found that he had squared the judge and packed the jury, but that at the last moment he offered you £26 on account, what ought you to do? I am but a poor lawyer, but I should strongly advise you to accept the money without prejudice." That was Kettle's last appearance in politics. A few days later he was killed in action while fighting with the British Army.

But the Headings of Agreement came to nothing; Lloyd George's ambiguities had created a fundamental misunderstanding which came to light only after weeks of discussion. Redmond, to whom the "two nations" theory of Ireland was as abhorrent as it was to any of the Sinn Fein leaders, had at first assumed that partition would be temporary and that there would be a final Irish settlement after the war; but Carson had been confidentially told by Lloyd George that partition would be permanent. To add to the confusion the Unionist members of the Cabinet, headed by Lord Lansdowne, rejected the proposals outright and told Lloyd George that they refused to consider themselves bound by them. In all the circumstances Redmond felt bound to withdraw his own approval of the Headings of Agreement, and the attempt to carry out the Home Rule Act in wartime was abandoned. But Lloyd George stayed in office. He declared that the settlement had been wrecked by extremists on both sides, and he dismissed his pledge to resign with the explanation that it was vital for him to stay in the Cabinet because of the grave state of the war.

From the British Government's point of view the negotiations had not been entirely unsuccessful, for they had at least shown the United States that Britain was seriously trying to solve the Irish problem. Their effect on Ireland was twofold. With Lloyd George's promise in his files, Carson knew that he could always keep the six counties permanently separate from any scheme of self-government for the rest of Ireland. Ulster's opposition to all-Irish Home Rule was thus confirmed and strengthened. In the south Redmond was seen to have made one more bid for Home Rule and to have failed again. The prestige of the "Old Party" dwindled, and it began to be clear that the motive power for winning Irish self-government would have to come from Ireland herself, and not from her representatives at Westminster.

3

While the negotiations over the Headings of Agreement were still in progress the final trial in connexion with the Easter Rising was held in London at the Old Bailey. On June 26 Sir Roger Casement, who had been confined in the Tower of London since his arrest, was accused of high treason "without the realm of England", in accordance with a statute enacted in the reign of King Edward III. He was defended by Serjeant A. M. Sullivan, of the Irish Bar, with two juniors from the English Bar, T. Artemus Jones and Professor J. H. Morgan, and with an American lawyer, Francis Doyle, as adviser for the defence. The prosecution was led by F. E. Smith (by then Sir Frederick Smith), the Attorney-General, who had with him Sir George Cave, the Solicitor-General, Archibald Bodkin and Travers Humphreys.

A famous picture by Sir John Lavery, the Irish artist, shows the Old Bailey during Casement's trial: the bearded Sullivan is addressing the three judges, Lord Reading, the Lord Chief Justice, and Justices Avory and Horridge, while Casement watches from the dock and F. E. Smith sits upright in the row in front of Sullivan, ready, it seems, to interrupt his learned friend on the least provocation. It was a dramatic scene, but the issue of the trial was never really in doubt. There may, indeed, have been a technical flaw in the indictment: Casement was charged with committing treason abroad, and Sullivan maintained that the statute of Edward III was actually drafted to avoid this kind of charge, and referred only to treason committed in England in support of the King's enemies abroad. But apart from this technicality it was clear that Casement, who was a British subject, had gone to Germany when Britain was at war with her and had not only tried to make Irish prisoners give up their allegiance to Britain (and in a number of instances had been successful) but had also negotiated with the German Government for the dispatch of arms, and if possible, armed forces—to be used against Britain in Ireland.

The charge of treason was irrefutable, and it was irrelevant for Casement to claim that he should have been tried in Ireland, where in fact there was no court capable of trying such an offence. He made, indeed, a neat debating-point in his speech from the dock when he compared the Irish with the Ulster Volunteers, and commented: "The difference between us was that the Unionist champions chose a path they felt would lead to the Woolsack, while I went a road I knew must lead to the dock." It was clever of Casement to forecast so accurately that F. E. Smith would one day sit on the Woolsack as Lord High Chancellor of England, but his defence was in vain. The jury returned the inevitable verdict of Guilty; Lord Reading put on the black cap and passed sentence of death by hanging.

The story of Casement's trial has been confused by its connexion with the notorious "black diaries" containing a long record of homosexual misconduct over many years. These diaries, which were said to have been found in luggage that Casement had left behind in London, have sometimes been declared to be forgeries; but since they were placed on view in the Public Record Office, London, in 1959 it has been generally (if not universally) recognised that they are in Casement's handwriting, though this does not, of course, prove that he actually committed the misconduct he described. His curious association with the Norwegian sailor Christensen is also regarded as convincing evidence of his homosexual tendencies. But the diaries did not affect the course of the trial; though F. E. Smith tried to persuade Sullivan to read them, in case he wished to put in a plea of Guilty but Insane, Sullivan flatly refused to have anything to do with them.

The debatable point about the diaries is whether or not they had any effect on the refusal of the British Government to advise the King to grant Casement a reprieve. Certainly the Government's handling of the diaries both during and after the trial was not to its credit. Their discovery was confidentially described at a conference of London editors, and copies of the diaries or extracts from them were shown to the King himself, to many influential people and to American Press correspondents in London. The apparent intention was to spread the story of Casement's immorality so that Ireland could never hail him as one of her honoured martyrs, and most probably the Government hoped also to influence public opinion against an agitation for his reprieve. None the less, several petitions were sent to the Home Secretary, and Randall Davidson, Archbishop of Canterbury, was one of many prominent men who had doubts about the wisdom of hanging Casement. He had met Casement frequently and felt sure that his treason was the result of mental unbalance. He also knew about the diaries, and he thought they provided an additional reason for commuting the sentence of death to one of life imprisonment. In a long letter to the Lord Chancellor he urged the Government to advise a reprieve, and he pointed out that:

"Ireland, America and possibly other countries would find people to make mischievous capital of the execution, and far more so if they could (as they would) spin a tale to the effect that after hanging a 'political prisoner' the authorities had been privy to the trumping up of an infamous story about the man's immorality, an accusation with which he had never even been confronted—far less had the accusation been proved after proper investigation."

The Cabinet duly debated the Archbishop's arguments, but decided in the end that the execution must take place. In his last days in prison Casement, whose mother had been a Roman Catholic though she had married into a Protestant family, was admitted to the Catholic Church and received Holy Communion. On August 3, the day of his execution, a small crowd of some 200 people waited in the roadway outside Pentonville prison. When the bell tolled to announce that Casement had been hanged they gave a little cheer and went quietly away. The mission which began when Casement shaved off his beard to sail to Norway was ended at last. The number of those executed for their share in the Easter Rising had reached its final total of 16.

CHAPTER XI

Sinn Fein Resurgent

I

AFTER THE FAILURE of the Headings of Agreement Ireland returned to the system of government which Asquith himself had declared to have broken down. A new Chief Secretary was appointed—this time a Unionist M.P., Henry Duke—and though Ireland was still under Maxwell's martial law, there was a gradual return to civil administration. In November Maxwell was recalled. Dublin Castle was again in command.

But Ireland had barely settled down after the Rising before she was again disturbed by ominous hints of conscription. When the principle of compulsory military service had been introduced for the rest of the British Isles earlier in the year, Redmond's influence had been strong enough to ensure that it was not applied to Ireland, where he knew that it would cause serious trouble. The English Unionists, however, deeply resented Ireland's exclusion, and they were supported by their Ulster colleagues, who would have been happy to see Ulstermen conscripted so long as the measure was applied to the whole of Ireland. The feeling that the rest of Ireland was not doing her fair share in the European War became stronger in the north-east after the slaughter of the Ulster Division in the Battle of the Somme in July, 1916—a disaster which was felt in Ulster to be the province's own "blood sacrifice" in the cause of the Union.

The autumn revival of plans for conscription in Ireland was bitterly opposed by Redmond. In his own constituency of Waterford he said that conscription would be resisted in every village in Ireland, and that if Britain tried to enforce it she would create "a scandal which would ring through the world". At the same time he was constantly pressing the Government to release the Easter Week prisoners and internees. He argued that their prolonged detention could lead only to renewed unrest, and that an amnesty should be granted quickly if it were to have any healing effect on the Irish situation. But the Government, preoccupied with the European War, was in no hurry to take Redmond's advice.

The continued detention of nearly 2,000 men, most of whom had had no trial, was not only creating bad feeling in Ireland; it was also strengthening Republican sentiments among the prisoners and internees themselves. In the convict prisons, where the sentenced men were doing their penal servitude, and still more in the big internment camp at Frongoch, where there were 1,800 men who had not been tried, men who knew little about the real inspiration of the Easter Rising were taught the Sinn Fein gospel by their better-informed fellow-prisoners, so that they emerged in the end as convinced and devoted revolutionaries, ready to take up the struggle for Ireland's freedom.

It was during this period of mass imprisonment that de Valera's position as leader of the revolutionary movement became firmly established. As the only surviving senior commandant of Easter Week he was an obvious candidate for the leadership, and his authority was strengthened by a curious incident in Dartmoor prison. It was here that the Irish prisoners were lined up one morning for inspection when a number of new arrivals came down the iron stairs into the hall. Among them was Eoin MacNeill, and in view of his efforts to stop the Rising, many of the Volunteers were doubtful whether to treat him as friend or renegade. De Valera had no hesitations. Loyalty to the former Chief of Staff overruled all his other feelings. In flat disobedience of prison rules, he stepped out of the ranks, turned to face his fellow-prisoners and gave the command: "Irish Volunteers! Attention! Eyes left!" The Volunteers gave their salute, MacNeill's status was assured and de Valera was hurried off by outraged warders to a separate cell, from which, however, the prison governor discreetly released him later in the day.

From that day, it is said, his authority was unquestioned, and when he and other prisoners were moved from Dartmoor to Lewes gaol he was formally elected leader of the prison committee. At Lewes, where he was active in organising strikes against unfair treatment, no proposal was ever discussed by the prisoners without first putting the question, "What does Dev think about it?" In this gaol, with the help of a friendly governor who got him a copy of Poincaré's four-volume book on quaternions, de Valera was able to resume his mathematical studies, but he also found time to think deeply about the future of Ireland. His comrades remembered afterwards that in prison discussions he tended to regard Dominon Home Rule as a more realistic objective than an independent Republic.

Farther west Constance Markievicz was serving her sentence in the women's prison at Aylesbury and finding, in her odd way, a certain satisfaction in her position. After her court-martial she had said delightedly to a friend in Kilmainham gaol: "Have you heard the news? I have been sentenced to death!" Though her sentence had been commuted to penal servitude, she was still happy to feel that she was suffering for "Ahland's" sake. "All my life, in a funny way, seems to have led up to the last year," she wrote to her sister Eva, "and it's all been such a hurry-scurry of a life. Now I feel that I have done what I was born to do." Few, however, of those who had known the lovely Constance Gore-Booth in the Irish hunting-field would have guessed that she was born to carry heavy cans up the winding stairs of an English gaol, reciting long passages in Italian from Dante's *Inferno* as she did so; or to be on friendly terms there with the notorious blackmailer, prostitute and gangster's moll known as Chicago May, who was later to say that Countess Markievicz was "the grandest woman I ever met".

The Irish prisoners in convict gaols were few in number compared with the great mass of untried internees who were concentrated at Frongoch, a disused distillery near Lake Bala, in North Wales, where the old buildings and new wooden huts had been used earlier in the war as a camp for German prisoners. It was here that Michael Collins, then a boyish-looking young man of 26 with a great fondness for organising sham fights or plunging hilariously into wild games of football, first became prominent among the Irish revolutionaries.

Collins was born in 1890 at Woodfield, Clonakilty, county Cork, and was the youngest of eight children of a farmer who had married, at the age of 60, a handsome girl of 20. He was educated at National Schools, where he was prepared (like many other West Cork boys of his time) for the examination for boy clerkships in the English Post Office; and his education was entirely in English, for although his father and mother were bilingual, neither Michael Collins nor any one of his brothers and sisters was taught Gaelic. At 15 he passed his examination and went to join his sister Johanna, also a postal clerk, in London, where he first worked at the West Kensington post office. Here he met many other Irish boys, became a keen member of the London branches of the Gaelic Athletic Association and the Gaelic League, and took up the study of Gaelic, though his leisure hours were so much occupied with sport and work for Civil Service examinations that he could not give much time to it. He was brought still closer to the Irish-Ireland movement in 1909, when he was sworn in as a member of the Irish Republican Brotherhood, and when a company of Irish Volunteers was established in London in 1914 he was one of the first to enrol.

By this time he had left the postal service, and, after

working first for a firm of stockbrokers, he had found a job in the Lombard Street office of the Guaranty Trust Company of New York; but on visits to Dublin early in the war he had met MacDermott and Clarke and had begun to dream of an Irish rising. Yet it was only in January, 1916, when he realised that as a resident in Britain he would soon be called up for military service, that on MacDermott's advice he returned to Ireland. His employers gave him an extra month's salary because he told them he was going to "join up", and they had no idea that the active service he had in mind was in the Irish Volunteers, not in the British Army.

Back in Dublin, Collins was engaged by Craig, Gardner and Co., the Dame Street chartered accountants, and in his spare time was soon in the thick of I.R.B. and Volunteer activities. He made a particular impression on Joseph Plunkett, who chose him as *aide-de-camp* for the Rising, and he fought in the G.P.O. After the surrender he escaped court-martial because he was unknown to the Dublin Metropolitan Police detectives who picked out the prisoners for trial, and he thus suffered the lighter penalty of internment.

It was at Frongoch that his flair for leadership first became visible. He was not yet "the big fellow" (as he was later to be called, in contrast with de Valera, "the tall fellow"), for at that time he seemed to be rather slight in his build. But his fellow-internees soon found that he had a lively mind, an agile body, a rather juvenile fondness for swearing and a slightly uncertain temper, though when his temper had worked itself out he would revert to his usual cheerful manner and engaging smile. They found, too, that he had considerable talent for organising resistance to unpopular orders, though some of the older internees, who wanted a quiet life and as little trouble as possible, had little use for him and called him a crank and a firebrand. In quieter moments Collins went back to his study of Gaelic and read Irish history.

But the Frongoch internment could not last indefinitely. During the summer and autumn of 1916 many of the internees were released as there was no evidence against them, and as Christmas drew near there were only some 600 left. A change in the British Government hastened their release, for on December 4 a long campaign by Lord Milner, Carson, Bonar Law and their friends to depose Asquith was given the final touch that made success certain by a vigorous leader in *The Times* written by Geoffrey Dawson, the editor. On the following day Asquith resigned and was succeeded by Lloyd George, who was soon making vague promises of new action to bring peace to Ireland. As an earnest of his good intentions he released the last 600 Frongoch internees just before Christmas. Only the men serving sentences in convict prisons remained in English hands.

2

The men from Frongoch found ample evidence of Ireland's new mood when they came home at the end of 1916. Much of Dublin, even in the centre of the city, had escaped damage in Easter Week. At the Abbey Theatre, for instance, not a pane of glass had been broken, though houses lay in ruins on the other side of the street; but the burnt-out G.P.O. and the devastated shops of O'Connell Street still bore grim witness to the defeat of the Easter insurgents. Yet everywhere there were signs of the resurgent spirit of Sinn Fein. It was already clear, in the phrase quoted later by Winston Churchill, that "the grass soon grows over a battlefield, but never over a scaffold".

This was a new Dublin indeed. Postcard portraits of the Easter Week leaders were shown in shop windows all over the city. Old Sinn Fein pamphlets had been bought so eagerly that there were none left in the bookshops a month after the Rising, and worn and tattered copies were now being passed carefully from hand to hand. Tom MacDonagh's "last and inspiring speech" had been freely sold as a broadsheet until the Castle had belatedly suppressed it.

Girls going to Mass had printed cards inside their prayer-books bearing the names of the 16 Easter Week martyrs (for Casement and Thomas Kent of Cork had taken their place at the side of the Dublin dead). Street urchins were playing a game called "Rebels' camp" and were singing cheeky parodies of well-known songs. What sounded like "Tipperary" turned out to have the different words of "It's a wrong, wrong thing to fight for England". The tune of "Rule Britannia" was borrowed for a tribute to those "gallant European allies" who did so little for Ireland: "Rule the Kaiser, the Kaiser rules the world, Never, never shall the Irish flag be furled." Music-hall performers had only to end their acts by waving an Irish flag to be sure of rapturous applause. Often, too, both young and old could be heard proudly singing "Who fears to speak of Easter Week?", set to the tune of the old Fenian song, "Who fears to speak of '98?"

The ecstatic welcome given to the ex-internees in this new Dublin was a clear warning to any English politician who thought that the Easter Rising would soon be forgotten. In these days there was only one test of virtue for Irishmen: were they "out" in Easter Week? If they were, then nothing was too good for them, and theirs were the only voices that people wanted to hear when committees assembled or meetings were held. Easter Week, as Sean O'Casey was to say afterwards, "became the Year One in Irish history and Irish life".

In the first months of 1917 steps were quietly taken to revive the revolutionary movement. In its usual cloud of secrecy the Irish Republican Brotherhood was reorganised, and Collins was given a place on the Supreme Council. The first moves were taken towards reforming the Volunteers, and Griffith, who had also been released from his internment, resumed the publication of *Nationality* as a weekly paper. Now it was no longer the organ of a small minority; all southern Ireland read it and studied the Sinn Fein doctrine. Griffith began where he had left off: week after week he declared that the independence of Ireland was the only solution of the Irish problem and that both partition and conscription must be steadily opposed, but he also introduced a new note by insisting that Ireland must be allowed to put her case before the Peace Conference which would be held at the end of the European War. This demand was in curious contradiction of the Sinn Fein policy of self-reliance, for had it been granted Ireland would have been relying not on herself but on the judgment of other countries.

The resurgence of Sinn Fein was shown unmistakably at a by-election in North Roscommon to elect a member of the British House of Commons. Sinn Fein decided to fight the election and astutely chose the venerable Count Plunkett as candidate. Plunkett, scholar, poet, antiquary and Count of the Holy Roman Empire, had been director of the National Museum of Ireland until he had been arrested and deported after Easter Week, though his only apparent connexion with the Rising was that he was the father of Joseph Plunkett and of two other sons who were sentenced to death and had their sentences commuted to ten years' penal servitude. He was clearly a respectable figure, and he had the impressive and fiery support of Father Michael O'Flanagan, the tall young curate of Crosna, who presented the Sinn Fein case at meeting after meeting in his deep musical voice. This was Father O'Flanagan's first appearance on the electoral scene: he had the satisfaction of seeing Count Plunkett elected by 3,022 votes against the Nationalist candidate's 1,708 and an Independent's 687. It was a sweeping victory for Sinn Fein, but like all subsequent Sinn Fein M.P.s, Count Plunkett declined to take his seat at Westminster. His place, he said, was in Ireland, for it was there that the battle for Irish liberty was to be fought.

For the time being, and indeed for many months to come, it was a bloodless battle. Dublin Castle was again trying to keep Sinn Fein down by the old coercion tactics. There were occasional swoops on Irish-Ireland organisations, after one of which Terence MacSwiney and Tomas MacCurtain, of Cork, and Sean T. O'Kelly were among 26 men deported to England; youths were fined or imprisoned for singing the Republican "Soldiers' Song" or "Who fears to speak of Easter Week?"; and the flying of the Republican tricolour and the wearing of Volunteer uniform were forbidden. But the British Government was increasingly perturbed by the new signs of Irish unrest, since it was still afraid of the harmful effect of Irish troubles on American sentiment; and Lord Northcliffe, who was then in close touch with Lloyd George, spoke fervently of the need for an Irish settlement when he talked to the Irish Club in London on St. Patrick's Day.

British anxiety about the United States was largely relieved on April 4, 1917, when the American President, Woodrow Wilson, declared war on Germany; but it was still necessary for Britain to conciliate the big Irish population in the United States, which had considerable influence on American policy. President Wilson himself saw that new moves were needed in Ireland. He told Walter H. Page, the United States Ambassador in London, to explain to Lloyd George that "if the American people were once convinced that there was a likelihood that the Irish question would soon be settled, great enthusiasm and satisfaction would result, and it would strengthen the co-operation which we are now about to organise as between the United States and Great Britain".

Lloyd George hardly needed the Ambassador's prodding, for he was genuinely anxious to clear up the Irish trouble. At the end of April he began new talks with the Irish Party leaders, and before they were over another Irish by-election had shown that swift action was needed to check the spread of Sinn Fein. In South Longford the Sinn Feiners had chosen an absentee candidate—Joseph McGuinness, who was serving a sentence in Lewes gaol—and one of their slogans was "Put him in to get him out". This was an area where the "Old Party" was particularly strong, and where, too, the influence of the "separation women"—wives of soldiers serving in the British Army, who felt that their separation allowances would be threatened by a Sinn Fein victory—was thrown vehemently against the Sinn Fein candidate. But McGuinness won. After two recounts he had a majority of 29. The *Manchester Guardian* described the South Longford result as the equivalent of a serious defeat of the British Army in the field.

In the middle of May Lloyd George made a new offer to Redmond. He was ready, he said, to introduce a Bill for the immediate application of the Home Rule Act to Ireland, but excluding the six counties of north-east Ulster for five years, after which the issue would be reconsidered by Parliament. If this was not acceptable he suggested that a Convention of Irishmen of all parties should be assembled for the purpose of producing an agreed scheme for Irish self-government.

Redmond rejected the Home Rule offer. It smacked too much of the ill-fated Headings of Agreement, and he suspected that any temporary partition of Ireland would prove to be permanent. But he thought that the idea of an Irish Convention had "much to recommend it", and he readily accepted the proposal on behalf of the Irish Party. Lloyd George acted at once. On May 21 he announced in Parliament that the Convention was to include representatives of all political parties in north and south, including Sinn Fein, but that the bulk of the membership would come from local councils, the Churches, the trade unions, and commercial and educational interests, so that it would provide "a real representation of Irish life and activity in all their leading branches". Preparations for the Convention were immediately put in hand, and to allow it to meet, as Bonar Law said in the House of Commons, "in an atmosphere of harmony and goodwill", the Government decided to release all Irish prisoners serving sentences for their part in the Rising.

Most of the prisoners landed at Dun Laoghaire on the morning of June 18. Cheering crowds welcomed them in Dublin, where Volunteers kept order in the streets, Sinn

Fein flags were openly displayed and the police kept discreetly in the background. De Valera, whom so few of the onlookers had ever seen before, was the hero of the morning's demonstration. The tall, austere ex-commandant, in whom Lady Gregory was later to trace a resemblance to Abraham Lincoln, was proudly acclaimed with a new revolutionary song:

> 'Twas in Kilmainham prison yard our fifteen martyrs died
> And cold and still in Arbour Hill they are lying side by side,
> But we will yet pay back the debt, for the spirit is still alive
> In men who stood through fire and blood with Convict 95.

There was a more familiar figure to welcome later in the day, when Constance Markievicz, gay and smiling, arrived by the evening boat and was escorted through the city by a vast procession of men and women.

That night, while bonfires were lighted on hills all over Ireland, de Valera was already at work. With other Sinn Fein leaders he drafted a message, in the name of the provisional Government of the Irish Republic, to the President and Congress of the United States, denouncing the "English conspiracy against Ireland", proclaiming the right of small nations to independence, and concluding: "We are engaged and mean to engage ourselves in practical means for establishing this right."

The British Government's conciliatory gesture had achieved nothing. Ireland had still, indeed, her fervent Home Rulers. Only a few weeks after her triumphant return Constance Markievicz was attacked by a Nationalist crowd in Clare and was gallantly rescued by the R.I.C. But Lloyd George's Convention was doomed before it began. The resurgent spirit of Sinn Fein had now a leadership which could fully exploit the country's new mood.

CHAPTER XII

A Match to the Fuse

I

THE IRISH CONVENTION held its first sitting on July 25, 1917, and its last on April 5, 1918. Most of its meetings were held in the Regent House of Trinity College, Dublin, though it also held sessions in Belfast and Cork. It clarified the Irish position by reaffirming the measure of disagreement between north and south. It showed the United States that the British Government was doing something, at all events, to promote an Irish settlement. It brought back into Irish politics the significant figure of Erskine Childers, who was seconded from the Royal Flying Corps to be one of the secretaries of the Convention. But its ultimate effect on the Irish situation amounted to nothing at all.

Its futility was implicit in the terms on which it was set up. Lloyd George promised to accept its report, even if it were not unanimous, provided that it revealed "substantial agreement" on a constitution "for the future government of Ireland within the Empire". "Substantial agreement" was exactly the kind of ambiguous phrase that Lloyd George was so fond of using, and it may be doubted whether he knew himself what he meant by it. Indeed, at one stage during the Convention's meetings a deputation went to ask him to clarify a particular point, and though he appeared to have done so, no two delegates could ever agree afterwards either on what he had meant or even on what he had said.

The Convention was also doomed by its composition. Its 95 members included mayors and chairmen of public bodies, together with almost every prominent Irishman outside party politics; but its weakness lay on the political side. Sinn Fein, which was offered five seats, declined to take part in it; William O'Brien's small All for Ireland Party also refused to be represented; and though the Southern Unionists were helpful and conciliatory (so conciliatory, in fact, that they thoroughly alarmed Carson) the Ulster Unionists came in with their hands tied, being committed to consultation with Carson and their council in Belfast before giving their votes on important issues. With Sinn Fein absent and Ulster unyielding, the Convention had no hope of reaching a settlement that would satisfy all Ireland. Moreover the choice of Sir Horace Plunkett as chairman was hardly a happy one. He was a great Irishman, but as chairman he was accused of wasting time and exerting no real authority over the Convention.

While the Convention was still preparing for its first meeting Sinn Fein had another by-election victory. Willie Redmond, John Redmond's younger brother and the very popular Nationalist M.P. for East Clare, had insisted, though he was 56, on taking a commission in the British Army so that he could serve with an Irish Division; and in June, 1917, he died of wounds while serving with the Irish Guards in France, where he had recently won the D.S.O. for conspicuous gallantry and devotion to duty. De Valera was chosen as Sinn Fein candidate for the ensuing by-election.

At that time de Valera was by no means the accomplished speaker he became in later years. He spoke slowly and at great length, and he both amused and exasperated his colleagues by his habit of bringing out the commonplaces of separatist philosophy as though they were the results of his own original thought. He was unknown in East Clare when the campaign began, but he came to it with the prestige of having been the last commandant to surrender in Easter

Week, and his obvious sincerity more than compensated for the drabness of his speeches. The police reported that his followers used a good deal of intimidation in persuading people to vote for him—a practice which was widely followed in the general election of 1918. But intimidation could not account for the magnitude of his victory when the result was announced on July 11. De Valera polled 5,010 votes, and his Nationalist opponent—a Clareman and a K.C. —only 2,035. He was thus the third Sinn Fein M.P. to be elected to the British House of Commons, though like the others, he declared that he had no intention of taking his seat there. A great meeting, at which the crowds stretched from O'Connell Street to College Green, was arranged to welcome him back to Dublin. One of the speakers was Thomas Ashe, a fellow-prisoner in Lewes gaol, who said movingly: "We had heard whispers in prison that a new Ireland had arisen, but we never dreamt anything like the reality we have seen."

A month later the Nationalist M.P. for Kilkenny died, and at the by-election Sinn Fein won again. This time the successful candidate was another ex-prisoner from Lewes—William T. Cosgrave, a Dublin alderman who had served in the Rising at the South Dublin Union and was a tougher fighting man than anyone might have guessed by looking at his light hair, blue eyes and mild, unaggressive face. De Valera, who had suggested that Cosgrave should stand, was at his side at the declaration of the poll, and reporters recorded that there was "frantic enthusiasm" as the two men shook hands.

Propaganda was the principal Sinn Fein weapon in the summer and autumn of 1917, though the Volunteers continued to drill and even appeared in the streets in their officially forbidden uniform. In secret a new constitution for the I.R.B. was being worked out by Michael Collins and Diarmuid Lynch, with the help of Ashe and Con Collins. Michael Collins had also become secretary of the Irish National Aid Association, which helped the dependants of men killed in the Rising and imprisoned Sinn Feiners, and this kept him a little apart from the main stream of Sinn Fein and Volunteer activities. De Valera had now left the I.R.B., and the first signs of division were becoming apparent between the I.R.B. men, who looked to Collins as their leader, and the Sinn Feiners like Brugha and de Valera, who had either left the Brotherhood or had never belonged to it.

In the meantime the police were trying desperately to check the new wave of Sinn Fein activities, though they were anxious to avoid any open clash with the Volunteers. The carrying of weapons in public places was prohibited by a Dublin Castle proclamation on July 28; more arms raids were carried out by both the police and the military; and many of the men released from Lewes and Frongoch were imprisoned again for making seditious speeches. One of these was Ashe, who was sentenced on August 20 to a year's hard labour for attempting to cause disaffection among the civil population. He was sent to Mountjoy gaol, where one of his fellow-prisoners was Austin Stack, the Kerry Volunteer leader who had been at Tralee when Casement landed. Together they decided to organise a hunger-strike in support of their demand that they should be treated as political prisoners, and the gaol authorities retaliated by submitting the prisoners to forcible feeding. After a week of this treatment Ashe collapsed and was taken to hospital, where he died within five hours. At his inquest a coroner's jury affirmed that death had been caused by his treatment in gaol and censured the Dublin Castle authorities and the deputy governor of Mountjoy.

The funeral of Thomas Ashe on September 30, 1917, was the clearest sign of the resurgence of the Easter Week spirit that had yet been given. Regulations about the wearing of uniform were ignored, though the streets of Dublin were full of proclamations describing the penalties to be inflicted on anyone who wore it. After lying in state, first in the Mater Hospital and then in the City Hall, with a Volunteers' guard of honour around it, the body was placed in a coffin covered with a Republican flag and taken in funeral procession to Glasnevin cemetery.

The dense crowds lining O'Connell Street saw first a small advance guard of uniformed Volunteers, then about 200 Catholic priests with gleaming top hats, and immediately after them the hearse, flanked by Volunteers with rifles reversed and followed by an officer with drawn sword. Then came a long stream of cars and carriages, including those of the Lord Mayor and Catholic Archbishop of Dublin, and after them an immense procession of representatives of all the patriotic organisations, including the I.R.B. (under the pseudonym of the Wolfe Tone Memorial Committee), Gaelic Leaguers in national costume, members of the Gaelic Athletic Association carrying hurleys, a detachment of the Redmondite National Volunteers led by Colonel Maurice Moore, and even the Dublin Fire Brigade mounted on their engines with Sinn Fein brassards on their arms. In all some 20,000 to 30,000 people followed the hearse, together with several bands; for the most part the crowds watched in silence, and one of their few demonstrations was a burst of hand-clapping when Constance Markievicz went by in her Citizen Army uniform. The Dublin police took no action as the forbidden uniforms were flaunted before them, and an English visitor, Douglas Goldring, overheard an English staff officer's comment: "Oh, yes, we do just the same in India. We always give the natives a free hand with their religious rites!"

When the coffin was laid in the grave at Glasnevin a guard of Volunteers fired three volleys over it, but this time there was no panegyric as there had been when O'Donovan Rossa was buried. The funeral had been organised by the I.R.B., and it was an I.R.B. representative, Michael Collins, who stood at the head of the grave in his uniform of vice-commandant of the Irish Volunteers. Few of the onlookers knew the name of this handsome young officer who spoke two short sentences, first in Gaelic and then in English, as the sound of the volleys died away. His English words were: "Nothing additional remains to be said. That volley which we have just heard is the only speech which it is proper to make above the grave of a dead Fenian."

Though the firing of blank cartridge by uniformed men in a public place was a flagrant breach of several Dublin Castle regulations, the British authorities took no action over the funeral and burial of Thomas Ashe. But they were shocked by his death, and at once made a number of changes in the treatment of Sinn Fein prisoners. They began also to make use of what was generally known as the "Cat and Mouse Act", which had been introduced in England at the time when suffragettes were going on prison hunger-strikes. This allowed the Government to release prisoners who were weakening themselves by refusing food and to re-arrest them later when they had regained their strength. It was an effective measure, and although Sinn Fein prisoners still went on hunger-strike from time to time, there were no more deaths from this cause until 1920.

Britain was particularly anxious to avoid trouble in Ireland while the Convention was sitting, and the Castle turned a blind eye to the opening of Sinn Fein clubs all over the country. Even on October 25, when resurgent Sinn Fein held its first Ard-Fheis, or national convention, the Dublin police watched good-humouredly as 2,000 delegates from these clubs poured into the Mansion House to draw up a new Irish constitution.

The agenda for the Ard-Fheis had been drawn up with considerable care, for the split which later bedevilled Irish politics was already in evidence in 1917. There were, in fact, two schools of thought among the revolutionary leaders. There were those who held that the Irish Republic had been finally established by the proclamation of Easter Monday, and now, hallowed by the blood of its martyrs, was beyond all challenge and needed no ratification by popular vote; there were others who thought that the proclamation could not be taken to have overruled ordinary democratic procedure and that the people of Ireland must be allowed to choose their own form of government. These two views appeared to have been reconciled in a formula devised by de Valera and unanimously accepted by the committee which drew up the agenda for the Ard-Fheis. It declared: "Sinn Fein aims at securing the international recognition of Ireland as an independent Irish Republic. Having achieved that status the Irish people may by referendum freely choose their own form of government." This formula, however, was more significant than it may have appeared at first sight. The old Sinn Fein movement had aimed solely at the independence of Ireland, and was even willing to go back to the Renunciation Act as a first step towards that end. The new Sinn Fein was formally committed to insistence on an Irish Republic.

The question of changing the movement's name had been discussed before the Ard-Fheis, but since the Rising had become popularly known as the Sinn Fein rebellion, all champions of Irish independence were usually known as Sinn Feiners and the new separatist M.P.s had been returned as Sinn Fein candidates, the case for keeping the old name was felt to be overwhelming. But the Volunteers among the delegates thought that the new Sinn Fein should have a new leader. Griffith might well have been re-elected in spite of the Volunteers' opposition, but he realised that a closely contested election would cause a disastrous split in the movement. The other possible candidates were Count Plunkett and de Valera, who at this time was backed by the I.R.B. To avert a contest both Griffith and Plunkett stood down. De Valera—"a man," said Griffith, "in whom you will have a statesman as well as a soldier"—was unanimously elected President of Sinn Fein.

The Ard-Fheis was divided, however, over the position of Eoin MacNeill. Some of the delegates had never forgiven him for his countermanding orders before the Rising, and when he was proposed for membership of the Sinn Fein executive Constance Markievicz moved that his name should be struck off the ballot-paper. Once again, as in the hall of

Dartmoor gaol, de Valera stood by his old chief, who, he declared, had not acted otherwise than as a good Irishman. In the result MacNeill headed the poll for the executive; Griffith and Father O'Flanagan were elected Vice-Presidents, with Cosgrave and Larry Ginnell (a Nationalist M.P. who had left the party to join Sinn Fein) as honorary treasurers and Austin Stack and Darrell Figgis as honorary secretaries. The Ard-Fheis decided that Sinn Fein should fight every Irish seat at the next general election for the British House of Commons, and that successful candidates should regard themselves as an Irish constituent assembly. In his final speech to the Convention de Valera first used the words which were so often quoted in later years: "We are not doctrinaire Republicans."

On the following day the Irish Volunteers held a secret meeting at Croke Park, the Dublin football and sports ground. De Valera was elected President, so that the leadership of the military and political wings of the independence movement was now united in one man, though otherwise the organisation of the Volunteers was separate from that of Sinn Fein. Cathal Brugha was appointed Chief of Staff, but it was significant that three members of the I.R.B. gained important positions on the executive. Michael Collins became Director of Organisation, Diarmuid Lynch Director of Communications and Sean McGarry General Secretary, so that the I.R.B. was as well placed as it had been before the Rising to exert a powerful influence on Volunteer policy. Collins soon made his mark in his new post. Training was organised systematically, and Collins at once showed the insistence on efficiency and contempt for laziness in his subordinates which were to gain him some unpopularity among more easy-going colleagues. He became so active, indeed, that de Valera suspected him of "organising more than the Volunteers".

Drilling was the Volunteers' chief activity in the winter of 1917–18, though bodies of masked men made occasional raids for arms on isolated country houses. Sometimes these raids were made in Dublin itself. Frank Gallagher was one of a party of Volunteers who went to the house of a British Provost-Marshal in Haddington Road, successfully pretended to be a plain-clothes squad of the Dublin Metropolitan Police and persuaded the guileless Provost-Marshal to give them his collection of rifles and revolvers "for safe keeping", so that there would be no danger of their falling into the hands of raiders.

As the Irish Convention was still sitting at Trinity College, there was a lull in political developments, though Sinn Fein gave a demonstration of "self-reliance" by taking action to improve food distribution among the poorer people. That winter a minor food crisis was threatened in Ireland, owing to the heavy exports of cattle, oats and butter to England; and though Sinn Fein could do little to stop this trade, which was very remunerative for Irish farmers, it took an unofficial census of food supplies and set up co-operative markets for selling potatoes to poor families at cost price. In Clare, Sligo and the neighbouring counties the Sinn Fein clubs seized grazing-lands belonging to large estates, cleared them of cattle and leased them out for tillage—an entirely illegal activity which still went on in spite of frequent arrests of the ringleaders. These efforts to improve food supplies increased the popularity of Sinn Fein, but there was still no indication that it had sufficient public support to give it victory in a general election. Indeed, as spring came its influence seemed to be waning, for it lost three by-elections—in South Armagh, Waterford and East Tyrone—and uninformed observers were tempted to think that it would soon die out.

The Waterford by-election was caused by the death of John Redmond in a London nursing-home on March 6, 1918. He was 61, and his health had given way after 36 years of political work and the additional burden of trying to steer the Irish Convention to a practicable conclusion. At his graveside at Wexford John Dillon, who succeeded him as leader of the Irish Parliamentary Party, said that "those who today misunderstand him will, in time to come, understand the greatness of his life and work and the unselfishness of his career". It had been in the end a tragic, unrewarded career. Home Rule, which all southern Ireland except the small minority of separatists had wanted so eagerly before the war, had seemed to be in Redmond's grasp until the opposition of Ulster wrecked his life-work; his denunciation of the two nations theory of Ireland had not been strong enough to overcome the British Government's growing belief that partition was the only solution of the Irish problem; and in his last months he feared that the impetuosity of the Sinn Fein leaders would bring about that very partition which they, like he, wished to avert.

By dying when he did, Redmond was at least spared the disappointment of witnessing the utter failure of the Irish Convention. Its final report was adopted by only 44 votes to 29, and there were many abstentions, so that its plan for an all-Ireland Senate and House of Commons with an executive responsible to them could not be said to be backed by any "substantial agreement". Perhaps the most important result of the Convention was its creation of a permanent split between the Southern Unionists, led by Lord Midleton, who had come to believe that Home Rule with safeguards was the best policy for all Ireland, and the Ulster Unionists, who voted consistently against all proposals for an Irish Parliament.

In any case the Convention's labours were forgotten almost as soon as it had issued its report. For on April 16 the British Government was given power by the House of Commons to impose conscription for military service in Ireland. Collins, de Valera and others were setting a slow fuse for an eventual explosion. It was Lloyd George who put the match to it.

2

The decision—not to impose conscription on Ireland, but to be empowered to impose it if necessary—had been made by the British Prime Minister with much reluctance. The objections to trying to force unwilling Irishmen into the British Army were fully recognised. Earlier in the war Asquith had made the point that conscription was permissible in England only because it was based on the universal assent of the English people; but clearly no such assent existed in Ireland. It was felt, too, that conscription in Ireland would not produce the desired results. Only three months earlier Sir Auckland Geddes, Minister of National Service, had explained that Ireland was excluded from a new Bill extending the range of compulsory service because the Government considered that "to have included a proposal to apply compulsory military service to Ireland would not have helped on the war". The Ulster Unionist M.P.s insistently demanded conscription for all Ireland, but it was only when Germany's March offensive on the Western Front made the Government decide to call up still more men in England, Scotland and Wales that the compulsion of Irishmen was regarded as a practical possibility.

Even then the Cabinet hesitated. Both Lloyd George and Bonar Law were doubtful, and Duke, the Chief Secretary for Ireland, said bluntly that they might as well enlist Germans. General Sir Bryan Mahon, the Irish-born G.O.C. of the British forces in Ireland, and General Sir Joseph Byrne, head of the R.I.C., both thought it would be difficult to impose conscription, and they warned the Cabinet that they would need more troops and that bloodshed and suffering would certainly follow. Even Carson, whose opinion was sought, though he was not then a member of the Cabinet, was against it. Unlike the Ulster back-benchers in the Commons, he thought that the Government would get little return from conscription in Ireland, and that any advantage would be outweighed by the resulting disturbances.

While Bonar Law hesitated, other Unionist members of the Cabinet put up a strong case for conscription in Ireland. They insisted that there would be bad feeling in Britain if the young manhood of Ireland was left untouched while the conscription age-limit for the rest of the British Isles was raised from 50 to 55, as proposed in the new Bill under consideration. They said, too, that the British trade unions would resent the continued exclusion of Ireland while their own members were being called up in increasing numbers; and another point, which was urged outside the Cabinet by the influential Sir Henry Wilson, was that the call-up of Irish young men was essential for the full restoration of law and order in Ireland.

It was only after much heart-searching and because he could not dispute the urgent need for all available manpower that Lloyd George gave way to his Unionist colleagues, but at the same time he devised a characteristic compromise. He proposed that conscription and Home Rule should be introduced together: the new Bill, therefore, would not actually apply conscription to Ireland but would give the Government authority to apply it at any time when it might seem to be necessary; and simultaneously the Government would press on with a new Home Rule Bill, in the hope that it would be in operation before the first Irishman was called up for military service. In the meantime yet more efforts should be made to get voluntary recruits in Ireland.

In his usual exuberant way Lloyd George told Cecil Harmsworth, Lord Northcliffe's brother, that he would resign if he could not get a Home Rule Bill through; but only a man of Lloyd George's mercurial temperament could have thought it would be possible to rush through Parliament in a week or two a new Bill that would be acceptable to all shades of Irish opinion. It was on this improbable and insubstantial basis that the new conscription Bill, including powers for its application to Ireland, was introduced in the House of Commons on April 9.

Its impact was immediate. The promise of an early Home Rule Bill made no impression on the Irish Nationalist M.P.s; and when the conscription Bill was passed by 301 votes to 103 they left the Commons under Dillon's leadership and went back to Ireland to organise an anti-conscription campaign. Dr. J. P. Mahaffy, the old Provost of Trinity College, used to say that "in Ireland the inevitable never happens, the unexpected always". The events of April, 1918, bore fresh witness to his wisdom. A few weeks earlier nothing could have been less probable than the Nationalist M.P.s would line up with Sinn Fein. Thanks to the British Cabinet's decision, this was now to happen, and the explosion touched off by the threat of conscription was to reverberate long after the need for Irish recruits had ceased with the end of the European War.

CHAPTER XIII

Sinn Fein Ascendant

I

BY THE SPRING of 1918 they had a new song in southern Ireland. One verse ran:

When we were little children Johnny Redmond was a fool,
He bade us to be satisfied with something called Home Rule,
But we have learnt a thing or two since we went to school,
  And we'll crown de Valera King of Ireland.

And another:

Up, de Valera! He's the champion of the right,
We'll follow him to battle 'neath the Orange, Green and White,
And when next we challenge England we'll beat her in the fight
  And we'll crown de Valera King of Ireland.

The song reflected de Valera's growing authority since his return from gaol in the previous June. He was not a typical Irish revolutionary: Oliver Gogarty once described him as looking like "something uncoiled from the Book of Kells", and Sean O'Casey observed that no one could imagine de Valera rushing round a hurling field, dancing a jig, drinking in a Dublin bar or "swanking" in the green kilt and saffron shawl affected by ardent Gaelic Leaguers. Yet his fervour and his courage were rallying young Ireland solidly behind him. An English newspaper correspondent reported that the young men were prepared to follow blindly "this tall, stern man in his early thirties with angular features and blazing eyes".

The threat of conscription gave de Valera his first big opportunity for showing his powers of political leadership. Two days after the Irish M.P.s had walked out of the House of Commons Larry O'Neill, Lord Mayor of Dublin, summoned an anti-conscription meeting at the Mansion House. It was attended by Dillon and Devlin for the Parliamentary Party, de Valera and Griffith for Sinn Fein, Tim Healy—a lively Parliamentary veteran who had sat for various Irish constituencies since 1880—as an Independent, William O'Brien for the All for Ireland League and three representatives of the trade unions. De Valera was the dominant figure. It was he who drafted an anti-conscription pledge to be circulated to every parish in the country; it was he who was chiefly responsible for the conference's firm statement that "the passing of the Conscription Bill by the British House of Commons must be regarded as a declaration of war on the Irish nation" and that "the attempt to enforce it will be an unwarrantable aggression, which we call upon all Irishmen to resist by the most effective means at their disposal". He was also one of the deputation which went that evening to Maynooth, where the Catholic hierarchy was holding its annual meeting, to urge the bishops to make a statement sanctioning resistance to conscription.

Hitherto the hierarchy had taken little part on either side in the development of the Sinn Fein struggle. It had viewed with some alarm the tendency of many younger priests to become ardent Sinn Feiners, and it had issued an instruction warning priests against "dangerous associations" and "organisations that plot against the Church or lawfully constituted authority". The conference had no idea what kind of reception its delegates would get at Maynooth, and Tim Healy was rather surprised at the assurance with which de Valera set out on the mission. When de Valera confidently observed that he had spent all his life among priests, the sceptical Healy retorted: "But have you lived all your life among bishops?" In fact, de Valera's assurance was justified. One of the bishops said afterwards that when de Valera entered their assembly it was "as the descent of the Holy Ghost upon them".

After hearing the deputation the hierarchy drew up its own anti-conscription manifesto, in which it stated:

> "An attempt is being made to enforce conscription on Ireland against the will of the Irish people and in defiance of the protests of its leaders. . . . We consider that conscription forced in this way on Ireland is an oppressive and inhuman law which the Irish have a right to resist by every means that are consonant with the laws of God."

At the same time it directed the clergy to celebrate a Mass of intercession on the following Sunday and to administer to their congregations the pledge drafted by de Valera, which said: "Denying the right of the British Government to enforce compulsory service in this country, we pledge ourselves solemnly one to another to resist conscription by the most effective means at our disposal." So resistance—though only to conscription, not to the whole system of British rule in Ireland—was officially sanctioned by the Roman Catholic Church. It was left to the faithful to search their consciences in deciding what means of resistance were "consonant with the laws of God".

The trade-union movement followed the bishops, and a 24 hours' general strike was called for April 23. Except in Belfast, the strike was solid throughout Ireland. Factories stood idle, shops and bars were closed, transport was stopped and visitors were annoyed to find that they could get no cars to take them to Punchestown races. It was now clear that southern Ireland had no intention of standing patiently by in the remote hope that conscription, when the Government chose to impose it, would be accompanied by Home Rule. New measures were needed to meet the changed situation.

Lloyd George's first move was to change the Government's chief representatives in Ireland. The Unionist Chief Secretary, Henry Duke, who had never liked the idea of conscription, was brought home to be made a Lord Justice of Appeal, and was replaced by a Liberal lawyer-politician, Edward Shortt. It was time, too, to appoint a new Viceroy. To succeed Lord Wimborne Lloyd George chose the redoubtable if at that time slightly discredited figure of Field-Marshal Lord French.

Lord French, who was later to become the Earl of Ypres, was then 65. Though born in Kent, he was of Irish ancestry, and after a few years as a naval cadet and midshipman, his career had been entirely military. He had won a great and deserved reputation as a dashing cavalry general in the Boer War, but his success was not repeated when he became Commander-in-Chief of the British Expeditionary Force in France in 1914. At the end of 1915 he was removed from his command, and was consoled by being given a home appointment as Inspector-General of the British Army. He had a pleasant personality and was said to be fond of pretty women, though allegations that he had entertained his women-friends at his G.H.Q. in France had been vigorously refuted. His appointment as Viceroy marked a significant change in the character of the office. In recent years the Viceroy had been largely a figurehead, but French's military seniority to the Commander-in-Chief of the British forces in Ireland made his power in times of disturbance greater than the Chief Secretary's.

When French was sent to Ireland the Government was afraid of another organised rebellion. It was resolved, however, that Britain should not take the offensive, and Sir Henry Wilson noted in his diary that at a dinner-party "Lloyd George impressed on Johnnie (French) the wisdom of putting the onus for first shooting on the rebels". French himself had high hopes that Home Rule would be established during his Viceroyalty, but in Ireland he was regarded as a military martinet sent to impose conscription. When he arrived in Dublin he stayed first at the Shelbourne Hotel, and as he stepped out of his car to enter it cries of "Up, Easter Week" and "Up, the rebels" came from excited waiters and chambermaids at the hotel windows. French was not perturbed. At dinner he asked the head waiter what Ireland meant to do about conscription, and was given the defiant reply: "Well, my lord, we are 70 men in this house. We have all made our peace with God. You may have our dead bodies, but you'll get nothing else." It must have been about this time that a British officer, newly arrived in Dublin, went into a D.B.C. (Dublin Bread Company) café and innocently asked a waitress what D.B.C. meant. The girl looked coolly at his uniform and answered: "Death before conscription."

French landed in Ireland on May 11, 1918. Within a week the whole situation was changed, for on the night of May 17–18 de Valera, Griffith, Count Plunkett, Darrell Figgis, Constance Markievicz, Joseph McGuinness, Sean McGarry and more than 70 other Sinn Feiners, including Maud Gonne and Mrs. Tom Clarke, were arrested and deported to English gaols. Michael Collins had been told of the coming round-up by a Dublin Metropolitan Police detective who was a spy for the Sinn Feiners, but though he had warned his colleagues, most of them were seized at their homes by soldiers or police. Collins himself escaped because he saw a military lorry at his door as he was cycling home; he promptly rode away and was able to spend the night at a friend's house which had been already raided. Cathal Brugha and Harry Boland were other prominent members of the Sinn Fein executive who escaped arrest. So de Valera, who had been in Ireland for barely eleven months since his return from Lewes gaol, was now to be out of the country again for another eight months. In his absence Collins became generally recognised as the chief organiser of the Irish resistance movement.

The reason for these arrests was given in a proclamation by French, stating that "it has come to our knowledge that certain subjects of his Majesty the King, domiciled in Ireland, have conspired to enter into, and have entered into, treasonable communication with the German enemy"; but his predecessor, Lord Wimborne, said he knew nothing of a German plot and did not believe there was one. The Government's "evidence", published later as a White Paper, was far from convincing.

Germany, it is true, had not forgotten Ireland. Throughout the European War there were rumours of German submarines putting in on the Donegal coast; a man on Tory Island had been heard to complain bitterly that a German sailor, who came ashore from a submarine occasionally to buy potatoes, had eventually got hold of the Department of Agriculture's maximum price order, "an' divil a ha'porth more than that would he pay!" Other stories of the same kind were circulating in England, such as that of the summer visitor to Galway who wanted to hire a boat and was told by a local fisherman that he could not spare one, as he was getting £3 a day from the Germans for dropping mines. When the visitor said he would try another fisherman who hired out boats he was told: "*That's* no good. *He's* getting £10 a week from the Government for fishing the mines up!"

Apart from such rumours and anecdotes it was true that pamphlets printed in Germany during the war had been found in Ireland, and that Devoy in America was still in contact with both Dublin and Berlin; but the only evidence of active German intervention in Irish affairs was provided by the arrest in April of Joseph Dowling, an ex-lance-corporal of the Connaught Rangers, who had been brought to Ireland in a German submarine and put ashore on the Clare coast in a collapsible boat. Dowling, who as a prisoner of war in Germany had joined Casement's Irish Brigade, had been sent by the German General Staff to report on the prospects for another Irish rebellion; but since his mission was Germany's own idea, it hardly revealed a plot by the Sinn Fein leaders. Perhaps it was just possible for the British Government to maintain that the various Irish–German contacts added up to a "German plot", and since an excuse was wanted for putting the Sinn Fein leaders

1. "Trust the Old Party, and Home Rule next year": John Redmond, leader of the Irish Parliamentary Party, addresses a Home Rule meeting at the Parnell Monument, Dublin, 1912. Six years later Redmond died, broken-hearted, as he saw all southern Ireland turning away from the Old Party to the Sinn Feiners.

2. "We won't have it": Redmond's counterpart in Ulster, the redoubtable Sir Edward Carson, K.C., proclaims at an Ulster meeting the North's determination never to accept Home Rule for Ireland. His hope then was to smash the whole project of Irish Home Rule; the idea of partition came later.

3. Sir Edward Carson signs the Covenant, City Hall, Belfast: The Ulster Unionists consolidated their opposition September 28, 1912, when 100,000 Ulstermen signed a covenant pledging themselves to resist Home Rule. On his left is Capt. James Craig, later Ulster's first Prime Minister and Lord Craigavon.

4. Crowds of Ulstermen making their way to the City Hall, Belfast, on Ulster Day to put their names to the Covenant.

5. Batons out in O'Connell Street: the baton charge by the Dublin Metropolitan Police, 1913, during the Dublin transport strike. Crowds in O'Connell Street are roughly dispersed after Jim Larkin, leader of the Irish Transport and General Workers' Union, had addressed a meeting of strikers and sympathisers. Three people were killed in the mêlée, and it was in consequence of these deaths that the transport workers decided to form the Irish Citizen Army.

6. Gun-running at Howth: Irish Volunteers line up at Howth harbour, July 26, 1914, to carry rifles away from the yacht *Asgard*, in which Erskine Childers, with his wife, Gordon Sheppard and Mary Spring-Rice, had brought a cargo of arms from Germany.

7. Gun-running at Howth: Mrs. Erskine Childers (with rifle in hand and wearing the red jumper which was the prearranged signal that all had gone well) and Mary Spring-Rice on board the *Asgard*.

8. Bachelor's Walk funeral: Jim Larkin (wearing broad-brimmed hat) at the head of an Irish Citizen Army detachment in the funeral procession for the three men killed in Bachelor's Walk, Dublin, after the Howth gun-running in 1914, when troops of the King's Own Scottish Borderers opened fire on a crowd of Dubliners who had been jeering and throwing stones at them.

9. Before the Rising: men of the Irish Citizen Army (who joined with the Irish Volunteers in the Easter Rising) on parade at Croydon Park, Fairview, Dublin.

10. Before the Rising: Irish Volunteers, with only bandoliers and haversacks to distinguish them from civilians, on parade in Croydon Park, Fairview, Dublin. Arthur Griffith, who became first President of the Irish Free State and died in 1922, is fourth from the right.

11. England's appeal: while the Irish Republican Brotherhood planned the Easter Week protest in arms, the English military authorities continued to call for Irish recruits for the British Army. The decorated tram was used for a recruiting parade in Dame Street, Dublin, in 1915.

12. Easter Rising: British troops man one of the improvised barricades thrown up by the insurgents in Easter Week, 1916, with the object of delaying the British advance.

13. Easter Rising: an insurgent prisoner being marched across O'Connell Bridge by his British captors.

14. After the Rising: Liberty Hall, headquarters of the Irish Transport and the General Workers' Union and of the Citizen Army, after its bombardment from the Liffey by the British gunboat *Helga*.

15. After the Rising: Ruins of O'Connell Street and Eden Quay.

16. After the Rising: the burnt-out shell of the General Post Office in O'Connell Street, which had been the insurgents' headquarters until it was made untenable by fire.

17. Countess and Labour leader: in the great gathering which followed the hearse of Thomas Ashe, the Irish Volunteer who died on hunger strike in 1917, were Countess Markievicz (née Constance Gore-Booth), the famous rebel who had been reprieved after being sentenced to death for her part in the Easter Rising, and Cathal O'Shannon, a prominent young Labour and trade union leader, who was later to be "on the run". They are seen talking at Glasnevin cemetery after the funeral—the Countess in uniform but without the plumed hat she wore in Easter Week.

18. The New Leader: as the only surviving senior Dublin commandant during the Rising Eamonn de Valera became head of both Sinn Fein and the Irish Volunteers after his release from prison in 1917. A year later, when southern Ireland was gravely disturbed by reports that Britain was proposing to introduce conscription for Ireland, de Valera was the principal organiser of the "No Conscription" movement. He is seen here addressing a big meeting at Ballahadreen, county Roscommon, in 1918.

19. Part of the crowd at Ballahadreen listening to de Valera's address.

20. G-men confer: two detectives of the G Division, Dublin Metropolitan Police, in informal conference outside the morgue in Store Street, Dublin, after attending an inquest. The tall man at the back facing the camera is Detective Hoey, and immediately on his right is Detective Smith. Both were shot dead shortly afterwards in the streets of Dublin.

21. Briefing the Auxiliaries: General Crozier, officer commanding the Auxiliary Division of the R.I.C., giving some of his men a briefing. The photographer who took this picture and the one above had to hide his camera behind a bystander's back, since he would have been arrested if he had been seen.

22. Mountjoy hunger strike, 1920: British troops, tanks and armoured cars cordon off the area round Mountjoy gaol, Dublin, to prevent riots by sympathisers during the hunger strike.

23. Searching for arms: British troops holding up a civilian truck in Lord Edward Street, Dublin. Such hold-ups were familiar scenes in Dublin in 1919–21.

24. "The sack of Balbriggan": remains of Clonard Street, Balbriggan, after the raid by Black and Tans on September 20, 1920.

25. Military raid: troops swoop on an Irish village to look for arms and Sinn Fein suspects.

26. Lord French's farewell, May, 1921: Before leaving Ireland Lord French inspects the Royal Irish Constabulary and the Auxiliaries in Phoenix Park. Immediately behind him is General H. H. Tudor, Chief of Police in Ireland, 1920–21.

27. Custom House on fire: as a dramatic gesture against the English, Irish Volunteers raid the Custom House, the administrative centre of Irish local government and one of Dublin's most beautiful buildings, in May, 1921. They held up the staff, poured petrol over the offices, and set it on fire.

28. Custom House battle: one of the British soldiers who were quickly summoned to the burning building, where they guarded the exits by which the Volunteers hoped to escape.

29. Custom House battle: Volunteer raiders and civilian bystanders put up their hands as British troops and Auxiliaries close in on the Custom House.

30. De Valera welcomed on his return to Ireland after talks with Lloyd George in July, 1921.

31. Truce negotiations between the British representatives and the Sinn Fein leaders began at the Mansion House, Dublin, in July, 1921, as a direct consequence of the moving appeal made by King George V at the opening of the Northern Ireland Parliament. De Valera and Griffith leave the Mansion House together after one of the meetings in October.

32. Ratifying the Treaty: Dail Eireann (sitting as the Southern Parliament) formally ratifies the Anglo-Irish Treaty at a meeting in the oak room of the Mansion House, Dublin, on January 14, 1922. De Valera and his supporters are absent from the meeting; Michael Collins is sitting opposite the Speaker, W. T. Cosgrave is on the extreme left of the front bench, and Griffith is next but one to him.

33. Open fighting between the new Irish Free State Government and the Irregulars—the anti-Treaty section of the I.R.A.—began on June 28, 1922, when Free State artillery bombarded the Four Courts, Dublin, where the Irregular commandant, Rory O'Connor, had taken up his headquarters. After two days' bombardment the Four Courts caught fire, and as the flames reached a store of ammunition a tremendous explosion sent up a great mushroom of smoke high into the air above the building.

34. Four Courts battle: the surrendered garrison of the Four Courts being marched away by Free State soldiers.

35. After the bombardment: Ruins of the Four Courts, July, 1922.

36. Attacking the Hammam Hotel: during the Four Courts battle other Irregular leaders and anti-Treaty politicians had made their headquarters in various O'Connell Street hotels, of which the Hammam was the last to remain in their hands

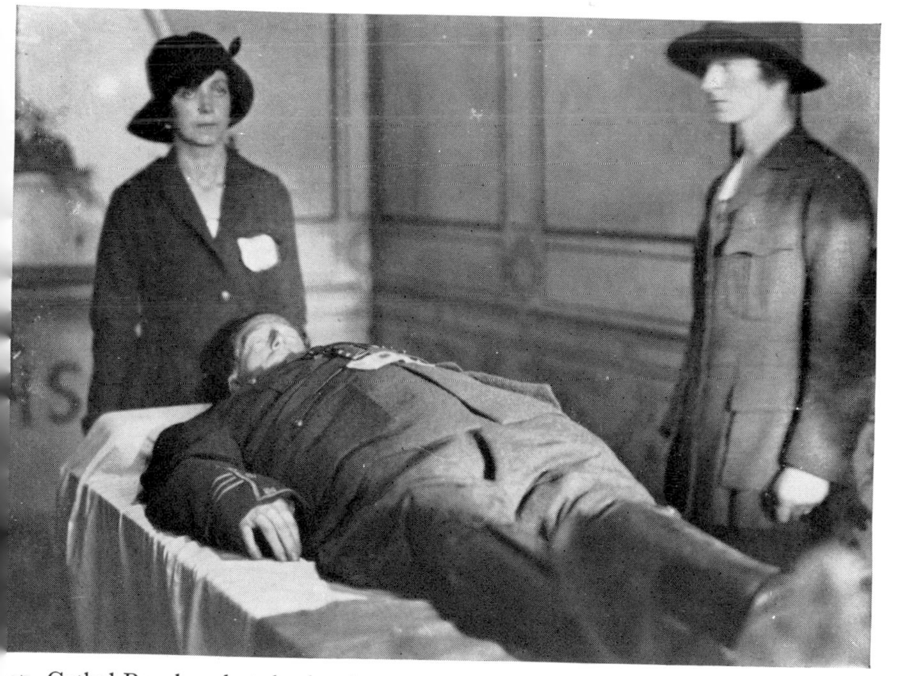

37. Cathal Brugha, shot dead as he came out of the burning Hammam Hotel with a revolver in each hand, lies in state in the Mater Hospital morgue.

38. Michael Collins in general's uniform at Portobello barracks, Dublin, taken over from the British in 1922.

39. The Free State takes over: General Sean MacEoin inspects a guard of honour as the newly formed National Free State Army also takes over barracks at Athlone from the British in 1922.

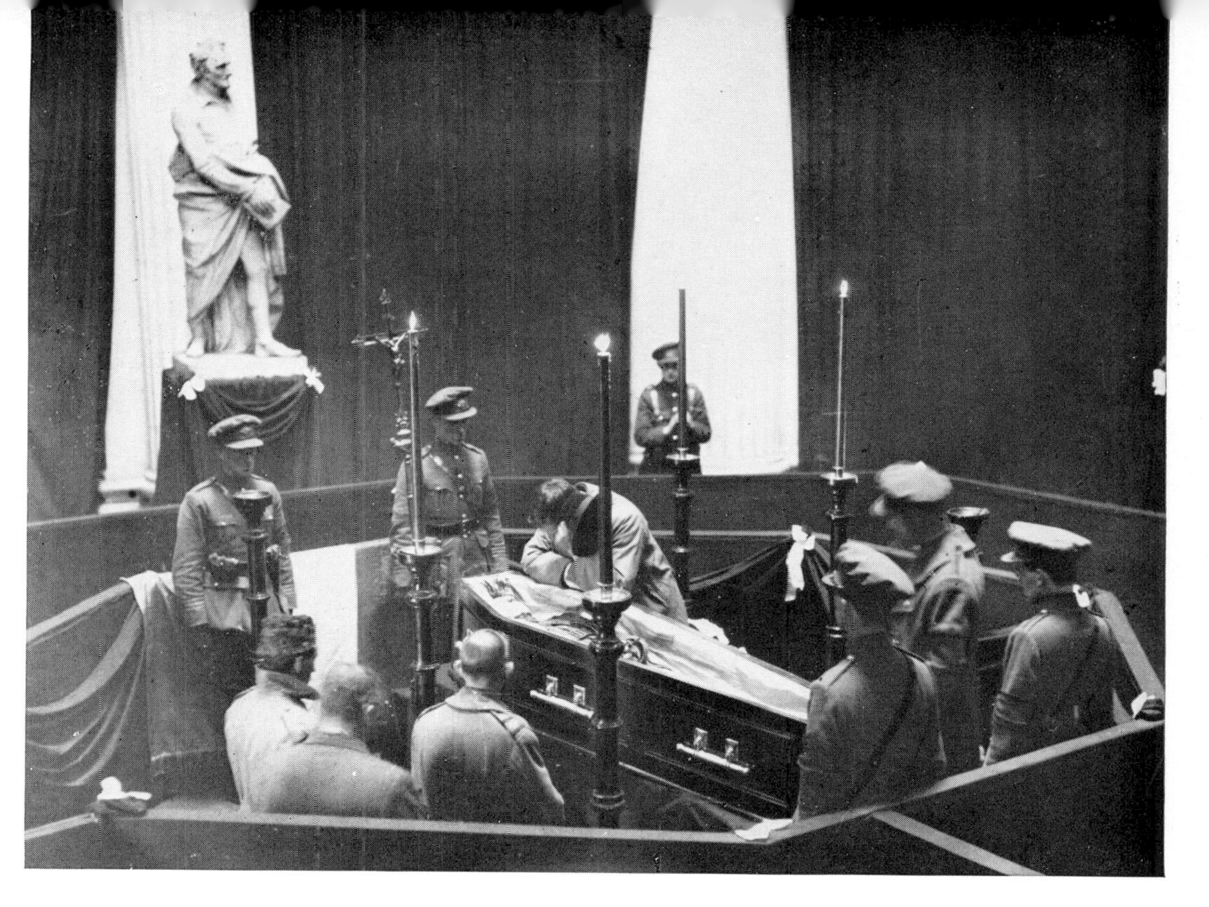

40. Lost leader: Michael Collins, killed in an ambush by Irregulars in county Cork in August, 1922, lying in state at City Hall, Dublin. His brother, Sean Collins, is kneeling beside him.

41. Guardians of the Free State: men of the new National Army dispersing t[h]
crowds at Ennis, county Clare, who had gathered to hear de Valera address [a]
anti-Treaty meeting. It was at this meeting that de Valera was arrested.

42. Irregulars' armoury: a Free State soldier examines a bomb factory captur[ed]
from the Irregulars in 1922 during the Civil War.

under lock and key again, the "plot" story was as good as any other.

With de Valera and most of his principal colleagues in English gaols the new Viceroy was able to settle down to a comparatively peaceful summer. The threat of conscription was temporarily shelved, and French issued a proclamation calling for further voluntary enlistment and expressing the Government's hope of "securing a contribution of men without resort to compulsion". The first target set was 50,000 recruits by October 1. Under the influence of this milder policy the frenzy of April seemed to be dying away, and Brigadier Hugo Headlam, the newly appointed Inspector of Infantry in Ireland, was able to tour the whole country in an official car without having any qualms about either his own safety or that of his charming girl driver.

2

The calm was only on the surface. After three defeats Sinn Fein resumed its triumphant career in by-elections, and Griffith, then interned in England, beat his Nationalist opponent by 1,200 votes at East Cavan in June. Father O'Flanagan was again active in this campaign, and was subsequently punished for his electioneering by the bishop of his diocese, who deprived him of all his faculties as a priest, including the right to say Mass. Moreover, though French's firm military rule appeared to have checked any immediate risk of a revolutionary outbreak, there was no cessation of activities and speeches which the British Government regarded as seditious. The police were so far immune from attack, but they felt, none the less, that they were living everywhere in an atmosphere of constant menace.

Decrees and prohibitions were the weapons first chosen by French for suppressing the independence movement. Sinn Fein, the Volunteers, the Cumann na mBan and the Gaelic League were all proclaimed as dangerous associations under the Defence of the Realm Act; their meetings were declared illegal, and so, too, was "the holding or taking part in any meetings, assemblies or processions in public places within the whole of Ireland". But meetings were still held, and were often broken up by the military or the police, who arrested the principal speakers. In all, about 1,100 arrests were made during 1918, and there were hundreds of police and military raids on private houses in search of arms or seditious documents.

One of the inflammatory speakers arrested in these months was Kevin O'Higgins, a 26-year-old law student and son of a doctor in Queen's County (now Leix), who had joined the Volunteers at Stradbally early in the war. At University College, Dublin, O'Higgins had been clever but idle, often choosing to spend the whole day on a stool in one of Mooney's bars instead of attending lectures; and while apprenticed at Cork to Maurice Healy, Tim Healy's brother, he had found political activity more enthralling than the routine of a solicitor's office. He was sentenced to five months' imprisonment for an offence which he himself described in some verses he wrote in Belfast gaol, beginning:

> I made a speech at Garryhinch,
> I urged the people not to flinch
> Before the threats of Viscount "Frinch",
>   So now I'm here!

One of his fellow-prisoners at Belfast was Austin Stack, who had been released from Mountjoy after Ashe's death and was subsequently re-arrested. Stack was impressed by this fearless, clear-thinking young man, who was at once an ardent Sinn Feiner and a Catholic who ordered his whole life by his religion. It was largely on Stack's recommendation that O'Higgins was chosen as Sinn Fein candidate for Queen's County in the general election later in the year.

The Volunteers were unaffected by the official ban on their work. Their own arms raids on private houses had been stopped by the executive's orders, and both in Dublin and in the provinces commandants devoted their efforts towards training an efficient fighting force. Collins was a hard-working Director of Organisation, and documents preserved from the period show his careful attention to detail. He is revealed, for instance, as having written twice to the Mid-Limerick Brigade to demand payment of 16*s*. 8*d*. for 100 copies of the Volunteers' magazine, *An-t-Oglach*. "A small sum—agreed," he wrote. "Yet multiply this apparently trivial amount by, say, 100—what have you? A largish sum. I do not request, I insist." Clearly the former employee of the Guaranty Trust Company had not forgotten his financial training.

An-t-Oglach was the successor to the *Irish Volunteer*, which had ceased publication after the Rising. It was a small four-page paper which came out twice a month and was edited then and for the following five years by Piaras Beaslai, except for an interval of a few months when publication was suspended because the editor was in prison. The first issue appeared on August 15, 1918, and Collins himself wrote some of the early articles; but perhaps the most startling contribution at that time was an article on "Ruthless Warfare", which was said to be written by "a leading Volunteer at present in prison". Beaslai later disclosed that the author was Ernest Blythe, a member of the Sinn Fein executive who was frequently imprisoned for making seditious speeches.

Collins had personally approved of Blythe's article, which called on the Volunteers to "acknowledge no limit and no scruple" in their resistance to any British attempt to impose conscription. "We must recognise," it said, "that anyone, civilian or soldier, who assists directly or by connivance in this crime against us, merits no more consideration than a wild beast, and should be killed without mercy or hesitation as opportunity offers." Irishmen were also included among the proposed victims of this ruthless warfare, for the article continued:

"The man who serves on an exemption tribunal, the doctor who treats soldiers or examines conscripts, the man who voluntarily surrenders when called for, the man who in any shape or form applies for exemption, the man who drives a police-car or assists in the transport of army supplies, all these having assisted the enemy must be shot or otherwise destroyed with the least possible delay."

These were savage words—quite as savage as the exhortations to destroy Sinn Feiners which appeared later in the R.I.C. *Weekly Summary* issued from Dublin Castle; and since the threat of conscription had brought up the Volunteers' strength to about 100,000, the influence of *An-t-Oglach* must have been substantial. Blythe, however, was not advocating an immediate shooting campaign; he was simply telling the Volunteers what they should do if, and only if, conscription were introduced.

Collins now added the post of Adjutant-General to that of Director of Organisation, and for the rest of 1918 he devoted himself to reorganising the Volunteers and building up a secret service through personal contacts among the police (particularly in the G Division of Dublin Metropolitan Police detectives), post office workers and gaol warders. Among his colleagues at the Volunteers' headquarters were Brugha, Richard Mulcahy, Beaslai, Rory O'Connor, Dick McKee and Eamonn Duggan. Brugha and Mulcahy, two Easter Week veterans, were respectively Chief of Staff and deputy Chief of Staff, but Mulcahy became acting Chief when Brugha was away in England making plans for reprisals there if conscription were introduced in Ireland. O'Connor, who was Director of Engineering, had a senior position in the Dublin Corporation engineering department, and had only recently been converted from Home Rule to Sinn Fein; McKee, the tall, dark and good-looking Commandant of the Dublin Brigade, was a printer by trade and had shown exceptional skill and energy as a Volunteer officer; and Duggan, Director of Intelligence, was a Dublin solicitor whose legal knowledge and personal shrewdness were especially valuable in such matters as the arrangement of bail for arrested Sinn Feiners. Most of these men were still able to lead double lives as workers earning their living and spare-time revolutionaries, but

Collins, who had lost his paid post as secretary of the National Aid Association, had no source of personal income. Presumably his friends and family came to his assistance, for he made no money out of his revolutionary activities.

The arrests in May had made bigger gaps in the Sinn Fein executive than at Volunteer headquarters. The political leadership was thus left largely in the hands of Harry Boland, who became joint secretary with Alderman Tom Kelly, a keen Sinn Feiner since 1905. As Boland knew he was wanted by the police, he at first went about Dublin in disguise, but he stopped doing so after hearing that a stranger had said of him: "I saw a man passing on a bicycle, with a false moustache and spectacles with no glass in them. I wonder who he was!" In any case the police seemed to have no eagerness to round up men who had been missed in May, and many "wanted men" safely attended the annual Sinn Fein convention at the Mansion House at the end of October.

By this time the British appeal for voluntary recruits in Ireland had clearly failed. Only about 9,000 had come forward, instead of the desired 50,000, and Lloyd George began to think seriously of making the Order in Council needed to introduce conscription. Strangely enough, the feeling in the Cabinet had now changed. Except for Milner, the Unionists were suddenly afraid of stirring up new trouble in Ireland, and Lloyd George found himself trying to impose the conscription plan on timorous colleagues who, as he angrily commented to Henry Wilson, had been "brave as lions" a few months earlier. While the Cabinet debated, the problem was finally solved by the end of the war. No Irishman had been conscripted; the only result of the long controversy had been to give a tremendous fillip to Sinn Fein, so that during the year the number of members of Sinn Fein clubs grew from 66,270 to 112,080. The conscription threat was, indeed, second only to the executions of the Easter Week leaders in creating a substantial backing for Sinn Fein among the Irish people.

An incident in Cork in the closing week of the European War suggested that it would not be long before the Volunteers turned from secret drilling to violent action. Denis MacNeilus, captain of a volunteers' cyclist company in the Cork Brigade, shot and seriously wounded a head constable who had come with other police to his lodgings to search for arms. He was arrested and taken to Cork gaol, and was rescued a few days later by a party of Volunteers who gained admittance to the gaol as visitors and then knocked out two warders and stole their keys. But the warning note sounded by this affair was scarcely heard amid the excitement of the armistice on November 11 and the preparations for a general election for all Great Britain and Ireland on December 14. Sinn Fein had pledged itself to fight every seat. It now had the chance of showing its growing strength.

3

The general election of December, 1918, was a triumph for Sinn Fein, though not the overwhelming and decisive triumph which it was later claimed to be. Sinn Fein entered the campaign with ample funds, which were generously supplied by Irish-Americans, but it was badly handicapped because most of its best-known men were in English gaols, and Robert Brennan, its director of elections, was arrested three weeks before the poll. Its election manifesto, too, was heavily censored by Dublin Castle. Yet even in its censored form the manifesto showed plainly that Sinn Fein policy was to secure the establishment of the Irish Republic; to withdraw Irish representation from the British Parliament and to deny the right of the British Government to legislate for Ireland; to set up a constituent assembly of the Irish M.P.s returned in the election; and to appeal to the Peace Conference for the establishment of Ireland as an independent nation. The manifesto condemned "the contemplated mutilation of our country by partition", which it described as one of "the ghastly results of a policy that leads to national ruin".

The issues, therefore, were squarely before the electorate, and the election was mainly a series of straight fights—in the south between Sinn Feiners and Nationalists and in the north-east between Sinn Feiners and Ulster Unionists, though the Nationalists, who had previously held more than half the seats in the nine counties of Ulster, were also active in many north-eastern constituencies. To avert the risk of losing Ulster seats to Unionists on a split vote, the Sinn Fein and Nationalist parties agreed to contest four seats each of the eight seats where there had been only a small Nationalist majority.

Many of the Sinn Fein candidates were in gaol, but in this election a candidate's absence in gaol was one of the best qualifications he could have. During the campaign and on polling day there was much intimidation by Sinn Fein. Most of the polling clerks were Sinn Feiners, and many electors believed that they would be victimised if they voted Nationalist. Often, too, the intimidation took a more direct form: Sinn Fein canvassers would knock at a farmer's door late at night and warn him that he had better vote Sinn Fein if he did not want to have his hay burnt and his cattle driven off. There was also a good deal of personation at the polling-booths, where the dead (so long as their names were still on the register) voted in large numbers, always on behalf of Sinn Fein. But though intimidation and personation gave Sinn Fein candidates more votes than they would otherwise have had, the general trend of the election was unmistakable. The threat of conscription had shaken the south and west of Ireland; the resultant feelings of unrest played into the hands of Sinn Fein, whose victory was always assured.

Before the dissolution of Parliament the Nationalists had held 68 seats, the Unionists 18 and Sinn Fein 7, the others being held by the All for Ireland Party and Independents. When the results were declared on December 28 it was seen that Sinn Fein had overwhelmed the Nationalists, the Ulster Unionists had also increased their strength and all the Independents had disappeared. The final figures were

Sinn Fein 73 (26 unopposed), Unionists 26 and Nationalists 6, of which 4 were in the Ulster constituencies covered by their agreement with Sinn Fein. Dillon, the Nationalist leader, lost his seat in East Mayo to de Valera. In 24 of the 32 counties only Sinn Fein candidates were returned.

As an indication of popular feeling the Sinn Fein success looks less impressive when the voting is analysed. Only 69 per cent. of the electors in contested constituencies actually voted, and of the votes cast only about 47 per cent. were for Sinn Fein. So an election held on the principle of single-member constituencies had the not unusual result of giving a great majority of seats to a party which did not, in fact, represent a great majority of voters. Even at that date a large section of the Irish population would still have been satisfied with Home Rule; in the country as a whole Sinn Fein remained a minority, and it is not true that at this election Ireland gave a clear vote for an independent Republic. Sinn Fein could, however, be well satisfied with the result, and it was left to Father O'Flanagan to make the slightly cynical comment: "The people have voted Sinn Fein. What we have to do now is to explain to them what Sinn Fein is."

CHAPTER XIV

The Shooting Begins

I

ON JANUARY 21, 1919, Lloyd George was attending the first meetings of the Peace Conference in Paris, where he was thinking more about Allied support for the White Russians against the Bolsheviks than about British support for the R.I.C. against the Sinn Feiners. In Dublin the Sinn Feiners who had been elected members of the British House of Commons and were not at the moment in English gaols were assembled in the Mansion House to set up the first Dail Eireann. Somewhere in England Michael Collins and Harry Boland were secretly completing their plans for the rescue of de Valera from Lincoln gaol, where he had been imprisoned after the "German plot" round-up. And on a country road in Tipperary nine young men, armed with rifles and revolvers, were waiting behind a ditch for a small convoy of R.I.C. and county council employees taking blasting explosives to Soloheadbeg quarry, about two and a half miles from Tipperary town and less than a mile from Limerick junction.

In the two years and eight months since the Easter Rising no policeman or soldier had been killed in Ireland. There had been cattle drives, attempted—and sometimes successful—raids on R.I.C. barracks, arms raids on country houses (until the Volunteers' executive stopped them) and occasional ambushes of small parties of R.I.C.; but apart from two or three incidents in which policemen were wounded the Volunteers could fairly claim that they were guiltless of bloodshed. On their own side, however, there had been a small death-roll, including two Volunteers shot dead in county Kerry during a raid on a police barracks and a Clare man killed by British soldiers who were dispersing an illegal meeting; and a number of Volunteers and civilians had been wounded in bayonet and baton charges when similar meetings were being broken up. But there had been few serious casualties on either side until the 3rd Tipperary Brigade started the shooting war at Soloheadbeg.

This brigade had been largely organised by Sean Treacy, a young man of 23 who was also a member of the I.R.B.; but it was later commanded by Seumas Robinson, who had fought in O'Connell Street during the Rising and had then gone to work on a farm in Tipperary. Robinson and Treacy led the ambush party on January 21, and among the others was Dan Breen, a daring young man who had run (with a friend's help) a primitive munitions factory in a small cottage at Donohill, four miles from Tipperary. There they had made a kind of hand grenade which had to be lighted with a match, until one day their factory had blown up and left them without raw materials for further work. The object of the Soloheadbeg ambush was to get explosives for making more grenades.

The explosives convoy was late. The Volunteers lay behind their ditch for five days until it arrived at the spot they had chosen for their attack. It was a very small convoy, consisting of a cart with a driver, another county council employee walking beside the horses and two policemen with rifles walking a little way behind. One of the policemen had been in Tipperary for 30 years, and the coroner said at his inquest that he had never known a quieter or more inoffensive man.

Robinson had given orders beforehand that no one was to be killed, but Treacy and Breen were too impetuous to be restrained by such an order. Breen said afterwards that they called on the policemen to surrender, but they can hardly have given them much time to make up their minds. Soon after the call to surrender Treacy fired; others followed suit, and the two constables fell dead. The Volunteers made off with the cart and the explosives and went into hiding for three months.

The significance of this episode is that it was the first of its kind, but it was not the signal for a general war of ambush and sudden attack. Indeed, the slaughter of two innocent policemen created feelings of horror throughout Ireland, and was denounced in Press and pulpit. When Griffith heard of it in his English internment, he grumbled prophetically: "If this sort of thing goes on, we will end up by shooting one another." But the Volunteers' executive gave the Tipperary Brigade its indirect blessing in the January 31 issue of *An-t-Oglach*, which stated that: "Every Volunteer is entitled, legally and morally, when in the execution of his military duties, to use all legitimate methods of warfare against the soldiers and policemen of the English usurper, and to slay them if it is necessary to do so to overcome their resistance." This sanction for slaughter was sponsored by Brugha, who, besides being Chief of Staff, was acting President of Dail Eireann.

Since the Tipperary men had waited for the convoy for five days it was merely a coincidence that they struck on the very day when the first meeting of Dail Eireann was being held in Dublin. Invitations to attend the meeting had been sent to Irish M.P.s of all parties returned at the general election; even Carson had received one—printed in Gaelic—which he kept as a souvenir. But only the Sinn Fein M.P.s were present. Since some of them had been elected for two constituencies, there were 69 representatives of the 73 Sinn Fein seats: of these 27 attended the meeting, 2 were absent ill, 5 were on missions abroad, 1 had been deported and 34 were in prison, their absence being noted, when the roll was called, by the clerk's monotonous repetition of "*Fe ghlas ag Gallaibh*" ("imprisoned by the foreigners").

Collins and Boland, who were actually in England, were recorded as being present to prevent people wondering where they were. Several of the M.P.s were theoretically "on the run", but at this stage of the Irish troubles the police still showed no anxiety to hunt down men who had once evaded arrest. Indeed, the Dublin Metropolitan Police kindly sent a guard to the Mansion House to protect the deputies.

The assembly took the name of Dail Eireann (Assembly of Ireland), and the deputies discarded their English title of M.P. to style themselves *Feisire Dail Eireann* (members of the Assembly of Ireland), a style which was later changed to *Taochta Dala* (deputy of the Assembly), the familiar T.D. of the present day. The first Dail was a good deal younger than most legislative assemblies: of the 69 elected members 33 per cent. were under 35 and another 40 per cent. were between 35 and 45. There were only two Protestants—Ernest Blythe and Robert Barton, a county Wicklow landowner who was a cousin and close friend of Erskine Childers, had held a commission in the British Army and had been converted to Sinn Fein after being put in charge of Easter Week prisoners in 1916. The only woman deputy was Constance Markievicz, who had been returned for the St. Patrick's division of Dublin. Since the 1918 general election was the first in which women were allowed to stand for the British House of Commons, and Constance Markievicz was the only woman returned for any constituency in the British Isles, she had also the distinction of being Britain's first woman M.P.; but Mrs. Sheehy-Skeffington, "Skeffy's" widow, could have shared the honour if she had wished, for she had been offered a seat and had refused it.

In accordance with the pledge in the election manifesto, no Sinn Fein M.P. ever sat at Westminster, though at a later date de Valera had doubts about the wisdom of this mass abstention. "There was one drawback in taking our representation away from Westminster," he once said to Robert Brennan. "Westminster gave us a platform we do not now have from which we could present our case to the world." As it happened, the Sinn Feiners' refusal to go to Westminster was much appreciated by the British coalition Government of Liberals and Conservatives, which had been returned with a big majority at the election; for obstructive Sinn Feiners might have caused considerable embarrassment in the Commons. Churchill wrote afterwards that "the two supreme services which Ireland has rendered to Britain are her accession to the Allied cause on the outbreak of the Great War and her withdrawal from the House of Commons at its close".

At its first session the Dail adopted a provisional constitution, under which it would have full legislative power and would exercise executive functions through a Ministry responsible to it, and then gave its unanimous approval to a Declaration of Independence. This stated that "English rule in this country is, and always has been, based upon fraud and force and maintained by military occupation against the declared will of the people", and that "the Irish Republic was proclaimed in Dublin on Easter Monday, 1916, by the Irish Republican Army, acting on behalf of the Irish people"; and after the dubious assertion that the Irish electorate had "seized the first occasion to declare by an overwhelming majority its firm allegiance to the Irish Republic", it went on to declare:

> "Now, therefore, we, the elected representatives of the ancient Irish people in National Parliament assembled, do, in the name of the Irish nation, ratify the establishment of the Irish Republic and pledge ourselves and our people to make this declaration effective by every means at our command. . . . We solemnly declare foreign government in Ireland to be an invasion of our national rights which we will never tolerate, and we demand the evacuation of our country by the British garrison."

The meaning of the declaration was underlined by Brugha. "You understand," he said, "that we have cut ourselves free from England. Let the world know it and those who are concerned with it bear it in mind. For come what may now, whether it be death itself, the great deed is done."

The Declaration of Independence was followed by the reading of a programme of democratic social reform, and the first public session of the first Dail ended after two hours. At a private session on the next day Brugha was formally appointed Acting Priomh-Aire (First Minister), a title which was usually anglicised as President. The post indicated, however, only the presidency of Dail Eireann, not of the Irish Republic; and since it was a tenet of the Irish Republican Brotherhood that its own head had always been nominal President of the Irish Republic, a curious duality of allegiance resulted. Until 1921, when de Valera was more or less formally recognised as President of the Republic, the I.R.B. still felt that its first loyalty was to its own chief, even though the Supreme Council abandoned all claim to executive authority when the Dail was established. But the bulk of the Irish people knew nothing of these nice distinctions. To them the presidency of the Dail was the supreme post in the Sinn Fein movement, and it was understood that Brugha was only a stand-in for de Valera. The immediate task, therefore, was to get de Valera out of prison. That was what Collins and Boland were doing in England.

2

Lincoln gaol, where de Valera was imprisoned, was a relatively easy prison to escape from, for there was a door in the exercise grounds which led to some fields, and if a key for that door could be made the path to freedom would be open. Sometime before Christmas, 1918, de Valera made the first moves towards getting it. The prison chaplain, for whom he served Mass, had a habit of leaving his keys lying about, and it was not difficult for de Valera to borrow them surreptitiously and make an impression in candle wax of the key which led to freedom.

Next came the problem of sending the pattern to friends outside the prison, and Sean Milroy, a fellow-prisoner, had the inspiration of making a Christmas card with the title of "Christmas 1917 and Christmas 1918". It had two drawings on it—one showing a drunk man trying to put his latchkey into his front door and saying "I can't get in," and the other showing a prisoner holding an enormous key—the exact size of the prison door key—and saying "I can't get out." This card was duly sent to Dublin, but since an explanatory letter, which had been smuggled out at the same time, was destroyed by a scared intermediary, de Valera's friends failed to understand that they were meant to make a key as shown in the second drawing. More messages had to be sent out to explain what was wanted. Two keys were made and sent to the prison inside cakes, but both were failures. At last a rough key and locksmiths' implements were sent inside more cakes, and one of the prisoners worked on this rough key until it would turn in the lock.

In the middle of January Collins and Boland went to England to supervise the proposed escape. They stayed with an Irish friend in Manchester, and with him they went to Lincoln on February 3. De Valera, Milroy and Sean McGarry were to make the escape, and everything appeared to be going smoothly until Collins, who had also brought a key, broke it in the lock. De Valera, however, was able to push it out with his own key and open the door, and the six men hurried across the fields to a waiting taxi. On their way they passed some soldiers, whom Boland greeted with a friendly "Cheerio, mates!"

From Lincoln they went to Manchester, where de Valera stayed at an Irish priest's house while Milroy and McGarry went on to Liverpool. But the problem of getting him back to Ireland was more difficult. The British Government was deeply concerned over his escape, of which it was quaintly rumoured that glamorous Sinn Fein girls had come over from Ireland to flirt with the guards while the prisoners got away. De Valera was being sought for everywhere, and it seemed safest for him to stay in England, where he moved on to Liverpool after three weeks in Manchester.

In the meantime Collins had gone back to Ireland with disturbing news: de Valera had told him that he had made up his mind to go at once to the United States, to win support and raise funds for the Republican cause. His colleagues were shocked. They felt it was his duty to stay in Ireland as soon as he was able to return there. "I told him so," said Collins, "but you know what it's like to argue with Dev. He says he has thought it all out while in prison, and he feels that the one place where he can be useful to Ireland is in America." In despair Brugha went to England to argue with de Valera himself, and at last persuaded him to make a short stay in Ireland before going to the United States.

Though de Valera had been rescued at the beginning of February, it was not until the end of March that he was able to go back to Ireland. In that month further sensational gaol-breaks delighted southern Ireland. Robert Barton, who had been arrested in February, escaped from Mountjoy, leaving a polite note for the governor saying he was obliged to leave because the accommodation was not all that he had expected; and a few days later 20 Sinn Fein prisoners climbed over a wall at Mountjoy in broad daylight, while their comrades seized and held the guards.

De Valera's freedom to return to Ireland was actually due to a severe influenza epidemic which was then ravaging both England and Ireland. When one of the Irish prisoners in Gloucester gaol died of influenza, Ian Macpherson, who had succeeded Shortt as Chief Secretary, decided to release all the Sinn Feiners then interned in England. It was assumed that this decision covered de Valera, and he returned quietly to Ireland, wisely rejecting a proposal that the Lord Mayor of Dublin should meet him "at the gates of the city" and escort him to the Mansion House. Though many of his admirers were disappointed that there was no demonstration for his homecoming, he was well advised to decline any ceremonial welcome. For the English garrison feared that his return might touch off another rising, and had filled the Dublin streets with infantry, cavalry, guns and tanks; aeroplanes roared overhead, and machine-gun posts on the roofs of Trinity College and the Bank of Ireland commanded Dame Street, Grafton Street and the approaches to O'Connell Bridge. When it was clear there would be no rioting the troops were withdrawn to barracks.

3

On April 1, 1919, Dail Eireann was at last able to meet in private session with a full mustering of Sinn Fein leaders. Sean T. O'Kelly was appointed Speaker, and de Valera was duly elected President of the Dail. He designated a Cabinet consisting of himself and eight Ministers—Griffith (Home Affairs), Collins (Finance), Brugha (Defence), Count Plunkett (Foreign Affairs), Countess Markievicz (Labour), Cosgrave (Local Government), Eoin MacNeill (Industries) and Barton (Agriculture). Laurence Ginnell, the former Nationalist M.P., was appointed Director of Propaganda—a significant appointment, since it showed that the Dail Government fully realised the importance of getting good publicity for its cause. It thus established a lead with which the British Government never caught up.

The new Cabinet at once began to carry out its declared intention of taking over the administration of Ireland from the British authorities—an intention which had not only been declared in the election manifesto but was also an integral part of Griffith's original programme for Sinn Fein. As Minister of Home Affairs Griffith took the first steps towards the establishment of Sinn Fein arbitration courts, which were later so extensively developed that for some time the King's writ ceased to run in the greater part of southern Ireland. Constance Markievicz's Department of Labour took over the settlement of industrial disputes; Barton, as Minister of Agriculture, set up a Land Bank to make loans to people wishing to buy land; and a particularly determined attack on British administration was begun by Cosgrave, as Minister of Local Government, and O'Higgins, as his Assistant Minister. Their object was to make their department the centre of Irish local government, and if councils declined to transfer their dealings to the Dail Ministry their correspondence was often re-directed to Cosgrave's headquarters by friendly postal officials. As his department got into its stride fewer and fewer letters and minutes from local councils reached the Custom House, which was the official headquarters of Irish local government; instead the councils' problems and requests were competently dealt with by Cosgrave and his staff.

Collins had the important task of financing the Dail Government's administration, but he still retained his posts as Adjutant-General and Director of Organisation of the Volunteers. Brugha, too, was Chief of Staff of the Volunteers as well as Minister of Defence—a dual appointment which underlined the new importance claimed by the Volunteers since the constitution of Dail Eireann; for since the Declaration of Independence was assumed to have made the Irish Republic a tangible reality, the Volunteers considered that they were now the authorised Army of the Republic and had the legal and moral right to kill the Republic's enemies.

Brugha's appointment also provided a new cause of friction between himself and Collins, whose temperaments had already proved to be incompatible in spite of the need for their close co-operation at Volunteer headquarters. Though Brugha was the official head both of the Volunteers and of the Defence Department, it was not long before the outside world, and particularly the United States, began to describe Collins as the Commander-in-Chief of the Irish Republican Army. Collins tried to put the misdescription right when it was drawn to his attention, but Brugha was both jealous and annoyed.

On April 10 the Dail met again in public session. It was a critical time. In the weeks after the Soloheadbeg ambush, there had been few serious clashes between Volunteers and British forces, but on the last day of March a British resident magistrate was killed at Westport, and a few days later an R.I.C. constable was killed at Limerick while a Sinn Fein prisoner was being rescued from the workhouse infirmary. De Valera had the choice between damping down the movement towards violence and encouraging it. He preferred to encourage it.

He did so by moving a resolution "that members of the police force acting in this country as part of the forces of the British occupation and as agents of the British Government be ostracised publicly and socially by the people of Ireland". In his speech elaborating the terms of the resolution he declared that the R.I.C. "are given full licence by their superiors to work their will on an unarmed populace. The more brutal the commands given them by their superiors, the more they seem to revel in carrying them out, against their own flesh and blood, be it remembered. Their history is a continuity of brutal treason against their own people."

This speech could be interpreted only as a direct attempt to stir up hatred of the R.I.C. It is notable because it was made a full year before the first of the Black and Tans arrived in Ireland; the men whom dc Valera was condemning were the original members of the R.I.C., the men whom Tom Kettle had jokingly dismissed as "an army of no occupation". It seems hardly likely that they had suddenly become the brutal sadists whom de Valera depicted.

A month later the Tipperary men were again in action. One of their number had been captured by the police and was being taken by train from Thurles to Cork. At Knocklong station, three miles south of Emly, a party of Volunteers, again commanded by Seumas Robinson, waited for the train to stop there, were directed by a spy to the compartment where their man was sitting, and at once opened fire on the escort of three R.I.C. constables and a sergeant. One constable was killed and the sergeant fatally wounded. After a hand-to-hand struggle on the platform the Volunteers carried their comrade away.

Again the attack was denounced in the Press, from the pulpit and in the House of Commons. The King and Lord French sent messages of sympathy to the bereaved relatives.

But now beyond all doubt the shooting had begun. More policemen were killed as the summer advanced, and isolated affrays in Clare, Tipperary and Limerick were set in a national context when detectives of the G Division of the Dublin Metropolitan Police were shot dead in the streets of the city. These Dublin killings were deliberately planned by the headquarters of the Irish Republican Army, as the Volunteers were now beginning to be called, with the authority of Brugha and Collins, who had become Director of Intelligence as well as continuing to hold his other posts. The Dublin G-men had been observing Sinn Fein and Volunteer activities for years, and knew most of the leaders by sight. Collins, who had spies among them to help him, resolved to eliminate the G-men as an active force, though with one possible exception (when he wrote to some prisoners in Mountjoy that he was personally "going to" a G-man who was later found shot) he did not do the shooting himself. As Collins's name became well known, he was often described as a gunman. In fact, he controlled and organised the gunmen, but it was not his finger on the trigger when an unsuspecting detective was ambushed and shot in a Dublin street.

De Valera was not in Ireland when Sinn Fein began its organised attacks on the police. A few weeks after his speech in the Dail he had carried out his resolve to go to America, and had been smuggled across the Atlantic as a stowaway. He landed in New York on June 28, the day the Peace Treaty after the European War was signed at Versailles.

CHAPTER XV

Pilgrim's Progress

THE DAIL GOVERNMENT set great store on American sympathy. It looked to the United States for financial help, which it knew would continue to come from the powerful Irish-American section of the population; it wanted moral support from the whole American public for Ireland's claim to independence; and it had also hoped that Woodrow Wilson, then in his second term of office as President of the United States, would help it to put Ireland's case before the Peace Conference. During the war Wilson had been the great champion of self-determination for smaller nationalities. It was not unreasonable, therefore, to expect him to take up the Irish cause.

De Valera's pilgrimage to America was concerned with the first of these objectives. Irish hopes of a hearing at the Peace Conference had been disappointed even before he arrived in New York. Sean T. O'Kelly had been sent to Paris to advance the claim for Irish representation at the conference; but although he had been supported by three commissioners from an American organisation, the Friends of Irish Freedom, who made a short stay in Ireland and went on to see Wilson in Paris, he soon knew that his mission was doomed to failure. When one of the commissioners reminded Wilson that he had promised to back every nation's right to self-determination, the President could only answer sadly: "You have touched on the great metaphysical tragedy of today. When I gave utterance to those words I said them without the knowledge that nationalities existed which are coming to us day after day."

The problem of self-determination was, in fact, a bigger one than Wilson had imagined, and Ireland's claim to separate representation at the Peace Conference was finally dismissed as part of a "great metaphysical tragedy". In any case the claim was always a thin one, since the Dail leaders, unlike the representatives of other nationalities whose cases were considered by the conference, had taken no part in the European War.

The collapse of the Peace Conference dream made it still more important for southern Ireland to build up close contacts with the United States; and the outward success of de Valera's visit seemed to bear out his contention that America was the place where at that time he could best serve Ireland. His public triumphs were impressive: he was made a freeman of New York and Chicago, was officially welcomed by the Governor of California and the Mayor of San Francisco, addressed both Houses of the Massachusetts legislature and was given a salute of 21 guns at Cleveland, Ohio. When he addressed a Chicago audience of 100,000 he could not begin his speech for 26 minutes because of the cheering. But there was trouble behind the scenes. The Friends of Irish Freedom had brought together the Clan na Gael, still led by John Devoy, the veteran Fenian, and the remnants of the United Irish League, under the leadership of Devoy's close friend, Judge Daniel Cohalan. Devoy and Cohalan regarded themselves as the principal organisers of Irish-American support for the Irish Republican movement, and they were at once on their guard when they found that de Valera was resolved to have his own way in America just as he had it in Ireland.

De Valera arrived in America with the double prestige of his heroism in the Easter Rising and his appointment as head of the Dail Government. In spite of his protests that he was only the President of Dail Eireann, he was hailed everywhere as President of the Irish Republic; and he was obliged to accept the title, though after the first occasion on which he had been so described at a public meeting he said with a laugh: "I wonder what Griffith will say when he reads that I came out in the Press as President of the Republic!" Four other members of the Dail were with him —Dr. Patrick McCartan, the official Dail envoy to the United States, Harry Boland, Diarmuid Lynch and Liam Mellows; and it was not long before there was more or less open friction between the Irish visitors and the leaders of the Friends of Irish Freedom.

From the outset Devoy was suspicious of de Valera's political views. As an old Fenian Devoy held that Ireland must stand out for nothing less than an independent Republic, but de Valera was given to speaking of Ireland's claim in terms of "self-determination", which might have meant no more than Dominion Home Rule—the more generous kind of Home Rule conceded by Britain to several of her former colonies. Devoy and Cohalan were further upset when de Valera insisted on their closing down the Irish Victory Fund, through which they had raised 1,000,000 dollars for Ireland and Irish causes within six months, so that he could start instead an official Irish National Loan (external). This loan had an original target of 5,000,000 dollars, which was later increased to 10,000,000 dollars, and subscribers were given registered bonds guaranteed by the Dail Government. It was a parallel issue to the Irish National Loan for home subscription, which Collins was busily organising in Dublin.

The issue of Irish bonds in America had been fully authorised by the Dail Cabinet, but Devoy and Cohalan deeply resented the supersession of the Irish Victory Fund. An impression of the rift created even as early as September, and of the Irish visitors' antagonism to the Devoy–Cohalan "gang", was given that month in a letter from Mellows to Nora Connolly. "I broke completely with the gang," he wrote. "Gang not pulling with de Valera. Want to run him. He won't be run. . . . Gang cold on bond proposition."

Devoy and Cohalan were neither the first nor the last in the Irish Republican movement to discover that de Valera would not "be run". But his insistence on the issue of bonds was fully justified by their successful reception. Though his colleagues in Dublin were well aware of his quarrels with Devoy and Cohalan, they still thought that his pilgrimage was making remarkable progress. At a private meeting of the Dail in October Griffith said that the centre of gravity of the political situation was for the present fixed in the United States. To England, however, the centre of gravity of the Irish problem seemed to be much nearer home, and to lie, in fact, behind those hedges in the Irish countryside where gunmen waited to shoot at British soldiers or Irish policemen.

CHAPTER XVI

Ambushes and Reprisals

I

WHILE DE VALERA was going in triumph from one American city to another and living the five-star-hotel life which made no appeal to him whatever, his colleagues in Ireland were beginning to organise the new phase of country-wide guerilla warfare which was to last for nearly two years. For the moment Ulster was in the background. Dail Eireann's claim to be an assembly for the whole of Ireland made no impression in the north-east, and at the 1919 Orange Day demonstration Carson showed that Ulster stood just where she had done before the European War. "If there is any attempt to take away one jot or tittle of your rights as British citizens," he told his audience, "I will call out the Ulster Volunteers. We are loyal men, the Government and the Constitution and the British Empire are good enough for us." Yet Ulster's position was not quite the same as it had been in 1914. The Unionist Press in Britain had lost much of its interest in her cause since it had ceased to be a convenient stick for beating a Liberal Government with; but the Unionists were the strongest group in the coalition Government, in which Lloyd George had not the whole of the Liberal Party behind him. Asquith, Sir John Simon and other leading Liberals were now in opposition, and were soon to show their disapproval of the Government's Irish policy.

The English Press was disturbed by the unsettled state of Ireland, and that summer an impressive outline of an Irish "new deal" was prepared by *The Times*, which was then edited by Wickham Steed, as Geoffrey Dawson had disagreed with Northcliffe and resigned. In June and July *The Times* published a series of 10 articles on "Peace in Ireland", and these were followed on July 24 by a four-column leader advocating the establishment of an Irish federation with separate legislatures for the south and the north-east.

Though Lloyd George and Northcliffe were no longer the close allies they had once been, Lloyd George gave the *Times* plan his careful consideration; but he remarked later in the year to his friend Lord Riddell, proprietor of the *News of the World*:

> "Northcliffe, who has been urging a settlement, would be critical even if I adopted his scheme in the main. He would say, 'You have left out a comma, and that comma is the most important thing in the whole scheme.'"

Oddly enough, a precisely opposite view was expressed by Wickham Steed, who said sourly to Walter Long:

> "We know enough of the Cabinet and of the Prime Minister to be sure that, if a scheme for an Irish settlement were inspired by God Almighty and were first published in *The Times*, it would be rejected by the Government because it had been published in *The Times*."

In the end Lloyd George turned down the federation proposal, and proceeded to work out a new Home Rule Bill of his own, which he hoped would be acceptable to Ireland as a whole, even though it would involve partition.

While Lloyd George was preparing his new Bill, which was to be called the Better Government of Ireland Bill, the Sinn Fein attacks on the R.I.C. and the Dublin G-men were beginning to gain momentum. In Dublin Collins recruited a small group of Volunteers who were known as "the Squad": these men gave up their civil occupations and devoted their whole time to the dangerous tasks that Collins, with Brugha's approval, assigned to them. In the provinces there were many raids on police barracks, and R.I.C. men were killed in ambushes in county Clare and county Tipperary. The death-roll was still small—18 policemen were killed from May 1 to the end of 1919—but it was growing ominously. One result of the new campaign was the closing down of a number of smaller police barracks in remoter parts of the south and west. Such barracks had become little more than death-traps, as their small garrisons could always be vastly outnumbered by local Volunteers.

In theory the Volunteers were now subordinate to Dail Eireann, for on Brugha's insistence they had been ordered to take an Oath of Allegiance, not only to the Irish Republic but also to the Dail. Some of the senior officers disliked the Oath: Seumas Robinson, for instance, took it with great reluctance, grumbling that "the Dail might go wrong and might accept less than a Republic". In practice, however, Collins remained the Volunteers' effective head, though he could not control the day-to-day movements of provincial commandants. It was one of these commandants in his own county of Cork whose action at Fermoy in September led to the first reprisal by Crown forces in Ireland.

The commandant was Liam Lynch, a taciturn, serious and bespectacled young man of 25, who came from a farming family in county Limerick and had been working since 1915 for a hardware firm in Fermoy, which was a British garrison town. He had joined the Volunteers in 1914, had been elected first lieutenant when the Fermoy company was reorganised after the Rising and had later become commandant of Cork No. 2 Brigade. On Sunday morning, September 7, a party of about 25 Volunteers, all wearing civilian clothes, assembled in groups of twos and threes near the Wesleyan Church at Fermoy, where they knew that a small detachment of the King's Shropshire Light Infantry would be coming to attend service. The 17 soldiers, who were carrying rifles but had no suspicion that they might be called upon to use them, were followed to the church by

Lynch in a motor-car. On their arrival Lynch jumped from his car, summoned his men by a blast on his whistle and called on the soldiers to surrender and give up their arms. When they refused, the Volunteers, some of whom were armed with revolvers, attacked them, and in the ensuing affray, in which the soldiers had no chance of firing back, one soldier was killed and four wounded. When a bugle-call raised the alarm in the barracks near by the Volunteers hastily jumped into motor-cars and escaped, taking with them the soldiers' rifles.

This well-planned assault on men who could never have expected to be attacked on their way to church was followed by the first of those unauthorised reprisals which were soon to be so familiar; but it did not take place until the following evening, when the troops had been further enraged by the inquest held on their dead comrade. Though the shooting had been unprovoked, the Fermoy Coroner's jury refused to return a verdict of Wilful Murder, and merely found that "the deceased man died from a bullet wound caused by some person unknown". It was because of this verdict, and not as an immediate consequence of the shooting, that troops from the Fermoy garrison burst into the town on the Monday night and wrecked the houses of tradesmen who had served on the jury. Neither their officers nor the R.I.C. intervened to stop the raid.

The Fermoy affair set the pattern in yet another way for the guerilla war. In the Easter Rising some of the Volunteers and the Citizen Army had fought in uniform, and many members of the Irish Republican Army still had their old grey-green Volunteer tunics. But they had long ceased to wear them except on great ceremonial occasions. In the new warfare the I.R.A. fought in civilian clothes, which gave them a big advantage in making surprise attacks and also helped them to escape after an ambush and mingle with passers-by as though they had nothing to do with any fighting.

Some of the officers still wore bits of their uniform: Tom

Barry, another notable Cork commandant, writes in his memoirs of wearing his Volunteer tunic as late as 1921, though Lynch had abandoned his own at the end of 1917 because, his biographer says, he found it "an unnecessary and foolish handicap on his activities". In effect, therefore, the only I.R.A. uniform was a trench-coat in winter—a garment which had the further advantage of allowing them to be sometimes mistaken for Auxiliaries or Black and Tans; and since trench-coats could also be worn by civilians, they could not be ranked as military uniform. In general, the war in Ireland was between uniformed soldiers and police on the British side and men in civilian clothes on the Irish. There was no precedent for this kind of warfare. The Irish sometimes claimed that the Boers had fought in the same way, but the Boers' slouch hats and bandoliers made them fully recognisable as belligerents, whereas the men of the I.R.A. (except when operating in flying columns) masqueraded as civilians until they actually drew their guns. It is not surprising that war fought by the Irish in this way was denounced as murder by the British.

Three days after the Fermoy reprisal Lord French proclaimed Dail Eireann an illegal association. But though the Dail could no longer hold public sessions, it continued to meet in private, and since all members were liable to arrest, the Cabinet took precautions against the possible capture of the whole body. Only part of the Dail assembled at any one time; other members received the formal summons to attend, together with a note saying that "as it is possible that this meeting will be suppressed and as some of the members must still be available to carry on the work the Ministry will be glad if you will abstain from attending".

At the same time the military and police began a still more intensive series of raids in search of arms and seditious literature, in the course of which they arrested any leading Sinn Feiners they encountered. On the very day when the Dail was proscribed there was a police raid on the Sinn Fein headquarters at 6, Harcourt Street, Dublin, where Collins had an office for his work as Minister of Finance. It was on this occasion that Collins made one of his many narrow escapes by climbing through a skylight on to the roof and so proceeding to the roof of the Ivanhoe Hotel, where he waited in safety until the raid was over. Many papers, including Griffith's *Nationality*, were suppressed after they had published the prospectus of the Irish National Loan, but by some oversight the authorities failed to suppress a small Sinn Fein weekly called *Young Ireland*. This now became the vehicle for Griffith's views.

Another propagandist newspaper made its first appearance in November. This was the *Irish Bulletin*, edited by Frank Gallagher and published in the form of cyclostyled sheets under the guidance of the Dail Director of Propaganda—a post in which Desmond Fitzgerald had succeeded Larry Ginnell and was soon to be followed by Erskine Childers, who had settled in Ireland with his American wife, herself a doughty champion of Irish freedom. The object of the *Irish Bulletin* was to provide destructive criticism of British Ministers' speeches and official British reports, to irritate Dublin Castle by publishing "top secret" Government documents which had fallen into Sinn Fein hands, and to give factual accounts (checked as far as possible by eye-witnesses' own stories) of attacks, ambushes and casualties on both sides and of brutalities committed by Crown forces. The paper was issued every day except on Saturdays and Sundays, and was sent through the post to 900 newspapers and to prominent people in England. The staff had the satisfaction of knowing that their handiwork was carefully studied and that *Bulletin* reports were quoted in the House of Commons, to the great disgust of the Chief Secretary.

In this autumn of 1919 the British authorities were making desperate attempts to save a rapidly deteriorating situation. The prisons were being filled with men and a few women sentenced for incitements to revolt or the possession of arms or seditious documents. Sinn Fein,

Cumann na mBan, the Gaelic League and the Volunteers were now officially suppressed in 27 counties, though even Dublin Castle must have known that it was farcical to attempt to disband the I.R.A. by proclamation. Ambushes and reprisals were becoming more frequent, and I.R.A. violence was followed by military destruction of shops and houses in Cork, Kinsale and Athlone. In several areas the I.R.A. made successful raids for arms: one of the most striking was a well-planned attack (without loss of life on either side) by Cork No. 3 Brigade on a British naval sloop lying in Bantry Bay, which was boarded and cleared of the contents of its armoury on the night of November 17 while its officers were on shore. At this time I.R.A. attacks on Crown forces were continually denounced in both the English and the Irish Press as criminal outrages. The general mass of the Irish populace probably shared the view of the Press and would have preferred the return of law and order to any dream of independence.

Another sensational ambush took place in December, when some of the Tipperary Volunteers co-operated in Dublin with Collins's "Squad" in an attempt to assassinate Lord French. Various plans for killing the Viceroy had been made and discarded at I.R.A. headquarters: one of the oddest of the rejected proposals was that of sending a pretty girl, whose brother was in gaol, to see French and to offer him, in return for her brother's freedom, an assignation at a house in Waterloo Road, where the I.R.A. would have been waiting for him. On some occasions ambushes had actually been laid, but had failed for one reason or another. Once Collins himself and Tomas MacCurtain had waited for the Viceroy, only to find that he had not taken his expected route. But on December 19 there seemed to be no possibility of failure. Collins had discovered that French was returning by train on that day from his country house near Boyle, in county Roscommon, and was due to alight at Ashtown Gate station, not far from one of the entrances to Phoenix Park, and drive from there to Viceregal Lodge inside the park. The attackers' plan was to wait at Ashtown Cross between the station and the park, to block the road with an old farm-cart immediately after the first car (which usually carried an armed guard) had passed, and then throw bombs and hand grenades at the car in which French was travelling.

Dan Breen and Sean Treacy were among the party of eleven who cycled out from Dublin to Ashtown Cross. But everything went wrong for them. An unsuspecting traffic policeman tried to clear them off the road, and when one of them threw a grenade at him the noise of the explosion warned the Viceroy's convoy to put on speed. The attackers had no time to carry out their plan of blocking the road. Instead they fired rifle-shots at the first car, gave the second the full weight of their bombs and grenades and then exchanged shots with an armed guard in the third car, which sped past to summon reinforcements. One of the I.R.A. men, Martin Savage, was shot and killed. Leaving his dead body behind, the rest of them cycled back to Dublin, where they soon learnt that their attack had been a complete failure. French had been in the first car, not the second, and had not been hurt; the second had contained no one but the driver, who had escaped with his life, although the bombs had forced the car off the road. So the only casualty was Martin Savage, who, it was revealed at the inquest, had been to Mass on the very morning of the ambush.

The I.R.A. considered that this attack was an act of war, and when the *Irish Independent* published a leader describing French's assailants as "assassins" a party of 20 to 30 Volunteers, led by Peadar Clancy, went to the newspaper's office with revolvers and held up the staff while they smashed the linotype machines. But the I.R.A.'s sensitivity about the use of words was not appreciated in England. There the assault on the King's representative in Ireland was regarded as an attempted murder, and one, moreover, which emphasised the need for swift and resolute action to restore Irish peace.

2

The British Government's new measures for Ireland took two forms—appeasement and coercion. Three days after the attempt on French's life a Bill for the Better Government of Ireland was introduced in the House of Commons. Early in 1920 posters appeared outside police stations calling for thousands of recruits to build up the strength of the Royal Irish Constabulary. The carrot and the stick were being offered to Ireland simultaneously—a procedure which G. K. Chesterton later derided in a pamphlet entitled *The Delusion of the Double Policy*.

Lloyd George's new proposals for Home Rule became generally known in Ireland as the Partition Bill, though in fact they left the way open for the establishment of one Parliament for the whole of Ireland. The Bill proposed to set up two Parliaments—one for the six north-eastern counties of Ulster (thus excluding Cavan, Monaghan and Donegal) and one for the other 26 counties. There was also to be a joint Council of Ireland, consisting of members nominated by the two Parliaments, which would be empowered to administer any all-Irish services that the two Parliaments might entrust to it; and it was hoped that this Council would help the six and the 26 counties to work harmoniously together, so as to create an atmosphere of goodwill in which they would ultimately agree to end partition. Both parts of Ireland would send a reduced number of M.P.s to Westminster, and the Imperial Parliament would retain control of the Armed Forces, foreign relations, Customs and Excise, the post office, merchant shipping and certain other matters. If, however, the two Governments should later agree to set up a united Parliament the post office was to be transferred to Irish control and a new arrangement for Customs and Excise was to be negotiated. Members of each Parliament would take the Oath of Allegiance used by Dominion Parliaments.

Except for the vital question of partition, this was a Bill

which most Irish people would have been ready to accept before the European War, and it was notable that the offer of Home Rule was now being made by a coalition Government in which the Unionists were predominant. But it came too late to be greeted with rapture by any section of the Irish population. The former Nationalists in southern Ireland had been taught by the Sinn Feiners to desire greater freedom and control of their own affairs than the Bill offered them; they regarded it also as a permanent establishment of partition, since they had little faith in the proposed Council of Ireland, and they bitterly resented the placing of Catholics in Ulster's six counties under what was certain to be a Protestant Government. The Southern Unionists and the Unionists in Cavan, Monaghan and Donegal felt that they were being betrayed by being left as a small minority in an area that would now be administered by and for Catholics. And even the Ulster Unionists had no enthusiasm for a Bill which superseded the Act of Union and gave them a Parliament for which they had never seriously asked. But Lloyd George was convinced that his plan would give Ireland the better government promised in the title of the Bill. He had now finally decided that the only solution of Ireland's problem was to divide the country and keep the two parts within the British Empire for external affairs, while allowing them a considerable measure of internal independence. This was the view he maintained as long as he remained at the head of British affairs.

Though sincerely hoping that his new Bill would appease Ireland, Lloyd George also realised that further coercion would be needed before it could be put into effect. In particular, it was urgently necessary to reinforce the R.I.C. There had been many resignations from the force since the Sinn Fein policy of ostracising the police had come into operation, and recruiting, which was still mainly among Irishmen, had been falling off because of I.R.A. intimidation of young men who wanted to join the force. The British Government decided, therefore, to open the ranks of the

R.I.C. to Englishmen, Scotsmen and Welshmen, and advertisements were issued at the beginning of 1920 appealing for recruits, who were offered the standard R.I.C. pay of ten shillings a day "and all found". The appeal came at a time when many ex-soldiers were still having difficulty in finding jobs in civil life, and it was readily answered. So at the very moment when Parliament was debating plans for the peaceful government of Ireland, a new phase of the armed struggle was about to begin. The Black and Tans were on their way.

CHAPTER XVII

The Coming of the "Tans"

I

IN THE INTERVAL between the decision to extend recruiting for the R.I.C. and the arrival of the first of the new recruits at Dun Laoghaire Sinn Fein won another victory at the polls. In the local elections held on January 15, 1920, 11 out of the 12 cities and boroughs of Ireland (all except Belfast) and 172 out of the total number of 206 councils returned Sinn Fein majorities. This time, however, the voting was by proportional representation, and the parties opposed to Sinn Fein were returned in considerable strength. For example, of the 80 members elected to the Dublin Corporation 42 were Sinn Feiners, 15 Labour, 12 Unionists, nine Nationalists and two Independents. The results showed, in fact, that although Sinn Fein was the most powerful and the most popular party, it had no overwhelming majority in the country as a whole. Indeed, even a sympathetic observer such as Hugh Martin, of the London *Daily News*, was able to calculate that the voting figures really showed an anti-Sinn Fein majority of 87,378.

But political theory was taking second place to violence in Irish daily life. In Dublin Collins's "Squad" was still striking at the G-men of the Metropolitan Police; but the detectives were on his trail, and in the middle of January they raided the house where he was living, and just missed him. The raid had been ordered by W. C. F. Redmond, Assistant Commissioner of the D.M.P. A few days later two shots were fired at Redmond as he was walking along Harcourt Street, and he fell mortally wounded, while his assailants ran away without any hindrance from the passers-by. The "Squad" had struck again; the removal of yet another police official who knew the I.R.A. leaders by sight made it easier for men "on the run" to move about Dublin without fear of recognition. After Redmond's death Dublin Castle offered a reward of £10,000 for evidence that would lead to the conviction of the killers of five members of the D.M.P. (including the prominent G-men, Hoey and Smith) and nine of the R.I.C. It was never claimed.

The public were not only reluctant to interfere openly with I.R.A. attacks; they were also unwilling to come into court to give evidence about them. When Lord Justice Ronan opened the North Tipperary Assizes in March he commented that since the last Assizes the police had on their records two murders, two attempts to murder, three cases of wounding, four of robbery and attempts to rob, three of arson, three of killing and maiming cattle, 13 of malicious injury, 12 of writing threatening letters, four raids for arms, two attacks on police barracks and one of firing into a dwelling-house; yet in spite of what he called "a terrible record of crime", only three trivial cases were presented for him to try. He drew the conclusion that people either sympathised with the offences or were too terrorised to give evidence. His second supposition was probably the right one. Witnesses were not so reluctant to appear in cases where there was a chance of ascribing guilt to the R.I.C., which suggests that they were less frightened of the constabulary than they were of the I.R.A.

Two incidents in March, 1920, illustrate the contrast in public reactions to different kinds of outrage. In the first, which occurred on the night of March 19, Tomas MacCurtain, Lord Mayor of Cork and commandant of the Cork No. 1 Brigade, was killed in his house by a party of masked raiders. In the second, a few days later, Alan Bell, an elderly magistrate, was dragged from a Dublin tram-car and shot.

MacCurtain, who was killed on the morning of his thirty-sixth birthday, had been an assiduous Gaelic Leaguer, a Cork organiser of the Fianna Eireann, a one-time member of the I.R.B. (which he had left, however, after the Rising, because he thought there was no further need for a revolutionary secret society) and a prominent Volunteer since 1914, though the countermanding orders of Holy Week had prevented him from taking any part in the Rising. He had been interned in Reading gaol in 1916, re-arrested two months after the general release of internees and deported to England for a further period of four months. Since his return he had been one of the three Volunteer commandants for county Cork, and had been elected Lord Mayor of the city after the recent elections. His career, in fact, was similar to that of many other leading Sinn Feiners, and from the British point of view there was nothing to suggest that he was either more or less dangerous than any of the others. He was shot dead, however, by a body of masked men with blackened faces who entered his house about 1 a.m. on March 20, and it was at once believed in Cork that the R.I.C. had killed him.

Because of this belief 31 civilians were willing to give evidence at the Coroner's inquest, and between them they built up a formidable indictment of the R.I.C. Evidence was given that a party of men had been seen leaving the police barracks in King Street, that they had been joined by others on their way to MacCurtain's house, and that they had approached and entered the house without interference from the ordinary police patrols. A button from a policeman's cape had been found in the roadway outside the house, and empty cartridge cases, of the type and calibre used in police revolvers, had been picked up not far away. The jury found the civilian witnesses convincing, declared that the killing had been done by members of the R.I.C. "officially directed by the British Government", and brought in a verdict of Wilful Murder against Lloyd George, French, the Chief Secretary, District Inspector Swanzy and other officers and members of the R.I.C.

On the face of it, this seems to be one of the earliest of the many authenticated cases in which Sinn Feiners were shot out of hand by the police; but there were several curious points about the death of MacCurtain. For one thing, the Cork military had been given orders to arrest him early that morning, and a military party actually arrived at his house at 2 a.m., only to find him dead. MacCurtain's killers presumably knew of this intention, and acted when they did in order to forestall the soldiers. But were these killers the police or, as Lord French declared, Sinn Fein extremists who thought MacCurtain's policy was too moderate? There seemed to be no particular reason why the R.I.C. should have wanted to kill MacCurtain, whom Darrell Figgis regarded as holding a midway place between the extremists and the moderates; and although an R.I.C. constable had been killed by Sinn Feiners that very evening, the attack on MacCurtain was too elaborately planned to have been organised in a couple of hours as a hasty reprisal.

Perhaps the crucial argument which supports the inquest verdict is that the raiding party was not interfered with by the police patrols; and for that reason, in spite of the strange circumstances of the affair, the guilt of the R.I.C. may be taken to be established, though the jury was merely indulging in a flight of fancy when it suggested that the killing had been ordered by the British Government. Collins, at any rate, was so convinced of the R.I.C.'s guilt that he arranged for District Inspector Swanzy, who had been named in the inquest verdict, to be killed by Volunteers a few months later, when he had been transferred from Cork to Lisburn in county Antrim. In the meantime MacCurtain's death caused no weakening of Sinn Fein fervour in Cork, where his place as Lord Mayor and commandant of the Cork No. 1 Brigade was taken by a Republican of equally passionate sincerity, Terence MacSwiney.

The second of the month's momentous incidents occurred in Dublin a few days later, and this time there were no doubts about the identity of the killers. The victim was

Alan Bell, a magistrate who was working at Dublin Castle in association with Sir John Taylor, the Assistant Under-Secretary, and had been given the task of hunting down Sinn Fein funds in Dublin banks and taking possession of them. He was doing it so successfully that he had recently seized £20,000 from accounts in the Munster and Leinster Bank believed to be those of Sinn Fein depositors. But Collins was not prepared to see his fighting fund taken away from him. The order was given for Bell's "execution". On March 27, as he sat in a crowded Dun Laoghaire tram in broad daylight, half a dozen young men with revolvers boarded it and one touched him on the shoulder, saying, "Come on, Mr. Bell, your time has come." He was taken out and shot dead by the roadside. No one in the tram lifted a finger to protect or save him.

The Black and Tan terror had still to come, but already the Sinn Fein terror was so complete that Dublin citizens sat passive and inert while an elderly man was slaughtered before their eyes. This reaction to a gross outrage was very different from that of the Cork witnesses who were so anxious to give evidence against the R.I.C. The contrast showed that Britain could expect little active co-operation from the Irish public in the restoration of peace in Ireland. It was also a sign, though Lloyd George was not yet prepared to recognise it, that the era of British constitutional rule in Ireland was ended.

2

At the end of this month of March, 1920, the first batch of new recruits for the R.I.C.—mostly ex-Servicemen who had enrolled in England, Scotland and Wales—landed at Dun Laoghaire. They were badly needed, for the strength of the R.I.C. had become fewer than 9,700, compared with the pre-war total of over 10,000, though their duties and responsibilities were more onerous than ever before. Because of a shortage of the dark-green cloth (so dark that it almost looked black) used for R.I.C. uniforms, the new members of the force at first wore khaki tunics and trousers with dark-green R.I.C. caps—a combination which caused a southern wit to call them the Black and Tans, borrowing the name from the famous hounds of South Tipperary and East Limerick. In due course the so-called Black and Tans were given the orthodox R.I.C. dark-green uniform, and were no longer distinguishable from older members of the force; but the name lingered, and since in country districts the inhabitants knew who were their old police and who were the new recruits, it was still possible to regard the Black and Tans as a separate force. In the end, indeed, the Black and Tans were rightly or wrongly accused of most of the violent deeds committed by Crown forces in Ireland, unless it was clear that they had been done by the military or the Auxiliary Division of the R.I.C., which came into being a few months later.

What sort of men were the Black and Tans? The Irish had no words too bad for them. Batt O'Connor, for instance, who was a friend of Collins, solemnly described them as having villainous looks and hardened, ruffianly faces, and William O'Brien, the old All for Ireland M.P., called them "desperadoes of the vilest type". Even a less partisan witness, such as Sir Christopher Lynch-Robinson, the last of the Irish resident magistrates, said that the first Black and Tans he saw at Trim, in county Meath, looked like a bunch of gorillas, with "india-rubber-looking faces, large ears, big fat lips" and "the blank uncanny expression of the cretin". It was constantly claimed that some or many of them were ex-convicts, but there is no evidence for the fantastic suggestion that the Government "scoured the prisons" and released the most desperate characters to be found there on condition that they would join the R.I.C. Yet stories of this kind were believed by Unionists as well as Sinn Feiners. Douglas Goldring, the English author, was told as gospel truth by a woman member of a southern Unionist family that a Cork man, who had been given a life sentence for murdering his wife and children, had been released after serving only a short part of his sentence and enrolled in the Black and Tans with the pay of £7 a week and £1 bonus for every Irishman he killed. The story is obviously absurd, since the Prison Commissioners could never have agreed to such a release, and in any case the Black and Tans were paid the regulation R.I.C. wage of £3 10*s*. a week, not £7; but it is an instructive sign of the times that such a wild rumour could be widely believed in Cork, where women and children were terrified to be told that a convicted murderer was at large among them.

In contrast with the Irish view of the Black and Tans is Winston Churchill's statement that they "were selected from a great press of applicants on account of their intelligence, their characters and their record in the war"; and Sir Ormonde Winter, chief of the Combined Intelligence Services at Dublin Castle from 1920 to 1922, has recorded that "most of the candidates had been members of the forces, and the conduct of each one was carefully scrutinised by the police before enlistment". The R.I.C. code, which governed the selection of all recruits, bears out Sir Ormonde's statement, for it says clearly that "officers should exercise the greatest care in their selection of men for the constabulary, and should beware of recommending candidates with whose past history, as well as present habits, they are not familiar, nor should they recommend any, whatever may be their own conduct, whose parents, relatives or associates are of disreputable or suspected character".

Since recruits were being accepted at the rate of about 300 a month (1,500 attested from January 1 to May 31, 1920) police inquiries may have been less thorough than usual, and Douglas V. Duff, who joined up later, has recorded that he was asked only to produce two references; but it is at least clear that no one was admitted to the force without some kind of testimony to his good character. The recruits who crossed to Ireland with Duff included dock labourers, clerks, farm workers, youths straight from public schools and universities and even a colonial police officer on leave, all in all a fairly representative cross-section of English young men. If this picture seems at variance with the savage deeds of the Black and Tans it should be remembered that only men who were in search of excitement and danger would have joined the force at such a time, and that such men would be predisposed to acts of violence and brutality when they found themselves in lawless and unsettled surroundings. Moreover, men who had formerly been subject to strict military discipline found conditions much laxer in the R.I.C., where the only serious penalties for misconduct were dismissal and loss of pension. These penalties had little deterrent effect on men who had joined the force only for a limited term.

Undoubtedly some men of criminal type slipped through the net of police inquiries and joined the Black and Tans. These were the men who used their position to commit thefts and robberies and were guilty of such atrocities as that of tying captured Sinn Feiners to the back of a lorry and trailing them in the road as the lorry moved off at high speed. But in general the ferocity which the Black and Tans were soon to display throughout Ireland was the almost automatic reaction of hardened ex-soldiers to a situation in which at any moment they were liable to be bombed or shot in the back by some seemingly harmless young civilian who would then vanish behind a hedge or be lost in a city crowd. Sinn Fein had begun the terror by their ruthless attacks on the police; the Black and Tans were soon to show themselves adept at retaliating with a counter-terror.

Besides sending the Black and Tans to Ireland Lloyd George made a number of important changes in the higher civil and military posts. General Sir Nevil Macready, son of a famous actor, was persuaded to give up his London post as Commissioner of the Metropolitan Police and go to Dublin as Commander-in-Chief of the British Forces in Ireland. Sir Joseph Byrne, the Inspector-General of the R.I.C., was relieved of his post, apparently because he disapproved of the new policy of meeting terror with counter-terror; Major-General H. H. Tudor was put in charge of the R.I.C., both old and new, and of the Dublin Metropolitan Police, and was instructed to organise an intelligence and secret service, which was put in the hands of Colonel Ormonde Winter.

At the same time, Sir John Anderson, who at the age of 37 was already regarded as one of Britain's leading Civil Servants, was moved from the chairmanship of the Board of Inland Revenue to become joint Under-Secretary at Dublin Castle, where he showed himself to be a courageous, patient and supremely efficient administrator during a very difficult period. His colleague was James MacMahon, a Roman Catholic who had been appointed Under-Secretary in 1918 but because of his religion had never been allowed to enjoy his superiors' full confidence. There was also a change in the post of Assistant Under-Secretary, where Sir John Taylor made way for Alfred W. Cope (generally known as "Andy"), who had been charged by Lloyd George with the special duty of working for an Irish settlement by peaceful means. He soon took the opportunity of discussing the Irish situation with Childers, who was taken to Dublin Castle after a raid on his house, and though this discussion came to nothing, it was not long before Cope became a useful secret intermediary between the Castle and the Dail Government.

Yet another striking character appeared at this time on the Irish scene: Sir Hamar Greenwood succeeded Ian Macpherson as Chief Secretary on April 3 and somewhat surprised the Irish by telling them that he "loved" their country. Greenwood, who was 50, had been born in Canada of Welsh parentage, and had come as a young man to England, where he had been called to the Bar and had entered Parliament as a Liberal. Before his appointment as Chief Secretary he had been Under-Secretary at the Home Office, and he was sent to Dublin as a tough careerist who could be relied upon not to lose his nerve. His subordinates found him a cheerful, energetic and agreeable chief, but

Ireland became the grave of his political reputation, largely because he was too ready to deny charges against Crown forces before they had been fully investigated. His mistaken zeal in attempting to cover up British acts of violence gave the Irish a new phrase for telling a lie—"telling a Greenwood".

Amid all these changes French remained the Viceroy.

3

While the first of the Black and Tans were settling in at their depôt, and were learning with some surprise that they were expected to attend lectures on law, the I.R.A. celebrated Easter by burning nearly a hundred Inland Revenue offices all over the country from Belfast to Cork. It was all done very neatly: young men with revolvers entered the various offices, politely held up the tax collectors and demanded their keys, and then took all the books and papers out of the safes, piled them on the floor and set the buildings alight. Simultaneously other groups of young men were setting fire to many of the smaller police barracks which had recently been evacuated, as the British had begun to concentrate the R.I.C. in the larger barracks.

This successful operation was a new proof of Collins's genius as an organiser. Its planning must have involved the exchange of messages and messengers all over Ireland, but Dublin Castle received no warning from any spy or informer. Once again, as in Easter Week, 1916, the new Irish revolution was notable for the absence of informers, though the ruthless slaughter of anyone who was even suspected of giving information to the British was a practical deterrent that few were likely to overlook. As the struggle went on, many dead bodies, often of Irishmen who had served in the British Army, were found by the roadside, shot by the I.R.A., with a label attached to them bearing the words: "Convicted as a spy. Spies and traitors beware." This was a grim warning to possible informers, though it did not, of course, provide any shred of proof that the man who was killed had really been spying. These killings of Irishmen by Irishmen were an effective part of the Sinn Fein terror.

Two days after the burning of the tax offices some 100 Sinn Fein prisoners in Mountjoy gaol began a mass hunger-strike to compel the authorities either to treat them as prisoners of war or to release them. The strike began on Easter Monday, April 5, and among the prisoners' leaders were Peadar Clancy and Frank Gallagher. The amount of actual hardship involved in a hunger-strike is debatable: some years later, when Gallagher wrote a book about the Mountjoy episode, Ernest Blythe, who had practical experience of hunger-striking, was inclined to scoff at it and told Lady Gregory that there was no suffering in such a strike—"one just lies there without pain". But the Mountjoy prisoners soon began to grow weak through their voluntary starvation. After a few days crowds of relatives and other sympathisers gathered outside the gaol, and the prison doctor, who either did not know how long men can live without food or was trying to bluff the prisoners into surrender, told Gallagher: "I can't keep some of your men alive another day." He was quite mistaken. The prisoners went on living, and were heartened by visits from Larry O'Neill, Lord Mayor of Dublin, and Arthur Griffith, who was acting President of the Dail during de Valera's absence in America; but appeals to the Viceroy for clemency brought only the formal answer that he could not modify the prison rules and that all the men had been warned about the consequences of their conduct. This official attitude was amplified in the House of Commons by Bonar Law, who said that the Government was obliged to arrest men on suspicion in Ireland to prevent crime, and that "it would be perfectly futile to do it if men are to be released because they choose to refuse food". The Government, he said, had counted the cost, and there was no possibility of a change in its attitude.

In the end, however, the Government gave in. On behalf of the national executive of the Irish Labour Party Tom Farren, the chairman, and Tom Johnson, the English-born acting secretary, called a general strike for April 13 in support of the Mountjoy prisoners: and the Catholic hierarchy issued a public statement declaring it was "their solemn duty to call the attention of everyone to the appalling tragedy that seems imminent in Mountjoy prison". Faced by the breakdown of civil life owing to the general strike, the Government released the prisoners unconditionally when the hunger-strike had lasted ten days. It was not until later in the year that the Government at last decided to make Irish hunger-strikers take the full consequences of their actions.

In the early summer of 1920 more troops were sent to Ireland, bringing the total number up to about 60,000. But in spite of the presence of this vast army of occupation, the I.R.A. continued their attacks and sometimes laid ambushes for the military. Typical engagements of the time were those at Ballylanders, in county Limerick, where a force of about 60 men from the East Limerick Brigade, armed with rifles and grenades, overwhelmed the small police garrison of five men, and at Kilmallock, in the same county, where some 300 to 400 Volunteers forced the police to evacuate their barracks, though they suffered heavy casualties in doing so. Men of a Scottish regiment were ambushed near Ennis, and seven prisoners were taken, but the most sensational blow against the British troops, and one which entailed no danger to the Volunteers, was the capture of a British brigade commander, Brigadier-General C. Lucas, and two colonels when they were having a few days' fishing holiday near Fermoy at the end of June.

This was another of the surprises planned by Liam Lynch, the enterprising commandant of Cork No. 2 Brigade. He had set one precedent by attacking British soldiers on their way to church; he was now the first I.R.A. commander to track down British officers while they were engaged in sport. Once again Fermoy suffered because of his enterprise: some of Lucas's troops broke windows in the town as a reprisal, and a resident was killed in the raid. The troops, however, need not have feared for their brigadier's safety.

Lynch had let the two colonels go, after one had been wounded in trying to escape, and though Lucas himself was kept prisoner, he was treated with perfect courtesy and was even allowed to go on with his fishing. After five weeks he escaped.

In this month of June Irish affairs had repercussions in both America and India. In the United States Devoy and de Valera were still at loggerheads. They had been publicly in conflict in February when de Valera had said in a newspaper interview that Ireland might be satisfied with the same sort of defence agreement with Britain which then existed between the United States and Cuba. Devoy, who stood for absolute independence for Ireland, fiercely attacked this Cuban proposal in the *Gaelic American*, and said of de Valera in a letter to a friend: "His head is turned to a greater extent than any man I have met in more than half a century." But de Valera went steadily on with his self-chosen task of raising funds for the Dail Government and of proclaiming the Irish cause on platforms all over the country. His speeches were inflammatory but austere: W. B. Yeats, who heard him speak in New York in May, described him as "A living argument rather than a living man. All propaganda, no human life."

It was in June that Devoy and de Valera had one of their most disastrous clashes. The resolutions committee of the U.S. Republican Party was meeting in Chicago to draft its programme for the presidential election later in the year, and Devoy had persuaded the committee to include a resolution about Ireland. It had been drawn up by himself and Cohalan on behalf of the Friends of Irish Freedom, and it affirmed the Republicans' "recognition of the principle that the people of Ireland should have the right to determine freely without dictation from outside their own governmental institutions and their international relations with other states and peoples". Such public support from one of the two great American parties—and the one, moreover, which actually won the presidential election—would have given valuable prestige to the Dail Government, but de Valera refused to accept it. This time he was more uncompromising than Devoy, and he insisted that the Republicans should put on record their unequivocal recognition of the Irish Republic. So the Devoy resolution was withdrawn; a rival one drafted by de Valera was put before the committee and rejected by 12 votes to one; and in the end the Republicans had no resolution of any kind about Ireland in their election programme. A few days later de Valera was equally unsuccessful in his efforts to persuade the Democratic Party to promise recognition of the Irish Republic. His attempts to gain official support for the Dail Government had now definitely failed.

The Indian episode, which occurred on June 28, was a mutiny of about 200 men of the Connaught Rangers at Jullundur in the Punjab. The mutineers had had letters from home telling them of British oppression; they declared that they were determined to stand by Sinn Fein, and they demanded the withdrawal of British troops from Ireland. There were about 90 active mutineers, and their resistance was overcome after some fighting in which two soldiers were killed and one wounded. The ringleader was shot after trial by court-martial, and others were sentenced to terms of penal servitude in England. The mutiny may have had less political significance than is usually attributed to it, for in the summer of 1920 the war-time separation allowances for wives of serving soldiers had been withdrawn, and there was general discontent among all troops in India, where mutinies also occurred among British troops who were not influenced by events in Ireland. Dissatisfaction over the separation allowances must have been at least a contributory cause of the Connaught Rangers' action.

CHAPTER XVIII

Terror and Counter-Terror

I

FOR MORE THAN a year since the killing of the two R.I.C. constables at Soloheadbeg in January, 1919, the I.R.A. had had much the better of their exchanges with the police and the troops. Ireland, it is true, was living under a police-state régime, which continued the now familiar routine of raids on private houses, forcible dispersals of meetings and arrests on suspicion of men who were kept in prison without being brought to trial; but Sinn Fein had built up a very effective terror, which ranged from the slaughter of policemen and alleged spies to the burning of coastguard stations and court-houses, the raiding of mails and even the shearing of girls' hair because they had been seen talking to soldiers or constables. Between January and December, 1920, 176 policemen were killed and 251 wounded. Attacks on the military were more hazardous and therefore less numerous, but 54 soldiers were killed and 118 wounded during the year. Casualties on the Irish side were very much smaller. a Sinn Fein statement reported 43 violent deaths of Volunteers and civilians in what were apparently the worst three months of 1920.

Three incidents in July indicate the ferocity of the Sinn Fein terror. At Bandon, in west Cork, an R.I.C. sergeant was ambushed and shot dead outside a church porch at the moment when he was entering the church to attend Mass.

A day or two later two armed Volunteers went to the County Club in Cork and shot dead Colonel G. B. V. Smyth, an R.I.C. divisional inspector, who had committed the heinous offence (in Sinn Fein eyes) of advising the R.I.C. to shoot first if they met any suspicious-looking person with his hands in his pockets on a country road at night. At the end of the month a gang of gunmen burst into the office of Frank Brooke, chairman of the Dublin and South-Eastern Railway Company, and shot him dead, though he had no direct connexion with either the police or the troops. This last outrage may not have been actually the work of the I.R.A. The terror gave thugs and criminals a useful cloak for their own misdeeds, and Brooke's killers may have been men who were paying off some old grudge.

Such crimes were possible because by this time the administration of British justice had virtually ceased in the south and west of Ireland. Even when policemen were killed in public no witnesses would come forward, and the general work of the British Courts had been largely taken over by the Sinn Fein Courts set up by Dail Eireann. All kinds of legal business were transacted in these Courts, and in spite of British attempts to suppress them, their organisation grew more elaborate from month to month. There were parish Courts for petty civil and criminal cases, monthly district Courts for more important cases, circuit Courts held in each district three times a year and presided over by one of four circuit judges, and finally a Supreme Court in Dublin. In spite of official disapproval, solicitors and barristers had to work in the Sinn Fein Courts, because there was little or nothing for them to do in the British counterparts. A Sinn Fein (or Republican) police force was also set up to support the work of the Courts. But no action was taken in them against Irishmen who killed policemen or soldiers, since such killings were held by the I.R.A. to be legitimate acts of war.

The British Government had now become well aware that it could not stop violence in Ireland under the existing rules of law, and a new Bill—hopefully called the Restoration of

Order in Ireland Bill—was introduced at the end of July and quickly put into effect. This measure gave wide powers to the military command, including authority to arrest and imprison without charge or trial anyone suspected of Sinn Fein associations, to try prisoners by court-martial, to hold witnesses in custody and imprison or fine them for failing to produce evidence, and to substitute military courts of inquiry for coroners' inquests. General Macready would have preferred to see the whole country put under martial law, so that he could have suppressed the Sinn Fein terror by purely military operations; but in default of such drastic action he was given some useful weapons in the new Bill.

On July 27 the Government inaugurated a small corps of ex-officers to serve as an Auxiliary Division of the R.I.C. The "Auxies", as the Irish were soon to name them, were never more than 1,500 in number, and they were officially and rather confusingly described as cadets—a term which gave the mistaken impression that they were mere youths. They were entirely distinct from the Black and Tans, and after a short period in which they wore khaki they were equipped with dark-blue uniforms and dark-green Glengarry caps. They were paid £1 a day, and like the Black and Tans, they were men who had joined up in search of danger and excitement. They made varying impressions on the people with whom they came into contact. To Sean O'Casey they were "sibilant and sinister raiders"; Frank Gallagher thought them "a wild and unmanageable terrorist corps"; their first commanding officer, Brigadier-General F. P. Crozier, later portrayed them as insubordinate, dishonest, sadistic and drunken; but Sir Christopher Lynch-Robinson, who had such a poor opinion of the Black and Tans, found the Auxiliary cadets "all young fellows of the Sandhurst type, very smart and debonair . . . extremely nice, friendly and well-behaved . . . a plucky, daredevil lot". They can best be summed up as a tough, hard-bitten corps, who reacted to the Sinn Fein terror by determining to make their own counter-terror even more formidable.

Some of the Auxies found Irish girl-friends, but it is interesting to observe that even General Crozier commented on the "almost total absence of sex offences". That, indeed, is one of the remarkable features of these troubled years. A traditionally "licentious soldiery" and the unruly Auxies and Black and Tans might have been expected to have left numerous accusations of rape behind them; but in fact this seems to be an offence which the British in Ireland were rarely charged with committing. Tom Barry, commandant of the Cork No. 3 Brigade, accused the Essex Regiment of all kinds of atrocities, yet when he made a detailed list of their misdeeds he could say only that they had "attempted" (presumably unsuccessfully) the rape of Irishwomen; and the British Labour Party Commission, which went to Ireland at the end of 1920 to find evidence of British misrule, could find no more serious example of sex crime than an occasion on which some Crown forces had raided a house where a girl was sleeping alone, had made her get out of bed and had ripped her nightdress from top to bottom. The American Commission on Conditions in Ireland, which sat in Washington in December, 1920, and January, 1921, and heard evidence from many Irish citizens (including MacSwiney's widow and sister and MacCurtain's sisters-in-law) gave the British forces an equally good record. It stated that "in no case has the crime of rape been specifically charged by Irish witnesses before us against the Imperial troops", and it gave great credit to the British High Command "for controlling the sensual licentiousness of its men".

The Labour Commission commented on the lack of reports of sex offences that "it was extremely difficult to obtain direct evidence of incidents affecting females, for the women of Ireland are reticent on such subjects", and probably there were a few cases of rape which were never reported. Lady Gregory noted in her diary in November, 1920, that "the family of the girls violated by the Black and Tans wish it to be hushed up", and added that "there has been another case of the same sort in Clare, but there also it is to be kept quiet". Yet if there had been any significant number of sex offences the industrious Irish propagandists would soon have found ways of publicising them, if only by discreetly calling the victims Miss X or Mrs. Y. In fact, however, even Mrs. Erskine Childers, who must have heard of all Britain's misdeeds through her husband's association with the *Irish Bulletin*, was apparently convinced that the chastity of Irish girls did not suffer during the years of the troubles. She told an American woman writer that she knew of no case in which a British soldier had betrayed a woman, though she made it clear that she attributed this fact to the virtue of Irish girls rather than to that of British soldiers.

With the coming of the "Tans" and the Auxiliaries life in southern Ireland began to assume the grim pattern which was to remain until the Truce was signed in July, 1921, and was then to be repeated with variations when the Free State Government was at death grips with the Irregulars in 1922 and 1923. It was a queer time. Only a small minority of the Irish population was actively involved in the struggle between the I.R.A., as agents of the Dail Government, and the British forces; other people went about their ordinary business and found amusement at races, dances and theatres until the British, who had imposed a curfew from midnight till 5 a.m., moved it back to an earlier hour and made theatre-going impossible. (But the curfew, exasperating though it was for the general public, at least provided some amusing incidents to lighten the Irish gloom. There was the story, for instance, of a Dublin mother going tremulously home with her husband and small son after the curfew hour, and fearfully invoking every saint in the calendar for protection. Suddenly challenged by a British soldier, she cried despairingly, "Jesus, Mary and Joseph!", and was reassuringly answered in a Cockney voice, "Pass, the 'Oly Family, all's well!" There was also the middle-aged prostitute who was brought before a military tribunal for being out after curfew and was formally asked if she "recognised the Court". "I do not," she replied in a puzzled voice, and then, as she scrutinised her officer judges, her eyes brightened, and she said cheerfully: "Wait a minute now! Ah, shure, I recognise the little major over there!")

Yet the conflict, in which so few of them at that time had any share, relentlessly imposed itself on the lives of all the citizens of Ireland. The usual transport for Auxies and Black and Tans was a Crossley tender—a Crossley motor chassis fitted with a wagonette body and capable of carrying eight to ten men with full equipment; and at any moment one of these lorries, loaded with fierce-looking men pointing their rifles at the passers-by, might roar through the streets, where also at any moment an apparently innocent civilian might take a grenade from under his coat and throw it at them. Then the police would open fire, and although as a rule neither they nor their assailant suffered injury, the unfortunate bystanders were often wounded either by the bomb or by the rifle bullets. Trams, too, were frequently held up and searched by soldiers or police. As soon as the alarm was given some seemingly respectable passenger might be seen taking a revolver from his pocket and slipping it down the front of a girl's blouse for safety until the search was over.

But it was at night that Irish men and women learned to dread the sound of the Crossley tenders, and to pray that the raiding parties in search of Sinn Fein suspects would not stop at their door. These raids were terrifying affairs, beginning with a loud battering on the door if the raiders were soldiers or a wanton smashing of its glass panels if they were "Tans". Then the occupants of the house would be lined up and their rooms searched, and anyone whose credentials were doubtful was taken away. The raiders rarely if ever captured any important men "on the run". Some of the houses where the I.R.A. leaders slept had hidden recesses, and it was in one of these that Austin Stack found refuge when soldiers raided his temporary home. A girl from another room got into his bed, so that the raiders would not find it warm but unoccupied, and Stack stayed safely in his hiding-place until they had gone. Even the country houses of the wealthy were not immune from British raids. On one occasion a party of Black and Tans rampaged through Dunsany Castle during Lord Dunsany's absence, and it is on record that as they were leaving the butler icily asked them: "Who shall I say called?"

Civilians had other hardships that summer, as well as raids on their homes and gun battles in the streets. Rail travel had become difficult, because drivers, guards and signalmen on the lines running west and south of Dublin refused to run trains carrying police or soldiers. Intending passengers often had long waits until either the men in uniform left the train or a more co-operative train crew could be assembled. Many of the railwaymen were dismissed, and on some lines traffic ceased altogether.

2

The month of July, in which Colonel Smyth and Frank Brooke were killed, was also the month in which the Black and Tans began the long series of destructive reprisals, sometimes involving the deaths of Irish civilians, which soon caused horror and indignation in England no less than in Ireland. Though in later months, when the Black and Tans were given regulation R.I.C. uniforms, they were no longer distinguishable at sight from the older members of the force, it became usual to ascribe all R.I.C. attacks to the "Tans", unless they were known to have been made by the Auxiliaries; but in fact both old and new members of the R.I.C. must have taken part in many of them, for there were still about 9,000 original members of the force and never more than 5,000 to 6,000 new recruits. All the R.I.C. were keyed up for their work by the publication from Dublin Castle of a paper called the *Weekly Summary*, which gave details of recent Sinn Fein outrages and in a ferocious leading article advised the new policemen to make Ireland "an appropriate hell" for Sinn Feiners. The violence of this publication was condemned by the Anglo-Irish journalist Robert Lynd, who wrote in the *Daily News* that its incitements had "had their natural result in making the Black and Tans feel towards their Irish 'enemies' as men feel towards wild beasts".

Galway and Tipperary were the first settings for Black and Tan reprisals. These tough recruits declined to accept quietly a state of affairs in which policemen were callously shot in the back by young men in civilian clothes; and it was soon their practice to ignore their officers' orders and retaliate on the villages which were thought to harbour the Sinn Fein killers. One of the first Black and Tan outbreaks was at Tuam, in county Galway, where two constables were ambushed and killed in July. In reprisal the Black and Tans looted public-houses (and drank their loot), raided shops and set fire to the town hall, while elsewhere in Galway they were said to have taken Sinn Fein youths out of their houses at night, stripped them and beaten them. In the same month at Newport, in county Tipperary, they began their practice of punishing the civilian population by destroying creameries; and there was a bigger reprisal at Templemore, in the same county, in August after the shooting of a district inspector. This time the police broke out of barracks in the evening and burnt the market hall to the ground, while troops joined the raiding party and fired rifles indiscriminately. The routine of Sinn Fein outrage followed by Black and Tan outrage began to take shape. Terror was now to be answered by counter-terror.

In most districts the troops had little to do with the more violent incidents of the counter-terror; Lord Russell of Liverpool, who served in Ireland in 1920 with the King's Regiment (Liverpool), has recorded that in spite of much provocation and anti-Army propaganda his men maintained excellent discipline and behaved with praiseworthy restraint. At Bandon, however, the Essex Regiment were accused of having tortured two of their I.R.A. prisoners by pulling out their hair and crushing their nails with pincers and pliers, the torturers, according to information sent secretly to Collins, being officers of Irish nationality. One of the prisoners went mad after his sufferings and remained insane for the rest of his life; the other was sentenced to penal servitude. After this incident the Cork No. 2 Brigade of the I.R.A. waged a ceaseless vendetta against the Essex Regiment, and Tom Barry, the commandant, ordered his men to shoot every soldier at sight, armed or unarmed.

Cork, where Barry and Liam Lynch commanded two very active brigades, was very prominent in this phase of the Anglo-Irish conflict. In August the new Lord Mayor of Cork, Terence MacSwiney, was arrested at the City Hall while presiding over an I.R.A. conference, and was charged with the possession of seditious documents. As soon as he was arrested he announced that he would go on hunger-strike. He began his strike immediately and continued it after he had been sentenced on August 16 to two years' imprisonment without hard labour and transferred to Brixton gaol.

There was trouble, too, at the other end of Ireland, where the old Ulster feud between Catholics and Protestants flared up in July and August. There had been rioting in Derry in June, and the garrison there had been strengthened in expectation of a Sinn Fein raid; and with these events in mind Carson made the emphatic declaration on Orange Day that "we in Ulster will tolerate no Sinn Fein, no Sinn Fein organisation, no Sinn Fein methods". A few days later there was a big mass meeting of Protestant and Unionist shipyard workers at South Yard, Belfast, where feelings of resentment against southern Irish workers who had found jobs in the north-east during the war helped to inspire an active campaign against Catholics and Sinn Feiners. Many were driven out of the shipyards, and there was rioting in Lisburn, Newtownards, Bangor and Derry.

The "pogrom" (as it was generally called) continued intermittently for several weeks, and was exacerbated by the shooting of District Inspector Swanzy (who had been transferred from Cork after the death of MacCurtain) at Lisburn on August 22 and of another R.I.C. man on September 25.

It was after this latter incident that three Sinn Feiners were dragged from their beds in Belfast and shot dead, more Catholic workers were driven from the shipyards, and their houses were burnt. Though the rioting died down in the autumn, it was still smouldering under the surface and was ready to flare up again in the following year. Catholics, both in Ulster and in southern Ireland, were particularly incensed by the official enrolment of an Ulster Special Constabulary, which gave Protestant civilians a share in keeping the peace. It was felt that Protestants who had taken part in the riots were being given Government sanction for their actions.

3

In the south the Black and Tans' counter-terror grew more intense from month to month. In September both England and Ireland were shaken by the somewhat exaggerated accounts of their raid on Balbriggan, a hosiery manufacturing town in county Dublin.

The origin of the Balbriggan affair was the killing by the I.R.A. of an R.I.C. district inspector and the wounding of a constable in the bar of a public-house. The assailants had used expanding bullets, which are forbidden by international convention because of the terrible wounds they inflict, but were frequently used by the I.R.A. when they had no supplies of ordinary bullets. The grisly appearance of their dead inspector's body aroused the fury of the police, and that evening between 100 and 150 Black and Tans set out from their Gormanstown depôt, three miles away, to punish Balbriggan for his death. It was a wild outing. Public-houses were looted and set on fire, private houses were wrecked and many of them, together with a stocking factory belonging to a British firm, were burnt, and two men, whom the Black and Tans thought to be I.R.A. officers, were killed. Irish propaganda described the affair as "the sack of Balbriggan", but in fact the damage, wanton though it was, was confined to one part of the town, and only one out of several factories was destroyed. Balbriggan was certainly not burnt to the ground. When Macready went there a few days later he thought that a person who did not know what had happened might have motored through the town without realising there had been a raid.

Balbriggan was a portent. It was followed in a few days by similar reprisals at Ennistymon and Lahinch (after five Black and Tans had been ambushed and killed with expanding bullets by the I.R.A.) and at Trim (after a raid on the barracks where a constable was wounded). So the long series of lawless, unofficial reprisals, in which the Black and Tans usually got drunk on liquor looted from public-houses, was now in full swing, and a loud chorus of disapproval began to be voiced in the English Press and House of Commons. Yet the Government, which had enrolled the Black and Tans to keep order in Ireland, declined to take action to check their own lawlessness. Even the die-hard Sir Henry Wilson condemned the reprisals, which he ascribed to lack of discipline, and said that they ought to be stopped at once. Of the Sinn Feiners killed at Balbriggan he said to Lloyd George: "If these men ought to be murdered, then the Government ought to murder them." But Lloyd George replied that the Government could not possibly take responsibility for such deeds. The reprisals were to be left to run their course unofficially.

Gun-battles between British troops and Volunteers were now almost a commonplace in the Dublin streets. One notorious encounter occurred on the actual day of the Balbriggan raid, when Volunteers (as usual in civilian clothes) attacked a party of British soldiers who were drawing bread rations from a bakery. They killed or fatally wounded six soldiers, but all the attackers escaped except a youth of 18, who was found hiding under the troops' lorry with an automatic pistol in his hand. This was Kevin Barry, a medical student and corporal in the I.R.A. He was taken prisoner and held for court-martial under the Restoration of Order in Ireland Act.

A few days later Treacy and Breen, two of the Tipperary

stalwarts, were nearly captured in Dublin in the house of Professor Carolan. The house was raided, and Carolan was accidentally killed, but Breen and Treacy escaped. Breen, who was wounded, found refuge in the Mater Hospital, a convenient sanctuary for injured I.R.A. men, since there was a Dublin Castle order that no hospitals were to be searched by the police or the military without special permission. (The reason, as Sir John Anderson explained to an exasperated police chief, was that if bandages were removed from a patient to identify him, and he subsequently died, the Government could be held responsible for his death; and though doctors and nurses were ordered to report to the Castle if they treated any cases for gunshot wounds, this order was consistently ignored.) Treacy stayed in Dublin to organise a rescue party to smuggle Breen out of hospital, but he was tracked down by the military, who sent two lorry-loads of troops to capture him at the Republican Outfitters' in Talbot Street. Finding escape impossible, Treacy fired at his pursuers, who shot him dead. His body was taken to Tipperary, where a funeral procession several miles long followed the hearse to his grave at Kilfeacle.

While the war of attack and reprisal went on an event of a different kind suddenly focused world opinion on Ireland. Through August, September and October Lord Mayor MacSwiney was still on hunger-strike in Brixton gaol, and more than one theory was advanced for his prolonged hold on life. One suggestion was that the priest who came regularly to see him hid food in his thick beard, but it is hardly likely that a man of MacSwiney's passionate integrity would have practised that kind of deception. A more plausible explanation is that the prison authorities put something colourless and tasteless—possibly glucose—into the water he drank, to give him at least a minimum of sustenance. For the Government did not want MacSwiney to die, though it was determined to establish the principle that Irish prisoners were not to be allowed to gain release by going on hunger-strike. In reply to an appeal by the British

Labour Party for MacSwiney's release Lloyd George declared that to set him free would be a betrayal of the loyal Crown forces in Ireland.

"Since the arrest of the Lord Mayor," he said, "15 officers have been brutally and treacherously done to death without even a chance to defend themselves. Surely the sympathy which has been given in such full measure to the Lord Mayor, whose condition has been brought about by his own deliberate act, is due to the bereaved widows and families of the murdered Irish policemen."

The responsibility for MacSwiney's ordeal was thus thrown on to the Dail Cabinet. But no order came from Dublin to tell MacSwiney to call off his strike or to end the hunger-strike being simultaneously carried on by 11 prisoners in Cork gaol. One of these men had already died, and another died on October 25, but it was MacSwiney's death on the same day, after fasting for 74 days, which aroused sympathy all over the world. This sympathy was fully expressed in the British Press; *The Times*, which had earlier insisted that it would be folly to allow him to die and had urged his release as an act of grace, commented on the day after his death: "We have never regretted and do not now regret the advice we then tendered." The logic of the Government's arguments was swept aside by humanitarian sentiments, and great crowds watched MacSwiney's funeral *cortège* passing through the streets of London. The Government prudently refused to allow the coffin to be taken to Dublin. Instead it was sent direct to Cork, and the day of the burial—October 31—was observed throughout southern and western Ireland as a day of public mourning.

On the following day Ireland had further cause for mourning. Kevin Barry had been tried by a military Court in October; the bullets left in his revolver corresponded with the bullet found in the body of one of the soldiers killed in the bakery affray; he was found guilty of murder and sentenced to death by hanging. A civilian hangman was sent for from England, and the execution took place at

Mountjoy on November 1, while hundreds of women wept outside the prison gates.

The sentence and execution illustrate the complexity of the Irish struggle. In the Irish view the I.R.A. were waging a war and Barry should have been treated, therefore, as a prisoner of war. But there was no precedent for a war in which combatants not only wore civilian clothes but also mingled with the public, and the British authorities had a case for claiming that killing by ambush in the Dublin streets was actually murder. Childers attacked this view in a letter to the British Press, and Griffith made a public appeal for Barry's life. Others pleaded that he should be reprieved because he was only 18, but since the dead British soldiers were only a year or two older, that plea could hardly have been expected to carry much weight. Though Barry's death caused great and understandable anger in Ireland, his execution was in accordance with the law enacted by the British Parliament.

In the middle of November the Dail Cabinet at last put a stop to hunger-striking. Griffith wrote to the new Lord Mayor of Cork, saying: "I am of the opinion that our countrymen in Cork prison have sufficiently proved their devotion and fidelity, and that they should now, as they were prepared to die for Ireland, prepare again to live for her." The strike was immediately called off, and there was no more hunger-striking during the Anglo-Irish conflict, though it reappeared in the Civil War. It was unfortunate that the Dail Cabinet had to wait for three men to die before admitting that hunger-striking had become a protracted form of suicide.

CHAPTER XIX

Bloody Sunday

I

IF THE IRISH leaders had been in a peace-making mood they might well have capitalised the feelings of sympathy for Ireland aroused in the autumn of 1920 by the deaths of MacSwiney and Barry. It was a propitious moment. Early in October Brigadier-General George Cockerill, a British M.P., had written a letter to *The Times* suggesting a truce in Ireland and the calling of a conference between representatives of the British Government and Dail Eireann. Throughout the year British newspaper correspondents had been closely following the Irish struggle, and Liberal journalists such as H. W. Nevinson, Hugh Martin of the *Daily News* and A. P. Wadsworth of the *Manchester Guardian* sent home reports which dismayed the public. Moreover, in the leader columns of the *Manchester Guardian* its editor, C. P. Scott, wrote article after article denouncing the use of "German methods of frightfulness" in Ireland, and his biographer reasonably claims that "Scott's pen was one of the chief forces in putting an end to the terror of the Black and Tans".

Conservatives, too, joined in the campaign against the lawlessness of British forces in Ireland. Lord Henry Cavendish-Bentinck, a Conservative M.P. of vigorous and independent mind, formed a Peace with Ireland Council, which sent General Sir Henry Lawson to report on the Irish situation and published anti-reprisals pamphlets by such influential writers as G. K. Chesterton and A. Clutton-Brock. (It was in one of these that Chesterton declared bluntly: "The whole world thinks that England has gone mad.") The small Labour Party steadily attacked Government policy in Ireland, and after unsuccessfully asking Lloyd George to set up an independent investigation into the conduct of the Crown forces it decided to send out its own Commission of Inquiry, which began an Irish tour in November.

Both youth and age were against the Government. Its Irish policy was condemned by the Oxford Union, where the debate was made memorable by a passionate address by W. B. Yeats, as guest speaker, who walked up and down the gangway between the benches haranguing and waving his arms at the undergraduates; and in the House of Lords old Randall Davidson, Archbishop of Canterbury, spoke forcibly against the Black and Tans. He denounced the Sinn Feiners' own outrages as "unutterably horrible", but went on to urge the Government to bring to an end the kind of reprisal in which "the disciplined forces of the Crown, appointed to suppress disorder, have themselves, though without definite superior authority and command, given terrible examples of the very kind of disorder which they are sent there to suppress". It was after this speech that Lord Curzon, Conservative leader of the House of Lords, admitted privately that the Government had no answer to the Archbishop's criticisms.

Far-sighted statesmen in Ireland could have used this wave of horror in England as an opening for forcing a satisfactory settlement. But the Dail President, de Valera, was far away from the scene of battle and had fixed no date for his return; Griffith hesitated to initiate a change of policy in de Valera's absence; and Collins's aims could have been summed up in Clemenceau's phrase during the European War—"*Je fais la guerre*." So the moment passed, and Lloyd George was left to press on with his Better Government of Ireland Bill and to hope that unofficial reprisals would somehow help to restore peace. He had previously called the Sinn Feiners a "murder gang"; at the Lord Mayor of London's banquet on November 9 he declared: "At last, unless I am mistaken, by the steps we have taken we have murder by the throat."

He was certainly mistaken. The execution of Kevin Barry had been the signal for many further attacks on policemen, which provoked the usual reprisals. Near Tralee five Black and Tans were killed in an ambush and two taken prisoner; in return the town was raided by police and military, who wrecked shops and houses with hatchets and crowbars and set fire to the County Hall, though without causing any fatal casualties. For days afterwards they held up normal life in Tralee while they were waiting for the return of the kidnapped constables. Their wait was in vain. Sinn Feiners had thrown the two men alive into the furnace of the local gas-works.

While the provincial leaders of the I.R.A. were waging their own ruthless war, not only in small ambushes but also in larger operations carried out by disciplined and organised flying columns, the leaders in Dublin were planning death and destruction on a still wider scale. Brugha was preparing to carry the Irish campaign into England by bombing and arson; Collins, who had now got rid of most of the Dublin detectives, was turning his attention to the Army's intelligence officers.

Some of these officers were then living in houses and hotels in various parts of Dublin, possibly because there was no room in the barracks for them, but more probably, as Collins assumed, because by living in the city and wearing civilian clothes they were better placed for picking up information about I.R.A. activities. Collins's efficient secret service gradually traced the addresses of these intelligence officers, and Dick McKee and Peadar Clancy, Commandant and Vice-Commandant of the I.R.A. Dublin Brigade, were ordered to arrange for them all to be killed on Sunday morning, November 21.

In the event neither McKee nor Clancy took part in the massacre. They were both captured by Auxies on the Saturday night and were taken to Dublin Castle, where they were put in the guardroom with a third prisoner, Conor Clune, a young man from county Clare who had been with some of the I.R.A. leaders at Vaughan's Hotel but was not involved in their plans. But though McKee and Clancy were prisoners, their arrangements were duly carried out. On the Sunday morning parties of Volunteers raided the houses where the officers were living and shot 14 dead, some in the presence of their wives.

In the course of the raids two Auxies who came to the rescue were killed also, but the I.R.A. killers escaped with the exception of one man, Frank Teeling, who was wounded and captured, and subsequently escaped from prison after being sentenced to death.

Of the 14 who were shot seven were officially recorded as being officers, three as ex-officers, two as members of the R.I.C. and two as civilians, and it may never be known how many of them were actually the secret agents whom Collins was seeking to remove. Certainly some were the right men, for General Crozier was told at Dublin Castle that morning that "Collins has done in most of the secret service people". Collins's own justification for the massacre was that the officers had all been directly or indirectly concerned with the killing of Irish citizens, and he told Crozier after the Truce: "I found out that those fellows we put on the spot were going to put a lot of us on the spot, so I got in first." Apart from some rather ambiguous statements in captured British documents, there appears to be no definite evidence either for or against these statements, but it is certain that some of the officers knew far more about the I.R.A. than Collins wished them to know. He therefore removed them.

It was the magnitude of the officers' killings on what came to be known as Bloody Sunday, combined with the brutally efficient organisation it revealed, which shocked Britain when the news became known. Yet Lloyd George did not think that the event called for a special Cabinet meeting, and Henry Wilson recorded Churchill's private opinion that the dead officers were careless fellows and ought to have taken precautions. It is, indeed, a mystery of Bloody Sunday that the residences of intelligence officers should have been so easily accessible to potential killers.

But Irishmen, as well as Englishmen, lost their lives on Bloody Sunday. McKee, Clancy and Conor Clune were killed in Dublin Castle: the Irish version of their deaths was that they were cruelly beaten up and shot against a wall, but the official British account, supported by Colonel Winter, Chief of the Combined Intelligence Services at the Castle, in his reminiscences written many years later, was that they were shot at breakfast-time while trying to escape. According to this account, a single sentry was left in charge of the prisoners while the rest of the Auxie guard went into an inner room for breakfast; the three men attacked the sentry, but before they were able to get away the other guards hurried back and after a hand-to-hand conflict shot them dead.

Irish historians generally regard the phrase "shot while trying to escape" as a euphemism for deliberate killing, but in view of the large number of Irish prisoners who at one time or another escaped or tried to escape it would have been little short of miraculous if none of them had ever been shot in such attempts. In this case McKee and Clancy had the best of reasons for wanting to escape at the earliest possible moment. They were the organisers of the slaughter of the British officers, and they must have felt sure that there was a strong likelihood of their complicity being discovered. Since, therefore, a death sentence probably awaited them if they stayed in captivity, they would have felt it worth while to risk their lives in an attempt to escape, and they would not even have been deterred by knowing that, if they had got out of the guardroom, they would have had more armed men to face in the Castle yard. Though Clune had no death sentence hanging over him, he would naturally have joined in his comrades' attempt. This explanation seems more likely than the Irish theory that the Auxies had the effrontery, after maltreating their prisoners, to take them out into the yard and shoot them in full view of any high official or senior officer who happened to be passing. In any case Sir John Anderson, who was not easily deceived, himself inspected the guardroom after the incident and was satisfied that the escape story was correct.

Another scene of slaughter on Bloody Sunday was the Croke Park football ground, where a crowd of some 6,000 to 8,000 people assembled in the afternoon to watch an important match. The military authorities thought it likely that the officers' killers would mingle with the football crowd to throw any pursuers off the scent, and they arranged to send a detachment of soldiers to Croke Park to search the crowd for weapons—a procedure which could easily have been carried out at the ordinary exits to the ground. As it happened, however, a party of Black and Tans arrived before the troops, and a shot was fired at them. In retaliation they rushed into the ground and recklessly opened fire on the crowd; the troops, arriving a little later and finding shooting in progress, also joined in the attack. The spectators were panic-stricken and rushed out wildly, so that the project for searching them was never carried out, though many discarded revolvers were found on the ground after they had gone. The only satisfactory part of this shocking affair was that the casualties, which might well have run into hundreds, were limited to 12 killed and 60 wounded, apart from those who were injured in the stampede for safety.

One immediate result of the Bloody Sunday shootings was to make British intelligence officers and undercover agents more careful where they lived. A member of the Dublin Brigade has recorded how "cabs, taxis and hacks were rushing to the Castle all day with spies, touts and their wives seeking safety"; such men were greatly handicapped in their secret service work when they could no longer live among the people. Six of the British dead were given a military funeral in London, where Lloyd George, Churchill and Greenwood followed the coffins up the aisle of Westminster Abbey. In Dublin Collins himself risked capture to attend a Requiem Mass for Dick McKee.

2

The Better Government of Ireland Bill had been given its third reading in the House of Commons on November 11, 1920, and it was introduced in the House of Lords on the day after England had heard of the Bloody Sunday killings. It was sponsored there by Lord Birkenhead, as F. E. Smith had now become, who spoke most generously of the Irish people and of the hope for a happier future. It would make, he said, "a shining page" in history if the coalition Government could succeed where O'Connell, Parnell and Gladstone had failed, and if Britain, after her victory in the war, "recaptured in a nobler conquest this island of incomparable beauty, and in doing so became reconciled to a people so individual in its genius, so tenacious in love or hate, so captivating in its noble moods".

That "nobler conquest" seemed very remote at a time when Britain, as Henry Wilson put it, had "handed over the government of Ireland to the Black and Tans", and the gunmen and flying columns of the I.R.A. were reacting with still greater vigour to the violence and ferocity of both Black and Tans and Auxies. During a tour of southern and western Ireland in November the veteran English journalist, H. W. Nevinson, heard many tragic stories of British misdeeds. He was told at Ardfert of a young girl being shot in the open road by a Black and Tan, at Killaloe of four captured youths killed on a bridge, at Shanaglish of the killing and mutilation of two brothers, and in Galway of the discovery of the body of Father Griffin, an Irish patriot, in a bog near Spiddal with a bullet in his head. He also heard at Gort of the wanton shooting by Black and Tans of a young wife, though he could not have guessed that the bereaved husband would later be highly indignant because the British offered him only £300 in compensation for his loss. Nevinson's tour convinced him that the property of Sinn Fein sympathisers was in constant danger, and doctors told him that there had been an alarming increase in cases of St. Vitus's dance and similar nervous ailments.

In this month Brugha's plans for carrying the war to England had their first results in Liverpool, where 15 warehouses were burnt by Irish incendiaries in a single night; but further arson was temporarily checked by the prompt action of the British police, who were able, with the help of papers found in Dublin, to round up and arrest more than a hundred people concerned in the plot. It was also at the end of November that the flying column of Tom Barry's Cork No. 3 Brigade engaged at Kilmichael a company of Auxies who were stationed at Macroom Castle, and wiped them out in the most devastating ambush of the whole conflict.

The Auxies at Macroom had effectively terrorised a wide area by raiding villages, beating up men whom they regarded as suspects and holding whole communities prisoner for hours at a time while young and old were lined up, questioned and searched. Barry determined to challenge them; with his flying column of 36 riflemen he chose a spot one and a half miles south of Kilmichael to wait for two lorry-loads of Auxies returning to barracks after their day's round-up. To confuse the enemy one of the ambushing party stood in the road wearing an I.R.A. officer's tunic, which on a dark November afternoon could be mistaken for a British uniform; and this ruse had the desired effect of making the first lorry slow down as it approached the ambush. The I.R.A. attack opened with a bomb, and as the Auxies in the first lorry jumped down on to the road they were exposed to a deadly fire and then engaged at close quarters with bayonets and rifle-butts. All nine of them were killed or fatally wounded within a few minutes, and the Auxies who had come up in the second lorry prudently offered to surrender. But one—or possibly more—of those who had thrown away their rifles in token of surrender then opened fire with a revolver, and the I.R.A. retaliated by shooting them all. In all, sixteen were killed outright, one who was wounded crawled to the side of the road and sank in the bog, and the eighteenth died later of wounds without recovering consciousness. A British official statement said that the dead bodies were mutilated with axes, but Barry has recorded that the I.R.A. had no axes and there was no mutilation. Three Volunteers were killed in the fight, which was soon followed by the establishment of martial law for the counties of Cork, Tipperary, Kerry and Limerick.

Martial law was proclaimed on December 10. On the next day a party of Auxiliaries was ambushed at Dillon's Cross, a few miles from Cork city, where one of them was killed and 11 wounded. This affair, coming so quickly after the bigger Kilmichael ambush which had enraged the Crown forces, was enough to trigger off a truly staggering reprisal. That night Auxies and Black and Tans surged into Cork, ordered the citizens to their homes before the official curfew hour and began a wild orgy of looting, wrecking, burning and drinking. They raided public-houses, took the contents of a jeweller's shop away in kitbags, looted other shops and set fire to the whole of Patrick Street, the City Hall and the Carnegie Library; and when the fire brigade tried to check the flames they cut the hoses with bayonets or turned the water off at the hydrant. The military, who were theoretically in charge of the city during the curfew period of 10 p.m. to 3 a.m., did nothing to stop the rioting. It was mainly a night of terror and vast material damage, which was later estimated at £3,000,000, and two Volunteers were shot by armed raiders in their home at Dublin Hill, outside the city. One was killed instantly, the other was fatally wounded.

When questions about the burning of Cork were put in the House of Commons Greenwood at first declared that neither the police nor the troops had anything to do with it, and that the inhabitants of the city had burnt it themselves.

But this was too much for anyone to swallow. After a few days a military inquiry into the responsibility for the fire was opened by General E. P. Strickland, commanding officer for the Cork district. Its findings were never published, but when a later British Government made a compensation settlement with the Irish Free State it agreed to accept liability for the destruction of a large part of Cork.

Only a few days later an Auxiliary shot and killed two men, one of whom was Canon Magner, parish priest of Dunmanway, on the open road near Bandon. The culprit was tried by a military Court, and found Guilty but Insane. This occurrence registered another black mark for the Auxiliaries, who were scattered about the country in 15 companies of 100 men each. Some of them had already been dismissed by their commanding officer, General Crozier, for various acts of indiscipline, though in general they seem to have been more amenable to command than the Black and Tans. Macready, at all events, declared that in spite of the utmost provocation the Auxiliaries "preserved a discipline beyond all praise".

By this time the bulk of the Irish people had only one wish—that both terror and counter-terror would be brought to an end and peace restored throughout the country. The I.R.A. had, of course, their supporters and admirers, in whose eyes they could do no wrong; among these the girls of the Cumann na mBan gave them particularly faithful backing. But others found Sinn Fein outrages no less shocking than Black and Tan reprisals, and though the Roman Catholic hierarchy refrained from making any joint pronouncement, individual church leaders expressed their "loathing and detestation" of the I.R.A.'s actions. Dr. Daniel Cohalan, Bishop of Cork, put this view most forcibly in his pastoral letter of December 19, in which he said that the killing of policemen was "morally murder and politically of no consequence, and the burning of barracks was simply the destruction of Irish property".

In some parts of Ireland families were homeless because

of the destruction of their houses by the Black and Tans, and the indiscriminate burning of creameries created local food shortages during the winter; but relief came from the United States, where an organisation called the White Cross raised nearly £1,375,000 for Ireland, mostly subscribed in America, though small sums came from England and Scotland.

Hopes of peace were still remote, though various negotiations were going on behind the scenes. An intermediary put Griffith in touch with the editor of *The Times* and an official of the British Foreign Office, but these talks collapsed when Griffith was arrested on November 26, leaving Collins to be acting President of the Dail in addition to all his other duties. Another peace approach followed in December, when Dr. Clune, Archbishop of Perth in Western Australia, went with messages from Lloyd George in London to Griffith and Collins in Dublin. He saw Griffith in Mountjoy gaol and had no difficulty in arranging an interview with Collins, but his intervention came to nothing. Lloyd George was not prepared to treat with the Sinn Fein leaders unless they would discuss terms on a basis "consistent with the unbroken unity of the United Kingdom", and he also insisted that all arms must be surrendered before peace talks could begin. These terms were unacceptable in Dublin. Clune went back to Australia and Ireland prepared to face, if necessary, yet another year of bitter warfare.

The arrest of Griffith, however, had an important effect on Irish developments. It brought de Valera home at last. For eighteen months he had thought he was serving his country better by staying in America and inaugurating the American Association for the Recognition of the Irish Republic than by resuming his place at the head of the Dail Government. But with Griffith interned he could stay away no longer. In the middle of December, 1920, he secretly sailed for Ireland, and he reached Dublin on Christmas Eve.

America had not changed de Valera. He had been away while the Sinn Fein Courts had been set up, while the Black and Tans and the Auxies had come to Ireland, while Collins had built up the I.R.A. into a small but deadly force, while MacCurtain and MacSwiney had died and the events of Bloody Sunday had shaken the world. Now without question he resumed his old authority, and his colleagues found him as stiff and as unsusceptible to argument as he had been in 1919. The New Year of 1921 saw him once more in command. From now on the first thing to be said about any new proposal would be the question put by his fellow-prisoners in Lewes gaol: "What does Dev think about it?"

CHAPTER XX

From Terror to Truce

I

THE CONFUSED STATE of British public opinion at the beginning of 1921 is illustrated by a conversation at Bishopthorpe, the Palace of the Archbishop of York, at an episcopal dinner-party in February. Of the four men present—the Archbishop himself, Dr. Cosmo Gordon Lang, the Bishop of Sheffield, Dr. L. H. Burrows, the Bishop of Durham, Dr. H. H. Henson, and the Bishop of Manchester, Dr. William Temple—each took a different view of the Irish situation. Dr. Lang thought there was no difference between Britain's actions in Ireland and those of Germany in Belgium during the European War. Dr. Burrows thought that the only hope for Ireland was to exterminate the Sinn Feiners. Dr. Henson was uneasy about what was going on, but felt that he could not oppose the Government's policy because he had nothing better to suggest. Finally, Dr. Temple considered that the whole affair should be submitted to the League of Nations. When four leaders of Christian thought had such conflicting attitudes towards Ireland it is small wonder that the general public felt dazed and baffled by the reports of outrages and reprisals in what they had once regarded as John Bull's other island.

The old Archbishop of Canterbury, however, had no hesitation in speaking out about Ireland. In a speech in the House of Lords on February 22 he again had no word of sympathy for the I.R.A., whose outrages he regarded as ten times worse than those of the Black and Tans, but he felt strongly that there was no justification for British reprisals. "You cannot," he said, "justifiably punish wrong-doing by lawlessly doing the like. Not by calling in the Devil will you cast out devilry." This was the attitude which was gaining more and more ground in England. The Government, as Lord Birkenhead told Archibald Salvidge, was still convinced that the Irish troubles could be cured only "by the assertion of force in its most vigorous form", but the influence of those journalists and pamphleteers who were calling for peace in Ireland was becoming stronger every month. Politicians of such varying temperaments as Philip Snowden, Asquith, Sir John Simon, Lord Robert Cecil, Commander Kenworthy and Sir Oswald Mosley spoke out against the Government, and the factual records of outrages given in the Sinn Fein propaganda sheet, the *Irish Bulletin*, made a considerable impression on many of the M.P.s who were sent a copy of every issue. The pressure of English public opinion was already becoming one of the most powerful factors working for peace in Ireland.

Yet Lloyd George was still able to make out a strong case for the Government's policy. In reply to a remonstrance by the Bishop of Chelmsford, Dr. J. E. Watts-Ditchfield, he wrote in April that there had been no "authorisation or condonation of a policy of meeting murder by giving rein to unchecked violence on the other side". Sinn Fein, he declared, had "inaugurated a reign of terror in Ireland which is certainly equal to anything in Irish history", and the R.I.C. had not begun to strike a blow in self-defence until over 100 members of the force had been "cruelly assassinated". "I recognise," wrote Lloyd George, "that force is itself no remedy, and that reason and goodwill alone can lead us to the final goal. But to abandon the use of force today would be to surrender alike to violence, crime and separatism, and that I am not prepared to do."

Lloyd George's arguments did not deflect the course of English public opinion, which gathered strength from the evidence that a peace party was also emerging in Ireland. Father O'Flanagan, who was still vice-president of Sinn Fein though the importance of the post had diminished since the establishment of a Dail Cabinet, had already sent Lloyd George a telegram saying that Ireland was ready to make peace. Galway County Council took a similar line when it discussed (though it did not actually pass) a resolution stating that the council viewed with sorrow "the shootings, burnings, reprisals and counter-reprisals now taking place all over Ireland", and requesting Dail Eireann to appoint three delegates to negotiate a truce. And all the time "Andy" Cope, the Assistant Under-Secretary at Dublin Castle, was busily establishing his personal contacts with the Dail leaders, and so preparing the way for the Truce which came in July.

Yet peace seemed far away at the beginning of 1921, and the first six months of the year were, indeed, the deadliest and most destructive of the whole struggle. On the Sinn Fein side the I.R.A. flying columns were particularly active, and before any major engagement Collins would send one of his staff officers—frequently Ernie O'Malley—to examine the local commander's plans. At the same time "shoot and run" attacks by Sinn Fein gunmen continued in the Dublin streets as well as in the country districts, and there were more cases of innocent civilians being injured by bombs thrown at British troops or police. On the British side there were nightly raids on private houses, from which suspected Sinn Feiners might be taken out and summarily shot, and in addition to unofficial Black and Tan reprisals, there were now authorised reprisals, or "official punishments", inaugurated by General Macready in the martial-law area. These included the destruction by explosives of houses and property belonging to people who were considered to be implicated in, or at any rate to have known about, ambushes of Crown forces. The practice was later abandoned because the local I.R.A. invariably burnt down the house of a Southern Unionist or other Government supporter in counter-reprisal, and since such houses were more valuable property than a villager's cottage, the real victims of the "official punishments" were the loyal friends of Britain. Tom Barry's Brigade, indeed, burnt *two* loyalists' residence for every Sinn Fein home destroyed.

One of the most successful Irish guerilla leaders in this phase of the war was Sean MacEoin, then known as "the blacksmith of Ballinalee", who had been appointed Vice-Brigadier and Director of Operations for Longford in the previous September. He had ambushed and caused heavy casualties among a large party of Black and Tans in November, and in January he was nearly caught in a small cottage near Ballinalee by an R.I.C. district inspector and ten constables; but in single-handed combat he escaped by first firing at the police and then throwing a bomb which killed the inspector and scattered the patrol. In February he and a dozen Volunteers ambushed an Auxiliary motor patrol in the same district, and the Auxiliaries surrendered after three of them had been killed and 12 wounded. This was the occasion when MacEoin (whom Macready described later as "a more cheery individual than most of his colleagues") brought a pleasanter note into the conflict by showing concern for the Auxiliaries' wounded and allowing their unwounded comrades to drive them away in one of their lorries.

A month later, however, MacEoin was spotted by the police on a visit to Dublin and was followed back to Longford, where he was arrested, wounded in the shoulder in a daring attempt to escape, and beaten up with rifle-butts. Because of the time taken for him to recover from his wounds, he was not tried until June 21, when a court-martial sentenced him to death. Fortunately for MacEoin his sentence had not been carried out before the Truce was signed.

It would be unrewarding to attempt any detailed survey

of these last six months of Anglo-Irish war. The Auxies were much in the news in February. They were involved first in the large-scale looting of a general store near Trim, in county Meath, as a result of which 26 of them were suspended, though they were later sent back to duty; and they were responsible also for the arrest in Dublin of two young Sinn Feiners whom they drove out to a field near Drumcondra, where the young men were found on the following morning, one dying and the other dead. At an official inquiry the Auxiliaries' company commander and two cadets concerned in these deaths were found Not Guilty of murder—a verdict which, in General Crozier's opinion, "was the last straw which broke the camel's back in Dublin". Parallel outrages by the I.R.A. in that month were the shooting of three unarmed soldiers who had been taken prisoner at Woodford, in county Galway, and the kidnapping and killing of unarmed soldiers of the Essex Regiment at Bandon, in county Cork—Tom Barry's area.

A much disputed outrage was the killing at Limerick on one night in March of the Mayor, George Clancy, a former Mayor, Michael O'Callaghan, and a leading citizen, Joseph O'Donoghue. In each case masked men burst into the men's homes and shot them dead. The Irish had no hesitation in saying that the killers were Black and Tans, and Mrs. O'Callaghan produced an impressive array of evidence in support of this claim. The British, however, stoutly maintained that they were not responsible, and were sure that the killers were I.R.A. gunmen, who had shot the Mayor and the ex-Mayor because of their laxity in fighting the war.

Certainly it would have been a senseless crime for the British to commit, since there had been no attacks on Crown forces in Limerick for several months, and it would have been folly for them to disturb a peaceful area. On the other hand, the quietness of Limerick was disturbing to I.R.A. headquarters, and the British had found the fragment of a letter from Dublin to the Limerick I.R.A., complaining:

"We have sent you 400 rifles. What are you doing with them?" All in all, there was a strong case for considering that I.R.A. extremists had decided to stir up trouble by getting rid of their too peaceable leaders and pinning the blame on the R.I.C.; but perhaps the only safe conclusion to be drawn about the Limerick murders is that there was enough circumstantial evidence to convict both sides of having committed them.

A Black and Tan outrage described by Sir Christopher Lynch-Robinson was the killing of the postmaster of Navan, a man who had nothing at all to do with politics: he happened to pass by while some Black and Tans were looting a shop, and since they feared that he might report them, they shot him dead and threw his body into the Boyne. Yet this was outdone in horror by the I.R.A. ambush of the members of a tennis party at the gates of a house near Lough Cutra, in county Galway, in May. The party consisted of Captain Blake, an R.I.C. district inspector, and his charming young wife, Captain Cornwallis, Mr. McCreery and Mrs. Gregory (daughter-in-law of Lady Gregory). When they left for home at the end of the afternoon's play they found the gates closed, and as Cornwallis got out to open them some 20 I.R.A. gunmen opened fire on the whole party. Captain and Mrs. Blake, Cornwallis and McCreery were killed; only Mrs. Gregory survived.

I.R.A. killings of so-called "informers" grew to a frenzy in these months. Between January 1 and April 30 the notice, "A warning to spies", was attached to 73 bodies found dead by the roadside. The word "spy" was interpreted with extraordinary latitude: any loyalist or non-combatant Irishman who happened to see some armed Volunteers and reported the fact to the British authorities was liable to be killed on the orders of the local I.R.A. commandant. Yet these same commandants had no compunction about sending out Cumann na mBan girls, whom the British would not suspect, to bring back reports of the movements of troops. This was precisely the kind of "spying" for which loyalists were killed, but the

I.R.A. must have felt confident that the British would not execute girls even if they were caught as spies.

Among the "informers" who were killed at this time were old Sir Arthur Vicars, formerly Ulster King-at-Arms, who was dragged out of his house and riddled with bullets, and Mrs. Lindsay, a plucky old lady of 70, living at Coachford, in county Cork, who had seen some I.R.A. men preparing an ambush and had passed on the information to the British military authorities. Mrs. Lindsay was not killed immediately. She was kidnapped by the Cork No. 1 Brigade and held prisoner while her captors tried to bargain with the British, offering to set her free in return for the lives of five Volunteers who had been sentenced to death at Cork. The bargain was refused. "While I would have gone to great lengths to save the gallant lady's life," Macready wrote later, "I could not listen to such a proposal, which would have resulted in the kidnapping of loyal or influential persons every time a death sentence was passed on a rebel." The men at Cork were executed, and the I.R.A. shot Mrs. Lindsay. The Cork No. 1 Brigade made another attempt at bargaining when they captured Major Compton-Smith, of the Royal Welch Fusiliers. This time they set his life against the lives of six Volunteers who had been sentenced to death. When their bargain was rejected they shot their prisoner.

Large-scale ambushes set by I.R.A. flying columns were more in accordance with the rules of war. For example, in an ambush planned by Liam Lynch a British military convoy was successfully attacked on March 5 at Clonbanin, on the main road from Mallow to Killarney, and the commanding officer, Brigadier-General H. B. Cummins, was killed in action. The I.R.A. had a special grudge against Cummins, for he was said to have been the first British general to take Sinn Fein hostages in his lorries. Tom Barry's Cork No. 3 Brigade ambushed converging detachments of British forces at Crossbarry, in the Bandon area, on March 19, and in three separate engagements inflicted casualties which were given as 39 killed and 47 wounded, captured dozens of rifles, a Lewis machine-gun and thousands of rounds of ammunition, and destroyed several military lorries. Actions like these had to be carefully planned, and the number of sizeable engagements in which the flying columns took part was not large; but there were enough of them to hold down a large body of British troops and to give some substance to the claim that the I.R.A. were fighting a legitimate guerilla war.

Brugha's plans for carrying the war to England were also being fulfilled in these months. In March and April buildings were burnt in Newcastle upon Tyne, South Shields, Manchester and Hyde, signal boxes were attacked near London and Manchester with the intention of wrecking trains, and hundreds of telephone wires were cut in various parts of England.

In all these months the character of the Irish conflict—that is to say, whether it was legally a war or was merely an endless succession of murders—was much in dispute, but now that de Valera was back at the helm he tried to clear up the doubts about it. He began by stating definitely that the I.R.A., whether acting in small parties of gunmen or in flying columns, was the agent of Dail Eireann. "One of our first Governmental acts," he declared, "was to take over the control of the voluntary armed forces of the nation. From the Irish Volunteers we fashioned the Irish Republican Army to be the military arm of the Government. This Army is, therefore, a regular State force, under the civil control of the elected representatives, and under organisation and a discipline imposed by those representatives, and under officers who hold their commissions by warrant from those representatives. The Government is, therefore, responsible for the actions of this Army." And in an interview with an American journalist in March he gave his complete support to the war of ambushes. If the British forces, he said, "may use their tanks and steel-armoured cars, why should we hesitate to use the cover of stone walls and ditches?"

This interpretation of the Dail's position was, however, de Valera's own, for the Dail itself never seems to have expressed an opinion on the fighting. Indeed, in a Dail debate in 1923 General Richard Mulcahy said emphatically that at no time did Dail Eireann accept responsibility for war against the British; the I.R.A., he declared, was left to act on its own initiative, and neither the political wing nor the public wanted the war. But in 1921 de Valera appeared to be speaking with full authority, and his remarks were given wide publicity.

The British Government never fully accepted the theory that England was fighting a war in Ireland. As late as May 21, 1921, Hamar Greenwood said that Britain's aim was to "pluck the last revolver out of the last assassin's hand". But between the time of that statement and the day when the Truce was signed the more realistic Lord Birkenhead had given his own opinion that the fighting in Ireland was, in fact, "a small war".

2

De Valera had returned to Ireland to find ominous signs of a split in the Dail Cabinet. At a later date he told William O'Brien that he had spent four years trying to keep the peace between Brugha, representing the old Fenian movement, and Griffith, representing the constitutional Sinn Feiners, and that nothing except the pressure of the Black and Tan terror could have kept them together so long; but this explanation left out of account the sharp jealousy which Collins's growing prestige aroused in some of his colleagues. Kevin O'Higgins thought that de Valera himself unconsciously shared this jealousy of Collins, and that was why he made the extraordinary suggestion that Collins, the mainspring of I.R.A. resistance, should give up his military duties and go to America. But this time de Valera did not have his own way. Collins refused, and stayed in Dublin.

Since Griffith was still interned, the real split in the Cabinet was between Collins, on the one side, and Stack and

Brugha, on the other. Stack, who was Minister of Justice, found Collins arrogant and overbearing, and was deeply offended when Collins said rudely: "Your office is a bloody disgrace, Austin." Brugha, as Minister of Defence, still felt that the I.R.A. was his personal responsibility, and still resented the fact that Collins was generally regarded as Commander-in-Chief. Both Brugha and Stack were also resentful of the secret influence that Collins exercised as head of the Irish Republican Brotherhood.

Collins was now at the height of his fame, and his personal prestige was strengthened by the many stories of his escapes and his almost miraculous immunity from arrest. He was said to be so much of a daredevil that he walked alone and unprotected through the streets of Dublin, though the British had put a price of £10,000 on his head and were searching for him everywhere, and that if he were stopped by the police he coolly bluffed his way out, as he certainly did on a famous occasion at the Gresham Hotel after dining there on Christmas Eve.

These stories were only partly true. Undoubtedly Collins had many daring escapes from capture, in which he was helped, as he well knew, by the fact that the British had only a poor photograph of him, and many of the searchers did not know what he really looked like. This was the explanation of a famous leg-pull which set all Dublin laughing. Some practical joker had told the British military authorities that Collins would be dining at the Shelbourne Hotel on a certain evening, and offered to point him out. The offer was gratefully accepted; on the appointed evening a group of soldiers advanced towards one of the tables in the big restaurant, and an officer seized one of the diners by the arm, saying portentously: "Michael Collins! Your hour has come!" But it was not Collins. The amazed diner, as guests at neighbouring tables saw with delight, was actually Mr. Foley, the Lord Mayor's secretary and a well-known figure in Dublin.

Yet Collins was not so unrecognisable as popular legend

has made him. Though most of the G-men who knew him well had either been killed or had resigned, some of the Dublin police still knew him by sight; but they knew also that it would be hopeless to try to arrest him. Edward Martyn, the old playwright and landowner, who still kept in touch with affairs though he was no longer an active Sinn Feiner, told Lady Gregory the secret of Collins's immunity: "He would walk down Grafton Street, but he always had an escort at hand, and if there was an alarm and he blew his whistle a hundred men would appear, and while a scrimmage was going on he would be far away."

The whistle and the hundred men may have been the elaborations of rumour, but the reality of Collins's escort was demonstrated to a young Black and Tan—Douglas V. Duff—who once spotted Collins in O'Connell Street and boldly marched up to him with an Auxie friend, announcing that he was under arrest and would be taken to Dublin Castle for identification. This guilelessness appealed to Collins's sense of humour. "Listen, boys," he said with a smile, "do you think I'm fool enough to walk about the streets of Dublin in broad daylight without an escort? Look around you! Do you see those three men near the fence there? Do you notice that couple on the edge of the pavement? Can you see those four men talking together just in front of them and that couple who are pretending to be interested in the shop-window?" The young policemen looked round, and saw that wherever they turned their heads there were men waiting and watching, all with their hands in their pockets and presumably ready to shoot at a second's notice. "If I raise my hand they'll shoot the pair of you," Collins went on, "and we shall be clear away long before anyone dares to make sure if you're as dead as you look. Now take my advice, my brave peelers, and go quietly. There's been enough blood shed in Ireland without shedding yours." The young men took his advice and went, having learnt that Collins's immunity from arrest was as well organised as everything else with which he was concerned.

De Valera's freedom from arrest was a different matter. Like the rest of the Dail Cabinet, he was theoretically "on the run", but the British Government had given orders that he was not to be arrested, since it was realised that there was no possibility of making peace with Ireland if the Dail President were in gaol; and unofficial envoys had no difficulty in getting in touch with him. Oliver Gogarty remembered an occasion when de Valera was using a doctor's house in Merrion Square as his supposedly secret hide-out and he was there summoned to the telephone by a voice which coolly asked: "May I speak to Mr. de Valera? This is Alfred Cope, speaking from Dublin Castle!" The Government was wise to let de Valera go free. For although the fighting was continuing with much loss of life on both sides, peace was in the air. The Better Government of Ireland Bill had now become law, and plans were being made for the establishment of separate Parliaments for Ulster and southern Ireland. General elections under British auspices were to be held in May. It was time for some fruit to be borne from Cope's private talks with Sinn Fein leaders.

3

The first direct British approach to de Valera was an unofficial one. Lord Derby, a peer of much influence in British politics, went on his own initiative to Ireland, saw de Valera on April 21 and had an inconclusive talk on the question of whether the Dail leaders would agree to negotiations without insisting that the principle of complete independence should be first conceded. A fortnight later, on Cope's suggestion, Sir James Craig came south to meet de Valera at a private house at Clontarf.

By this time Carson had stepped into the background, and Craig had become the effective political leader in Northern Ireland, as the six counties of Ulster were renamed under the Better Government of Ireland Act. He had agreed to be Prime Minister when the Northern Ireland Government was established. Elaborate precautions were taken to keep his meeting with de Valera secret until it was over, but nothing came of it. Craig said afterwards that de Valera had begun the discussion with a history lecture, taking half an hour to reach the era of Brian Boru and then proceeding to review all Ireland's grievances during the last 700 years. They ended by issuing a joint statement, saying merely that "Sir James Craig and Eamon de Valera held an informal conference at which their respective points of view were interchanged and the future of Ireland discussed". The only result of the meeting was to dispel Cope's hope that the two men might find some common ground for the basis of an agreement.

The deadlock between northern and southern Ireland was as insoluble as ever. Craig told the Ulster Unionist Association that he would go down into the grave sooner than betray by one single inch the rights of Ulstermen as British citizens; the Dail Government widened the split by encouraging a boycott of Ulster goods in the south and making no effort to restrain its supporters when branches of Ulster banks were raided and robbed, supplies of Belfast cigarettes seized from small Dublin shops and destroyed, and trains intercepted and raided if they had freight consigned from Ulster. But it was clear that the situation would be drastically changed, either for better or for worse, when the two Irish Parliaments were elected and partition was formally introduced.

"Where," asked that apostle of common sense, General Macready, "except in Ireland, or possibly in a South American Republic, could open rebellion, martial law, peace proposals and a general election be all running side by side at one and the same time?" It was a strange situation, but it was one which the British Government could not avoid. The elections were provided for in the Better Government of Ireland Act, and they had to be held, even though the election in Southern Ireland—now the official British name for the 26 counties—was sure to be won by the very men who were fighting against British authority.

Northern Ireland polled on May 19, and the rest of the country on May 24. On the earlier of these dates Lord FitzAlan of Derwent (formerly Lord Edmund Talbot, an uncle of the Duke of Norfolk) took office as Lord Lieutenant for both parts of Ireland. It was hoped that the appointment of a Roman Catholic as Lord Lieutenant would be regarded as a conciliatory gesture in the south, but the time had gone by when gestures of this kind could be of any significance. The only real importance of the change was that it removed Lord French from Viceregal Lodge after an arduous but unsuccessful term of office.

Northern Ireland was to have a House of Commons of 52 members, and was also to send 13 representatives to the British House of Commons. Though Catholics and Sinn Feiners had to face intimidation during the election, the result left no doubt that the six counties accepted partition. The Unionists won 40 seats, the Nationalists six and Sinn Fein six, including de Valera, Griffith and Collins among the successful candidates. Both the Nationalists and the Sinn Feiners declined to take their seats, and Craig began his long career as Prime Minister with a solidly Unionist House of Commons. Later, however, Devlin and the other Nationalist M.P.s changed their minds and took their seats.

Southern Ireland, as defined in the Act, was to have 128 members in its House of Commons and was entitled to send 33 representatives to Westminster. In agreeing to put no obstacle in the way of the election the Dail Cabinet insisted that it should be regarded as the election of the second Dail Eireann, not of a Southern Ireland House of Commons, and that members elected would sit in the Dail after taking the Republican Oath; but it was content to use the existing register and constituencies and the system of proportional representation provided for in the Act. The extent of intimidation in this election can be gauged from the fact that Sinn Fein candidates, many of whom were I.R.A. officers, were returned unopposed for every constituency except Trinity College, which returned four non-party members, also unopposed. But in view of the state of the country it is unlikely that the result would have been much different if anti-Sinn Fein candidates had dared to stand for election.

A fresh crisis was now at hand. The Act laid down that unless at least half the elected members attended the opening of the Southern Parliament and took the Oath of Allegiance to the King the Parliament would be dissolved and Ireland would be ruled by Crown Colony government. The Government was well aware that the Sinn Fein members would not attend, and in fact when the Parliament opened on June 28 only the four Trinity College members were present. But by that time the threat of Crown Colony government had receded, and a new approach to the Irish problem was being considered.

4

The day after polling in the 26 counties was marked by a sensational coup in Dublin. De Valera and his colleagues had been casting round in their minds for some daring stroke which would show that Irish warfare was by no means restricted to ambushes and shoot-and-run killings. The idea of an attack on Beggar's Bush barracks had been examined and prudently discarded, and finally the decision was taken to burn the Custom House, the finest of all Dublin buildings and the headquarters of the British Civil Service in Ireland. The aesthetic claim for the preservation of such a beautiful building was offset, in de Valera's opinion, by the argument that the destruction of the Civil Service records would loosen the British domination of Irish economy. The Custom House was therefore doomed, and Oscar Traynor, then commandant of the I.R.A. Dublin Brigade, was ordered to draw up a plan of attack.

By the simple device of brandishing a large envelope marked O.H.M.S. Traynor had no difficulty in gaining admittance to the Custom House, and he went over the whole building at leisure, taking note of where inflammable material was to be found. Another I.R.A. officer made a similar inspection, and an elaborate scheme was drawn up, involving an exact time-table and the cutting of outside telephone wires. On May 25 a large detachment of Volunteers entered the Custom House in the middle of the day, rounded up the staff and poured paraffin over every office in the building. So far everything was going according to plan.

By chance, however, a policeman passing on a bicycle saw the Volunteers at work and rode to Dublin Castle to give the alarm. A party of Black and Tans jumped into lorries and drove to the Custom House, where they covered all the entrances with their rifles until military reinforcements arrived. Some of the Volunteers managed to slip out; others, being met by rifle fire wherever they looked out, went back to the room where the staff were assembled and amused the girl typists by angrily upbraiding their officers for having got them into such a mess. Eventually troops entered the building from the roof, 80 Volunteers were taken prisoner and five were killed in resisting capture.

But the Custom House was on fire. That part of the work had been done well. The fire brigade was delayed because other Volunteers had raided the fire stations and taken away essential parts of the engines, and the building was well alight before the brigade arrived. Everything inside the Custom House was burnt to ashes, and the fire was still burning ten days later. The Civil servants, however, resumed their duties elsewhere. The most indignant of them was old Sir Henry Robinson, chairman of the Local Government Board, who had expected a raid some time previously and had asked for a military guard on the building, only to find it withdrawn without a word of explanation a fortnight before the raiders actually came.

The burning of the Custom House and the result of the election increased the confusion in which the British Cabinet found itself in the early summer of 1921. The Irish situation seemed to be growing worse; a single week in May had caused more British casualties than any other week since the Easter Rising. The strength of the British forces in Ireland then amounted to about 50,000—some 35,000 regular troops, 12,500 R.I.C., including the Black and Tans, and 1,500 Auxiliaries; but the Cabinet estimated that the only way to make sure of winning the Irish war was to raise an additional 100,000 troops and special police, together with thousands of armoured cars, and then to cover the whole of southern Ireland with blockhouses and barbed wire, so that great drives on the Boer War model could be made to round up the whole I.R.A. This was not an extravagant estimate, for in fact the I.R.A. vastly outnumbered the Crown forces. It may have been true, as Collins stated, that no more than 3,000 of them were actually in the field at any one time, but behind these 3,000 stood a total I.R.A. strength of over 112,000, so that the supply of reinforcements for flying columns was virtually inexhaustible. The I.R.A.'s weakness, of course, lay in its shortage of arms and ammunition, but its advantage in numbers was unmistakable.

Yet Lloyd George hesitated to call for the 100,000 men needed to conquer the I.R.A. British public opinion was still seething over the Black and Tan outrages, and he doubted whether it would accept a policy of unmitigated repression in Ireland. Sir Laming Worthington-Evans, who had succeeded Churchill as Secretary for War, was quite sure that Britain would not support increased coercion, and he was particularly perturbed because officers and men in the Regular Army were applying not to be sent to Ireland when they were ordered there. Churchill, who had become Secretary for the Colonies, thought that the threat of increased coercion should be accompanied by an offer of the widest possible measure of self-government. This was the policy towards which Lloyd George was leaning when the situation was dramatically changed by King George V's speech at the opening of the first session of the Northern Ireland Parliament on June 22.

The King had long been perturbed about reprisals in Ireland. In May his private secretary, Lord Stamfordham, had written to Greenwood, saying that, "The King does ask himself, and he asks you, if this policy of reprisals is to be continued, where will it lead Ireland and us all?" The visit to Belfast gave him the opportunity of speaking publicly about the Irish situation, and although his advisers at Buckingham Palace urged him not to run the risk of a journey to Ireland, he insisted on going, and courageously drove through Belfast with Queen Mary in an open carriage. General Smuts, the South African statesman, who was then in London, and Lloyd George had both had a hand in the preparation of the King's speech, in which he spoke of the "sorrow and anxiety" he had lately felt about Irish affairs.

> "I speak from a full heart [he said] when I pray that my coming to Ireland today may prove to be the first step towards the end of strife amongst her people, whatever their race or creed. In that hope I appeal to all Irishmen to pause, to stretch out the hand of forbearance and conciliation, to forgive and forget, and to join in making for the land they love a new era of peace, contentment and goodwill."

The effect of the King's intervention was immediate and striking. The great welcome he received on his return to London showed that he had correctly gauged the sentiments of the British people. On the next day he sent Stamfordham to Lloyd George to urge him not to miss "the psychological moment", and was informed that Lloyd George was already writing to Craig and de Valera to invite them to London. The Government, Lloyd George said in these letters, was deeply anxious that the King's appeal for reconciliation should not have been made in vain.

The decisive step had been taken. Though only two days earlier Lord Birkenhead, as the Government's spokesman in the House of Lords, had refused to consider the opening of negotiations with southern Ireland, the Government was now ready to begin discussions with the President of the outlawed Dail Eireann. Yet in spite of this astonishing change of front, de Valera approached the proposed meeting with his usual caution. He wrote to assure Lloyd George of his earnest desire to help in bringing about a lasting peace between Britain and Ireland, but added that he saw no avenue by which this peace could be reached "if you deny Ireland's essential unity and set aside the principles of national self-determination". In the same letter, written on June 28, he said that he was "seeking a conference with certain representatives of the political minority in this country", and he accordingly invited Craig, Lord Midleton and three other Unionists to a Mansion House conference. As Prime Minister of Northern Ireland, Craig naturally refused an invitation extended to him as a "representative of a political minority", but the others accepted, and to make the meeting more representative the British Government released Griffith, Barton, MacNeill and Duggan from prison to attend it.

The conference met on July 4 to arrange proposals for a truce to be held while Government negotiations were in progress. On the following day General Smuts, who had been told that the Sinn Fein leaders would welcome his advice, arrived in Dublin for talks with de Valera, Griffith, Childers and others. Taking South Africa as an example, he urged them to aim at Dominion status. "Make no mistake about it," he said, "you have more privilege, more power, more peace, more security in such a sisterhood of equal nations than in a small, nervous republic having all the time to rely on goodwill, and perhaps the assistance, of foreigners." His advice confirmed the Dail leaders in their decision to make a truce, and on July 8 Macready was invited to the Mansion House, where he arrived with his own truce proposals and a revolver in his pockets. Great crowds had been waiting in Dawson Street and its neighbourhood since the conference had begun. Many of them had fallen on their knees to pray that peace would come back to Ireland. When Macready appeared—a sure sign that a truce was coming—they burst into cheers for the commander of the English garrison in Ireland.

Details of a truce, which forbade attacks, provocative action or military manoeuvres on either side, were agreed, and the hour of 12 noon on July 11 was fixed for its coming into force. The British forces were at once ordered to take no action except for defensive purposes, but the I.R.A. kept to the strict letter of the agreement and were busily engaged in attacks on police, military and magistrates until the exact hour ordained for the truce.

The cessation of fighting was a great relief to the hard-pressed men of the I.R.A. flying columns and the Dublin Brigade, though a statement that Liam Lynch had told Collins that Cork could not go on with the war because of the shortage of arms and ammunition has been circumstantially repudiated both by Tom Barry and by Florence O'Donoghue, who was then adjutant of the Cork No. 1 Brigade. To some I.R.A. men, such as Barry himself, the truce seemed merely a temporary arrangement, which was unlikely to last more than a month. But Collins took a different view. When once the momentum of I.R.A. resistance had been checked, he felt that it would be impossible to start it again. If they tried to resume fighting, he told his friend Batt O'Connor, "in a fortnight all would be over". Much had still to be said and done before peace could be fully restored in Ireland. But the Anglo-Irish war ended when the truce of 1921 was signed at the Dublin Mansion House.

CHAPTER XXI

Delegates for London

I

IT WOULD BE wrong to imagine that every revolver in southern Ireland stopped firing as soon as the truce came into force. The I.R.A. headquarters honourably suspended all offensive action, but isolated gunmen in various parts of the country still attacked unsuspecting members of the R.I.C., and reports of occasional assaults on civilians by Auxies and Black and Tans were still received. In some districts the I.R.A. went round extorting funds for re-equipment, and a prominent Anglo-Irish landowner, Lord Bessborough, was incensed at having a notice served on him demanding a levy on his property "to maintain the Irish Army in any contingency which might arise owing to the breakdown of negotiations". At the same time the seeds of future trouble were being sown by the hero-worship given to the I.R.A. The fighting men, often wearing the Volunteer uniform they had discreetly put away during the actual war, were fêted everywhere. Many of them began to feel that they had won a military victory, and they found it hard to settle down to ordinary work on farms or in shops.

The truce was certainly a victory for Sinn Fein, but it was not a military victory. The people who boasted "We have beaten the British into the seas" were very wide of the mark; the real truth was stated by the I.R.A. Chief of Staff, General Mulcahy, in the Treaty debate in December, when he said frankly: "We have not been able to drive the enemy from anything but a fairly good-sized police barracks." The Irish victory, in fact, was one of public opinion: the vigour and pertinacity of the Irish stand for self-government—the old Sinn Fein policy of self-reliance—had made the people of England (and through them their Government) turn at last against measures of repression and decide to meet the wishes of southern Ireland as far as it was feasible to do so. But it must always be debatable whether this result could not have been more quickly achieved by an ordered programme of civil disobedience and peaceful non-co-operation towards the British authorities than by the long campaign of violence and destruction.

The second half of 1921 was dominated by political issues. Both Craig and de Valera went to London for separate talks with Lloyd George—Craig to maintain the rights already granted to Northern Ireland, de Valera to find a basis for an Anglo-Irish treaty. With him went Griffith, Barton, Count Plunkett and Childers, and Childers's English friends were shocked to see how much he had aged during his stay in Ireland. His hair had gone white, he was thin and deadly pale, and his old sense of humour had left him. It was clear that he, for one, would accept no compromise of any kind over Irish independence.

De Valera went along to 10, Downing Street on July 14 for his first meeting with Lloyd George. The British Prime Minister was in his element. As though he had never talked about taking "murder by the throat", he greeted de Valera as a brother-Celt, and was soon deep in a discussion of the precise meaning of Saorstat Eireann, which appeared at the head of the Dail Government's notepaper. Irish linguists differed over whether the broader Saorstat or the more abstract Poblacht was the better Gaelic word for republic, but Lloyd George was delighted to find that the literal meaning of Saorstat was Free State. The word, he remarked, would not need to be changed when a settlement was reached.

Like Craig at Clontarf, Lloyd George had to listen to much Irish history before he could bring de Valera down to practical details. "I made no impression," he told his private secretary afterwards. "I listened to a long lecture on the wrong done to Ireland starting with Cromwell, and when I tried to bring him to the present day, back he went to Cromwell again." The two men had several meetings, and it was at the third of these that Lloyd George produced a plan for Dominion Home Rule, which was set out in detail for de Valera to take back to Dublin.

It was a remarkable document. The British Government had gone far beyond the modest Home Rule proposals of the Better Government of Ireland Act. Ireland was offered Dominion status, which meant, it was said, that she

> "shall enjoy complete autonomy in taxation and finance; that she shall maintain her own courts of law and judges; that she shall maintain her own military forces for home defence, her own constabulary and her own police; that she shall take over the Irish postal services and all matters relating thereto, education, land, agriculture, mines and minerals, transport, trade, public health, health insurance and the liquor traffic; and, in sum, that she shall exercise all those powers and privileges upon which the autonomy of the self-governing Dominions is based, subject only to the considerations set out in the ensuing paragraphs."

These considerations included the granting of naval and air facilities to Great Britain, the continuance in Ireland of voluntary recruiting for the British forces, the limitation of the Irish Army to a size in conformity with that of military establishments in Britain, free trade between the two countries and a contribution from Ireland to Britain's war debt.

Such restrictions were certainly unprecedented in the conception of Dominion status, but they did not constitute any threat of British oppression of Ireland; and in general, the document offered southern Ireland a degree of freedom that could hardly have been dreamt of ten years earlier. But partition was to stay until the whole of Ireland agreed to abolish it. In the meantime any settlement "must allow for full recognition of the existing powers and privileges of the Parliament of Northern Ireland, which cannot be abrogated except by their own consent".

This was the offer which was formally made to de Valera on July 20. He flatly rejected it and said he would not even take it back to the Dail Cabinet. But when Lloyd George warned him, "You know that this means war? And you realise that the responsibility will rest upon your shoulders?" he at last agreed to take the document to Dublin, where the Dail Cabinet also rejected it.

Much correspondence had to be exchanged before a peace conference could be arranged, and the negotiations nearly broke down soon after de Valera's return to Ireland. Though the Dail Cabinet had turned down the British offer, it agreed to submit it to a meeting of Dail Eireann. To make this meeting fully representative, Dublin Castle announced that all imprisoned and interned members of the Dail would be released, with the exception of Sean MacEoin, who was still awaiting execution after his conviction for murder. De Valera at once stated that he would not go on with the negotiations unless MacEoin were released. "In British legal phraseology," he said, "he is termed a murderer, but for us, and I believe for the world, he is a heroic Irishman." Dublin Castle gave way, and MacEoin was released. Later in the month, when the Dail met in public session, he proposed the election of de Valera as President of the Irish Republic—a title then formally adopted (though without any clear definition of its meaning) to replace the older title of President of Dail Eireann. The proposal was seconded by Mulcahy.

At the same session a new Cabinet was elected, consisting only of senior Ministers. Its members were Griffith (Foreign Affairs), Stack (Home Affairs), Brugha (Defence), Collins (Finance), Cosgrave (Local Government) and Barton (Economic Affairs). Two of those who had previously sat in the Cabinet—Count Plunkett and Constance Markievicz—now became Ministers without Cabinet rank. Another of the Ministers outside the Cabinet was Kevin O'Higgins, who remained Cosgrave's assistant in the Local Government Ministry.

The Dail meetings that August were great re-unions of deputies who had long been separated by imprisonment or active service. One who returned after a long absence was Sean T. O'Kelly, who had been a Sinn Fein representative in Europe—alternately at Rome and at Paris—ever since his unsuccessful attempt to have the Irish case put before the Versailles Peace Conference in 1919. All the deputies took the Oath to "bear true faith and allegiance" to "the Irish Republic and the Government of the Irish Republic, which is Dail Eireann". In a private session, however, de Valera pointed out that he did not regard the Oath as relating to forms of government. In his own view he was pledged to maintain the independence of Ireland and to do the best for the Irish people, and he would keep himself free to consider each question as it arose. In public he again declared that he was not a Republican doctrinaire.

The Dail followed the Cabinet's lead and unanimously rejected Lloyd George's offer of qualified Dominion status. They did so, as de Valera explained in a letter to the British Prime Minister, because the restrictions were considered to "involve a surrender of our whole national position". After reading his letter to the Dail de Valera declared: "We cannot change our position because it is fundamentally sound and just, and the moment we get off that fundamental rock of right and justice, then we have no case whatever. No fight can be made except on that rock, and on that rock we shall stand."

2

In the following weeks more letters were exchanged between de Valera and Lloyd George—de Valera insisting that the southern Irish could attend a conference only if they were accepted as representatives of an independent sovereign State, Lloyd George retorting that to accept them on that basis was impossible, since it would imply that Britain was recognising the severance of Ireland from the Empire. Time after time in the correspondence Lloyd George declared that the basis of the British proposals was that Ireland should owe allegiance to the King and should remain a member of the British Commonwealth; from the terms of these letters, and from what he had gathered in his own talks with Lloyd George in London, de Valera knew that Britain would not agree either to the establishment of an independent Irish Republic outside the British Commonwealth or to the withdrawal from Northern Ireland (except with her own approval) of the powers bestowed on her by a British Act of Parliament. At one stage in the correspondence plans were actually made for beginning an Anglo-Irish conference in Inverness on September 20. These plans broke down, but at last an acceptable compromise was found. Irish delegates were to attend a conference in London, beginning on October 11, "with a view to ascertaining how the association of Ireland with the community of nations known as the British Empire may best be reconciled with Irish national aspirations". De Valera approved of this formula.

So far the main participants in the Anglo-Irish negotiations had been Lloyd George and de Valera. Yet when the Dail Cabinet met to appoint delegates to the London conference, de Valera announced that he was not going. Once again, as in 1919 when he decided to go to America, he was impervious to all argument. It was now his view that in times of crisis the President's place was at home; if in the end another British offer had to be rejected it would be better, he thought, for the rejection to come from someone like Griffith, who was known to hold moderate views, than from himself, who was regarded as an extremist.

The choice of delegates was no less significant than de Valera's refusal to be one of them. The five men chosen were Griffith, Foreign Minister, Collins, Finance Minister, and Barton, Minister for Economic Affairs, together with two lawyers, Gavan Duffy and Eamon Duggan. Erskine Childers was to be one of the four secretaries to the delegation. So de Valera kept with him in Dublin the two extremist members of the Cabinet—Stack and Brugha—and sent to London a middle-of-the-road delegation, with Childers to keep a cold and uncompromising eye on what they were doing.

Confusion at once arose over the delegates' status. Credentials drawn up by the Cabinet and ratified by the Dail described them as "Envoys plenipotentiary from the elected Government of the Republic of Ireland to negotiate and conclude with the representatives of his Britannic Majesty George V a Treaty or Treaties of association and accommodation between Ireland and the Community of Nations known as the British Commonwealth". Though these credentials were never officially accepted by the British Government, they could clearly be regarded as empowering the delegates to sign a treaty on their own responsibility. But subsequently, before they left for London, the Dail Cabinet gave them orders to submit to Dublin the complete text of any draft treaty about to be signed and to await a reply. The inconsistency of these instructions left it undecided whether the delegates were to act as effective plenipotentiaries or merely as London agents of the Dublin Cabinet.

A still deeper confusion was to cast a shadow over the coming weeks. The Dail Cabinet might have been expected to be quite clear about the extent of any concessions that the delegation could be allowed to make in London. In fact, the delegates began their London talks without any Cabinet lead on the fundamental issue at stake. Was it, as Brugha and Stack later maintained, unthinkable that any treaty should be signed unless it confirmed the complete independence of the Irish Republic proclaimed in Easter Week? Or were the delegates simply to "do their best for Ireland"

and extract the best possible terms from Britain even if these did not include the confirmation of the Republic?

No definite decision was taken on this vital point. De Valera was afterwards to stand firmly on the "rock" of the Republic, but he made a different impression on his colleagues when they were leaving for London. Griffith, who was as truthful a man as ever lived, said later: "When I was going to London I knew that neither I nor any other man could bring back a Republic, and he (de Valera) admitted to me that it could not be done." A delegation which entered negotiations without any clear demarcation of the line on which it could finally stand was heading for trouble from the beginning. It is not surprising that Collins wrote in a private letter shortly before the Treaty was signed: "The only names worth considering after this will be the names of those who have kept away from London." It was due to his own and Griffith's steadfastness that this gloomy prophecy did not come true.

CHAPTER XXII

The Treaty is Signed

I

THE FIRST SESSION of the Anglo-Irish negotiations was held at 10, Downing Street on October 11, 1921. Lloyd George tactfully avoided the problem of whether the two delegations should shake hands by genially waving the Irishmen to their seats, where they found themselves facing a formidable array of British political talent.

Lloyd George's chief colleagues were Austen Chamberlain, Lord Privy Seal, Leader of the House of Commons and leader of the Conservative Party (in succession to Bonar Law, who had retired through ill-health, though he was later to return to politics); Lord Birkenhead, Lord Chancellor, also a Conservative; and Winston Churchill, Secretary of State for the Colonies and, like Lloyd George, a Liberal. The other British delegates at the opening session were Greenwood, Chief Secretary for Ireland, Worthington-Evans, Secretary for War, and Sir Gordon Hewart, Attorney-General; the two secretaries were Thomas Jones, then Assistant Secretary to the Cabinet, a brilliant Welshman who had once been an economics professor in Belfast and was generally sympathetic towards Irish aspirations, and Lionel Curtis, exponent of a scheme for Commonwealth federation and joint founder of the influential quarterly, the *Round Table*. But the four principals overshadowed the others. Lloyd George had few equals in the subtle tactics of inducing opponents to leave their prepared defences and fight on ground of his own choosing. Chamberlain, who had been in politics all his life, was the perfect type of the experienced English Parliamentarian. Birkenhead, whom Ireland had known so well as F. E. Smith, had a clear and swift-moving brain, an unchallengeable legal knowledge and a manner of intervening in difficult issues with indisputable authority. Churchill, perhaps the least important of the four, was already a statesman of vast experience, though the Irish were inclined to regard him more as a typical British Imperialist than as a friend of Ireland.

Of the Irish who faced them only Griffith had a political knowledge and background that could in any way be matched with theirs. Collins had no experience of inter-Government negotiations, though he had matured remarkably during his years as Finance Minister and organiser of the I.R.A., and he was soon to show that he could hold his own even with Lloyd George and Birkenhead. Of the others Duggan and Duffy were good lawyers, but not of the standing of Hewart and Birkenhead, and Barton's knowledge of politics was confined to what he had learnt as a Dail Minister. Among the four secretaries Childers was well versed in every phase of Anglo-Irish affairs, and John Chartres, a Sinn Fein sympathiser who had been in charge of the index department of the London *Times*, was a valuable adviser on constitutional legal problems. But throughout the conference the overwhelming weight of political expertise was on the British side.

Though the delegates met at the first session as strangers, the coming weeks made them known to each other as personalities as well as political negotiators. In general, the Irish delegates, like Redmond before them, declined to accept English hospitality, though this did not prevent Collins from having many a drink with Birkenhead, who was attracted by Collins's vivid personality and delighted to hear his stories of narrow escapes. But a regular meeting-ground for English and Irish was provided at the hospitable

London home of the Irish artist, Sir John Lavery, and his charming red-haired wife, Hazel, an American girl who had a good deal of Irish blood in her and was distantly related to the Martyns of Galway. All the Irish delegates except Childers went to meals with the Laverys, and Lady Lavery often invited Churchill and other English politicians to meet them. At one dinner Collins and French were sitting on either side of their hostess—an encounter which made French comment urbanely, "London is the best place, after all, to meet people." Hazel Lavery's devotion to Collins caused much gossip in London society, but Collins, who was engaged to a girl in Ireland, had no idea that he figured so prominently in his hostess's romantic imagination.

These social meetings were an agreeable background to the heavy work of the negotiations, which began with seven plenary sessions between October 11 and 24. At these the general situation was discussed, and Lloyd George asked the Irishmen to state their objections to the terms offered by Britain. As the familiar ground was covered the Irish found themselves being pressed to say plainly whether they would pay allegiance to the Crown, accept membership of the Empire and allow Britain the naval facilities necessary for the defence of the British Isles.

It was in response to these questions that they produced a plan for so-called External Association drawn up by the Dail Cabinet under de Valera's guidance. The idea was that Ireland should be linked with the Empire yet not wholly a member of it.

> "On the one hand [the document stated] Ireland will consent to adhere for all purposes of common agreed concern to the League of Sovereign States associated and known as the British Commonwealth of Nations. On the other hand Ireland calls upon Great Britain to renounce all claims and authority over Ireland and Irish affairs."

In elaborating this suggestion, in response to Lloyd George's pressure, Griffith agreed that Ireland would accept the Crown as head of the association of States.

After the seventh plenary session the discussions were carried on in sub-conferences, in which the principal negotiators were Lloyd George and Birkenhead, on the British side, and Griffith and Collins, on the Irish. Agreement was always in sight on economic and financial issues, and even the thornier question of defence and naval facilities seemed unlikely to create any insuperable difficulties; but the vital matters at stake were allegiance to the Crown, adherence to the Empire and the position of Ulster.

The Irish were anxious that the conference should not break down over Crown and Empire, since they did not want to appear to be making symbols more important than the real concessions which Britain was offering; if a break had to come, they wished it to be on Ulster, so that they could be recognised as the champions of Irish unity against the obduracy of Craig and the north. Since the Government of Northern Ireland was already in being, they were attempting an impossible task in seeking guarantees for the "essential unity of Ireland"; but they stuck doggedly to their claim, and made so much headway that Lloyd George once proposed to reduce Ulster to local autonomy under an all-Ireland Parliament in return for Irish allegiance to the Crown. But Craig, when consulted about this proposal, would have nothing to do with it, and since there could be no question of coercing Ulster, a new approach had to be found.

This new approach emerged in the British proposal for a Boundary Commission, which would revise the boundaries between the six and the 26 counties so that the Ulster areas with Sinn Fein majorities could be transferred to the southern Irish Government. Griffith felt that this proposal, if faithfully carried out, might solve the unity problem. He imagined that Fermanagh and Tyrone, where there were Catholic and Sinn Fein majorities, would be transferred to the south, and Northern Ireland would be left with the four counties of Antrim, Armagh, Derry and Down; and since four counties would be too small a unit for satisfactory economic life, Ulster would be obliged to throw in her lot with southern Ireland. Thus the "essential unity", even if not provided for in the Treaty, would be certain to follow in due course.

Lloyd George did not seek to dispel this hopeful view of what might happen if a Boundary Commission were set up. His tactics, in fact, were to balance concessions on Ulster against allegiance to the Crown, and in private talks with Griffith he said that he needed some kind of reassurance about the Crown if he were to overcome the Conservative die-hards, who regarded the whole conference with the deepest suspicion. On October 30, when preparing his speech against a die-hard vote of censure to be moved in the Commons on the following day, he persuaded Griffith to agree that the Irish delegates would recommend recognition of the Crown if they were satisfied about everything else; and twelve days later Griffith further promised Lloyd George that "while he was fighting the Ulster crowd we would not help them by repudiating him".

Lloyd George took this to mean that the Irish would not break off the conference over Ulster provided that the Boundary Commission were to be established; and he drew up a draft of their conversation which was shown to Griffith and approved by him. This was the draft produced in the closing stage of the conference which made it impossible for the Irish to force the "break on Ulster" they had always intended to hold in reserve if they thought the final British terms were unsatisfactory.

2

Lloyd George was not exaggerating the danger of the whole conference being wrecked by the Conservative die-hards. Carson had always been against any negotiations with "the rebels"; and it was quite on the cards that the Conservative and Unionist Party conference, which was due to open in Liverpool on November 17, would decide to withdraw the party's support from the coalition Government, which would thus have been forced out of office. Two die-hard colonels, Gretton and Archer-Shee, were to move a resolution at the conference censuring the Government for entering the negotiations. It was clear that much would depend on the attitude of Sir Archibald Salvidge, who, as Conservative leader in Liverpool, was to be the conference chairman.

Salvidge had long been a stalwart champion of Ulster, and the die-hards naturally expected him to support them. But he was also an old friend of Lord Birkenhead, and he was quite ready to look at the Irish problem from his friend's point of view. After a week-end of reflection he issued a public statement saying that he would "decidedly refuse, whilst negotiations are in progress, to be identified with a revolt which will help neither Ulster nor the Unionist Party". Before this statement was published Birkenhead made a secret journey to Liverpool to win Salvidge over to the Cabinet's side. On reading what Salvidge had written he said that he could not have done it better himself.

The *Morning Post*, the accepted organ of the Conservative diehards, took a different view. It considered that Salvidge was letting Ulster down, and it assailed him bitterly in a leading article entitled "Salvidging Ulster". On the day when the Conservative conference opened long lines of sandwichmen paraded the streets of Liverpool displaying these two words on *Morning Post* contents bills, but this public attack had no effect on the conference's decision. Salvidge spoke for three hours. He denied that he was deserting Ulster and insisted that it would play into de Valera's hands to show disunity in the middle of the Treaty negotiations; and his arguments proved so convincing that the conference gave an overwhelming vote in favour of the Government's efforts to achieve a settlement. The die-hard attempt to wreck the Treaty talks was thus defeated, but Salvidge had to live through a trying period in which Orange Lodges condemned him in indignant resolutions and anonymous correspondents wrote abusive letters, of which one began: "You swine, how much has Michael

Collins paid you?" At the same time both he and Birkenhead were constantly assailed in the *Morning Post* for their "treachery to Ulster".

After the Unionist vote the Treaty negotiations entered their last phase. Discussions on the relation between Ireland and the Crown continued. Another memorandum on the virtues of External Association was presented by the Irish delegates, making the point that though southern Ireland was prepared to recognise the Crown as "head of the association", she could not do so in Ireland, since the nearness of England would give the Crown the opportunity of using powers which were obsolete in more distant Dominions. Finally, the Irish delegates were unexpectedly invited to put into the Treaty "any phrase they liked which would ensure that the position of the Crown in Ireland should be no more in practice than it was in Canada or in any other Dominion". This completely answered the objection in the latest Irish memorandum, and when the British representatives said they would try to modify the Oath of Allegiance it began to seem as though Dominion status on the lines suggested would give the Irish almost all the independence they had asked for—always excepting the actual name and form of Republic.

After making so many concessions without reaching complete agreement the British began to press for a definite end to the conference. On Thursday, December 1, Lloyd George presented his "final draft" of the British proposals—"final" in the sense that it was the last British offer, but not excluding revision on minor or even on major points. A few alterations were made immediately. Then on Friday the Irish delegates left for Dublin, taking the draft with them to show to the Dail Cabinet.

All seven members of the Cabinet were present at the meeting on Saturday morning—de Valera, Griffith, Collins, Barton, Brugha, Stack and Cosgrave, together with Duffy, Duggan, Childers and O'Higgins. Griffith spoke strongly in favour of accepting the draft Treaty as the best terms that

England would offer, and was supported by Collins and Duggan. Barton and Duffy, who had not been so closely in touch with the British Ministers, wanted to reject the draft on the grounds that the English were bluffing and could be induced to make still further concessions. Childers was also against it, and so, most vehemently, was Brugha, who remarked offensively that in choosing to carry out the main negotiations with Griffith and Collins "the British Government had selected their men".

Later, when the seven Cabinet Ministers continued the discussions alone, de Valera said he could not subscribe to the Oath of Allegiance or sign any document that would give Ulster power to vote herself out of the Irish State. Both he and Brugha felt that the draft did not guarantee the essential unity of Ireland, and Barton urged him to come back to London himself and take part in the final discussions. But de Valera did not go. Instead Griffith undertook that he would go back to London but would not sign the document, and would then bring it to Ireland again for submission to the Dail and if necessary to the Irish people.

On that understanding the delegates returned to London. They still hoped it might be possible either to secure Ireland's full demands for a Republic or to break off the conference over Ulster; but if the Oath of Allegiance still proved to be the crucial point it would be left to the Dail to take a decision before anything was signed. The position seemed clear at last, but in fact it was not. For the Cabinet had not considered one important possibility—that of the delegates being told either to sign at once or to face the threat of an immediate resumption of war.

3

On the Sunday evening, December 4, the Irish delegates were at Downing Street again, but the talks were abruptly broken off after Griffith had repeated the Irish demand for the principle of External Association and Duffy had unguardedly said: "Our difficulty is coming into the Empire."

Yet Lloyd George had not given up hope of a settlement. On the Monday morning he sent Thomas Jones to the Irish delegation's headquarters to ask if Collins, who had not been present at the Sunday meeting, would come to Downing Street for a private talk. Jones had a persuasive way with him; Collins went, and Lloyd George, after promising again to modify the Oath of Allegiance, spoke so forcibly of the assured enlargement of southern Irish territory through the Boundary Commission's work that Collins agreed to bring some of his fellow-delegates to Downing Street for further talks that afternoon.

He returned with Griffith and Barton. On the British side were the four chief negotiators—Lloyd George, Chamberlain, Birkenhead and Churchill. The main Treaty clauses were again considered, and though the offer to Ireland remained one of Dominion status (with the title of Irish Free State) and not of Republican independence, the Oath of Allegiance was modified to meet Irish susceptibilities. In the revised Oath Ireland came first and the Crown second: it provided for "true faith and allegiance to the constitution of the Irish Free State", and continued, "I will be faithful to King George V, his heirs and successors by law", without any mention of allegiance. With the Crown and Empire problems so nearly settled Lloyd George dramatically disposed of the Ulster issue by producing the report of his earlier conversation with Griffith, who had then shown himself to be satisfied with the promise of a Boundary Commission; and the Irish delegates realised that they had lost their chance of forcing a "break on Ulster". Other points were discussed and disposed of, but still the Irish were reluctant to sign the draft Treaty.

While they hesitated Lloyd George presented his ultimatum. He had promised, he said, to let Craig know the result of the negotiations by the following day; the delegates must sign the agreement for a Treaty now or else quit, and both sides would be free to resume whatever warfare they chose to wage against each other.

This was the contingency against which the Dail Cabinet had not guarded, and the Irish delegates, wearied by their long weeks of discussion, were not alert enough to realise that on this occasion, at all events, Lloyd George was bluffing. Craig, after all, had been waiting a long time to hear the result of the negotiations. He was a patient and good-humoured man, and he could surely have waited a few days longer. If Griffith had insisted that he must have three days' grace to take the draft to Dublin again Lloyd George would have had to give way. But the Irish were taken in. Magnetised by Lloyd George's Welsh wizardry, they were made to believe that it was now or never for a Treaty or the resumption of war.

Griffith's dilemma was acute. He had promised the Dail Cabinet not to sign the draft, but he had also made it clear all along that he would never break off the conference over the Oath of Allegiance. Yet since he had himself accepted the Boundary Commission proposal he could not break on Ulster, and he had either to break on the Oath or sign the draft. He decided to sign, and said he would do so, whether the rest of the delegates signed or not. This was the decision that made Austen Chamberlain say that Griffith "was the most courageous man I ever met".

Griffith's announcement was not enough for Lloyd George. All the delegates, he insisted, must sign. The meeting had begun at three o'clock, and it was now eight; there was little time left before the letter must be sent off to Craig. Lloyd George emphasised the urgency of the situation. His secretary, Geoffrey Shakespeare, was ready to leave for Belfast, and since it was too late for the boat train, it had been arranged for him to go by special train and destroyer; two letters had been written, one including a copy of the Treaty and saying it had been signed, the other announcing that negotiations had been broken off and that war with southern Ireland would be resumed within 72 hours. "The train is ready with steam up at Euston," Lloyd George declared. "Mr. Shakespeare is waiting. Which letter shall I send? I must have an answer by ten to-night."

It was a bitter moment for the Irish delegates. After settling an outstanding amendment to the draft they agreed to go back to consult their colleagues. Churchill recalled later that "Michael Collins rose looking as if he was going to shoot someone, preferably himself. In all my life I have never seen so much passion and suffering in restraint."

None the less, on his way back to the Irish headquarters Collins said he would sign the Treaty. Though it disestablished the Republic, he felt that Dominion status was the best that could be done for Ireland, and he preferred it to the resumption of a war in which, he was sure, the I.R.A. would be speedily beaten. Duggan, too, said he would sign, but two hours of painful argument were needed before Barton and Duffy would agree to do so. The odd thing about this argument is that the delegates made no use of a direct telephone line to de Valera which was always open. Lloyd George's wizardry had made them feel that they and they alone must deal with his ultimatum.

At Downing Street the British statesmen hardly expected to see the Irishmen again, and it was 11.30 p.m. before they returned with the news that they would all sign. Within two hours some minor points of drafting were cleared up and copies of the much revised Treaty were typed out and duly signed by both British and Irish. There had been no shaking hands when the negotiations began. But now the British Ministers walked round the table to shake hands with the Irish delegates, and Birkenhead said to Collins, "I may have signed my political death-warrant tonight," to which Collins replied with sombre foresight, "I may have signed my actual death-warrant." With the Treaty signed Geoffrey Shakespeare duly set off for Belfast in Lloyd George's best fur coat and with his cheerful assurance that: "If anything happens to you, you shall have a grave in Westminster Abbey." At the end of his journey he found the Northern Ireland Government relieved that the terms of the Treaty were not so bad as they might have been.

The negotiations were over at last. Ireland's protest in arms had won her a degree of freedom, including absolute control of her financial affairs, that Parnell and Redmond could never have thought possible. Indeed, in granting southern Ireland Dominion status and claiming only a modified Oath of Allegiance Britain had given concessions that would have seemed unbelievable to Lloyd George and Birkenhead themselves only a few weeks earlier.

They still seemed unbelievable to the Unionist die-hards. Henry Wilson called the Treaty "a complete surrender"; Carson said he had never thought he would live to see a day of such abject humiliation for Great Britain; the *Morning Post* called the Treaty "an abandonment and betrayal of British powers and British friends in Ireland", and when the Archbishop of Canterbury issued a thanksgiving message it bitterly commented: "PRIMATE'S THANKSGIVING: For the success of the Devil's work in Ireland, for the murder of hundreds of Loyalists, for the sorrows of widows and orphans, for the suffering of the homeless and bereaved, for treachery to God, King and Country, *We thank Thee, O God*." The Southern Unionists, who had long ceased to be die-hards and now stood for Home Rule with safeguards, were no less dismayed. Ulster, they felt ruefully, had got all that she had asked for, but the 300,000 southern Protestants were left in the lurch, and every pledge given to them had been broken. Their leader, Lord Midleton, thought that the Treaty was "one of the most deplorable desertions of their supporters of which any Ministry has ever been guilty".

In Britain generally and in most of the British Press the agreement was regarded as an honourable and generous one, which ended an intolerable state of affairs in Ireland and opened the way to a new era in Anglo-Irish relations. The signing of the Treaty, said the *Daily Telegraph*, was the greatest event that had happened in the internal affairs of the country for generations; the *Daily Mail* proclaimed, "God save Ireland." It is true that the British signatories were soon to be sharply punished by the Conservative Party for their temerity in making peace with "rebels": within a year Lloyd George was driven from power, Churchill went with him, and Birkenhead and Chamberlain, though Conservatives themselves, also followed their fallen chief into the political wilderness, from which, however, all of them except Lloyd George were to emerge in time to hold high posts in later Governments. But their unpopularity with many of their political colleagues had no effect on the fate of the Treaty agreement. That had been formally signed, and in England there could be no thought of going back on the Ministers' signatures. The position was very different in Ireland.

CHAPTER XXIII

Parting of the Ways

I

ON THE EVENING of December 6, 1922, de Valera travelled from Limerick to Dublin to take the chair at a Dante celebration at the Mansion House arranged by the Dail Ministry of Fine Arts. Though news of the signing of the Treaty had been too late for the Irish morning papers, its principal terms were published in the Dublin evenings, and Stack and Brugha, the two irreconcilables, were waiting at the Mansion House to show them to de Valera. He glanced at the papers, saw with dismay the clauses referring to Dominion status and the Oath of Allegiance, and was still reading them when Duggan, who had crossed from England that afternoon, entered the room and handed him a copy of the agreement. De Valera had little time to read it before going to the Dante meeting. It is on record that he sat impassively in his place, looking stonily before him and saying nothing except the few formal words with which he introduced each speaker.

This was the prelude to the great Treaty debate, which was to pass from the Cabinet to the Dail and finally to the streets and country roads of Ireland. Yet the first reactions of the Irish people were to give the Treaty a whole-hearted welcome. They saw that it meant the end of the Anglo-Irish war, the release of Ireland from British domination and the opening of an era of peace and prosperity, and they were grateful. Even some of those who were soon to condemn the Treaty acclaimed it joyfully at first. If Sean O'Casey has remembered correctly, Constance Markievicz "ran round telling people to be merry, for great was the Treaty brought back by the Irish delegates", and Harry Boland called it "the freedom that came from God's right hand"; and P. S. O'Hegarty recalls how a prominent Cumann na mBan young woman said cheerfully, "Ah, well, all for the best; no more war", but was soon denouncing the agreement whole-heartedly when de Valera gave the word to oppose it.

The Dublin pattern of general approval followed by a sharp division of opinion was reflected also among Irish-Americans in the United States. When the news of the Treaty came through they were all exultant, and arrangements were made for joyous celebrations. A banquet was held at the Shoreham Hotel, Washington, but H. W. Nevinson, the only Englishman to attend it, noted that although there were many triumphant speeches, there were also a few which sounded a critical note. The reason for the coolness of some speakers was soon explained. As Nevinson left the banquet he heard that a telegram had been received in Washington, saying bluntly: "Renounce Treaty. De Valera." This was enough to divide Irish-Americans just as the Irish themselves were divided. Some followed de Valera's lead; others, among whom was Devoy himself, thought that the Treaty was a notable milestone on the road to full independence, and vigorously supported Collins and Griffith.

It was not, however, until Thursday, December 8, that de Valera was able to take public action to denounce the Treaty, which he had disliked from the moment when he first saw it at the Mansion House. On Wednesday, while most of the delegates to London were on their way back to Ireland, he issued an ominous statement that "in view of the nature of the proposed Treaty with Great Britain, President de Valera has sent an urgent summons to the members of the Cabinet in London to report at once that a full Cabinet decision may be taken". The Cabinet meeting began on the Thursday morning and lasted till late at night; and at some period during the day de Valera found time to write a letter to the Press explaining his views to the people of Ireland. All the members of the Cabinet were present, together with Duffy, Duggan, Childers and O'Higgins, and the cleavage between those who thought that the Treaty was the best that Ireland could get and those who clung to the ideal of full Republican independence was revealed in every phase of the discussion. When at last a vote was taken (only Cabinet members voting) there was a majority of four to three in favour of the Treaty: Griffith, Collins, Cosgrave and Barton voted for it, de Valera, Brugha and Stack against it. Barton disliked the Treaty as much as its opponents did, but he felt that he was obliged to vote for it since he had signed it.

De Valera's own position was made clear in his letter to the Press.

> "The terms of the agreement [he stated dogmatically] are in violent conflict with the wishes of the nation as expressed freely in successive elections during the last three years. I feel it my duty to inform you that I cannot recommend acceptance of the Treaty either to Dail Eireann or to the country. In this attitude I am supported by the Ministers of Home Affairs and Defence. . . . The great test of our people has come. Let us face it worthily without bitterness and above all without recrimination. There is a definite constitutional way of resolving our political differences."

Before long de Valera was himself to depart from the constitutional way of resolving political differences, but his first task was to revise the agreement with Britain in a way which he thought would be acceptable to the people of Ireland. This revision caused much controversy: it was known as Document No. 2, and the first draft, which was eventually published without his consent, contained an Oath of Allegiance which differed very little from the Oath in the London agreement, except that it changed "to be faithful to King George V, etc." to "to recognise the King of Great Britain as head of the association". This Oath was omitted from the final version of Document No. 2, but in any case the document accepted the principle of association with the British Commonwealth, and thus disposed of the claim that the London agreement was bad because it had failed to secure recognition of an independent Irish Republic. Yet it was the condemnation by irreconcilable I.R.A. officers of this failure which was to lead in a few months to the tragedy of civil war.

De Valera led the opposition to the Treaty in the Dail debate which began, after two preliminary meetings, on December 19. In the same week in which Carson bitterly accused the British Government of having accepted the Treaty terms only because a revolver had been pointed at its head (and Birkenhead retorted that Carson's speech "would have been immature upon the lips of an hysterical schoolgirl") de Valera asked the Dail: "Are we in this generation, which has made Irishmen famous throughout the world, to sign our names to the most ignoble document that could be signed?" This was a remarkable description of a document which, as Griffith had pointed out only a short time earlier, had given Ireland equality with England, together with full powers of fiscal control, and had provided for the evacuation of Ireland by British troops after 700 years' occupation.

The debate in the Dail continued until December 22 and was then adjourned until January 3, when it went on for four more days until a vote was taken on January 7. The split was clear from the first day to the last. Against the Treaty were those who insisted that Ireland must demand a Republic and be ready to go to war again if it were not granted: among them were de Valera, Brugha, Stack, Childers, Liam Mellows, Seumas Robinson and all the women deputies, including Constance Markievicz, who brought an odd touch into the debate by quoting a wild rumour (which she may have invented herself) that Collins was to become engaged to Princess Mary of England. On the other side the leading supporters of the Treaty were

Griffith, Collins, Cosgrave, O'Higgins, Sean MacEoin, Eoin O'Duffy and Mulcahy, the I.R.A. Chief of Staff; their general arguments were that the Treaty was the best that could be obtained, that it brought real gains to Ireland and that it was a stepping-stone to complete independence.

Many bitter things were said in the debate. Mary MacSwiney, Terence MacSwiney's sister, said that Collins was "worse than Castlereagh" and contemptuously dismissed any thought of co-operation between the two sides in the Dail; Robinson sneeringly described Collins as only "a Fleet Street hero", and Brugha made a curious attempt to belittle Collins's immense services by saying that he was merely "one of the heads of a sub-section of my department". (The good-humoured Collins soon forgave Brugha for his attack, and observed a couple of days later: "Do you know,in spite of it all I can't help feeling a regard for Cathal.")

On the other side even the level-headed Griffith lost his temper. Stung by Childers's pedantic criticisms, he angrily rejoined, "I will not reply to any damned Englishman in this assembly"—an inappropriate outburst, since Childers had an Irish mother and had been brought up in county Wicklow, and in any case Griffith had just been speaking most courteously to another Englishman (Thomas Johnson, the Dublin trade-union leader), who had brought a deputation to the Dail to discuss the question of unemployment. Arguments for and against the Treaty were stated over and over again; the issue was clearly joined between the "doing their best for Ireland" deputies who believed that the Treaty would lead to full independence, and those who maintained that there was no such certainty, that it was dishonest to accept the Treaty with the intention of seeking to circumvent it, and that since the Republic had been set up in 1916 the delegates had no power to disestablish it. The unsettled question of whether the delegates were plenipotentiaries or simply agents had, of course, a profound bearing on the point of their authority to sign the Treaty.

To a great extent the opposition to the Treaty was based on the mistaken view that it represented a final and unchangeable settlement, a view which Griffith curtly dismissed by pointing out that it was "no more a final settlement than we are the final generation on the face of the earth". The opposition remained unconvinced, but it was not quite strong enough to gain the day. When the vote was taken there was a majority of 64 to 57 in favour of the Treaty. A deputy who was watching de Valera thought that the result took him completely by surprise.

The representatives of the people of southern Ireland had thus shown their approval of the Treaty, and it seemed clearly impracticable that de Valera should lead the Government which would have to carry it into effect. It was still possible, however, that the Treaty might be rejected by popular vote. De Valera therefore announced that he would resign the presidency, but would be willing to stand for re-election, and if he were re-elected would hold office—with a Republican Cabinet—until the people had a chance to express their view. This curious proposal came to nothing; the Dail rejected the motion for his re-relection by 60 votes to 58; Griffith was then elected President and formed a new Dail Cabinet, consisting of himself, Collins, Cosgrave, Duffy, O'Higgins and Mulcahy, who succeeded Brugha as Minister of Defence. Griffith's election led to a dispute over whether he was President of Dail Eireann or President of the Republic, as de Valera had come to be officially called. Griffith settled it by saying that he would occupy whatever position de Valera had resigned from until the people had the opportunity of voting about it.

Within a few days southern Ireland had a second Ministry, for the Treaty had laid down that the negotiations for putting it into effect should be carried out by a Provisional Government appointed by the Southern Parliament—the body elected in June which the southern Irish had preferred to regard as the second Dail. The obvious course of making the Dail Cabinet the Provisional Government was not taken; it was apparently thought that it would complicate the position if Griffith were head of both Governments, and Collins was therefore appointed chairman of the Provisional Government. Cosgrave and O'Higgins were members of both Ministries, which made it clear that they had become the most important men on the pro-Treaty side after Griffith and Collins. But though the Provisional Government was responsible for dealings with England, the departments of State were administered by the Dail Cabinet. Mulcahy, therefore, as the new Minister of Defence, remained responsible to Dail Eireann.

2

With the appointment of the Provisional Government the tempo of the British departure from southern Ireland began to quicken. On January 16, 1922, Dublin Castle was formally handed over to the new Government; the Irish Ministers were introduced to the senior Civil Servants, who noted that the new men looked pale, anxious and extremely young ("scarcely out of their teens"); and the evacuation of British troops from the 26 counties was begun to the strains of "Let Erin remember!" The Auxies and the Black and Tans were sent home, and the disbandment of the whole of the R.I.C. and the Dublin Metropolitan Police was put in train. An unpleasant aspect of the evacuation was that British soldiers and police were jeered and spat at on their way to stations and docks, and in some parts of the country they were ambushed and attacked by gunmen in flagrant contravention of both Truce and Treaty.

The Provisional Government made the City Hall its temporary headquarters, and Beggar's Bush—the first Dublin barracks to be evacuated by the British—became the Army's G.H.Q. To maintain civil order the Government began to recruit a new paid and uniformed police force known as the Civic Guard, who replaced not only the R.I.C. and the D.M.P. but also the Republican police who had been appointed in association with the Sinn Fein

Courts. In contrast with the R.I.C. the Civil Guard were unarmed, and they remained so even during the worst period of the Civil War.

Throughout the month Collins was in constant touch with Churchill, who, as British Colonial Secretary, was concerned with the detailed arrangements for the Irish change of status; and on January 21 he went to London to meet Craig at the Colonial Office. The two Irish leaders promised to help each other in every way. That night Collins and Churchill dined with the Laverys, who found them both in high spirits because of the new agreement with Craig.

But the shadows were gathering in Dublin. Influential support for the Treaty had come from the Irish Republican Brotherhood, which, under Collins's leadership, had told its members in the Dail that it was in Ireland's interests for the Treaty to be passed. Yet already powerful forces were massing in opposition.

De Valera and his supporters had formed a new political group—Cumann na Poblachta (the Republican Party). Childers had succeeded Mellows in the editorship of *An Poblacht*, which denounced the Treaty in every issue. The women of Cumann na mBan, many of whom had grown hard and bellicose during their long months of active assistance in preparations for I.R.A. attacks and ambushes, were almost solidly against the Treaty, and when Constance Markievicz was elected president of the organisation all pro-Treaty members were asked to resign.

The Cumann na mBan, indeed, played such an important part in inspiring resistance to the Treaty that before long the Provisional Government's opponents were described as the "women and Childers party". Yet in the end neither the women nor the politicians were the prime instigators of civil strife in Ireland. The direct threat to peace came from a group of irreconcilable officers in the Irish Republican Army.

CHAPTER XXIV

Brother Against Brother

I

THE ATTITUDE OF those officers of the I.R.A. whose actions led to the Civil War was summed up by Liam Lynch in the assertion: "We have declared for an Irish Republic and will not live under any other law." In theory there should have been no difficulty in reorganising the Army to meet the changed political situation. Mulcahy, as Minister of Defence, gave orders for the creation of a uniformed regular army, under the command of General J. J. O'Connell, and proposed that Volunteers who did not join it should stay in civil life as an army reserve. But in practice the smooth working of this scheme was frustrated by the emergence of a powerful anti-Treaty group among the senior officers of the I.R.A.

The leader of this group was Rory O'Connor, I.R.A. Director of Engineering, who had been a particularly reckless commander in the war with Britain, and among his supporters were Liam Mellows, I.R.A. Director of Purchases, Oscar Traynor, Commandant of the Dublin Brigade, and the two outstanding divisional commandants, Liam Lynch and Ernie O'Malley. Their view was that Dail Eireann had no right to approve a Treaty which disestablished the Republic, and that the I.R.A. therefore owed no further allegiance to the Dail. They proposed, therefore, to remove the I.R.A. from the control of the Dail Government, and to restore it to its earlier status as a Volunteer force under the command of its own elected executive.

Their first moves were in strict accordance with military formality. They asked Mulcahy to approve the holding of an Army Convention to consider the future of the I.R.A., and he agreed that such a convention should be held within two months of January 18. Mulcahy also gave them an undertaking that the Army should be maintained as the Army of the Irish Republic, though it is difficult to understand what such a pledge could have been meant to convey at a time when arrangements were already in hand for setting up a non-Republican Government.

The two months' gap before the holding of the proposed convention allowed recalcitrant I.R.A. officers in various parts of the country to take action on their own initiative against the Provisional Government, whose authority they refused to recognise. Armed bodies seized lorries and munitions belonging to the Government's new regular troops; O'Malley, Commandant of the Second Southern Division, raided an R.I.C. barracks at Clonmel as it was about to be evacuated and suppressed a local newspaper by breaking up the type and machines; and Liam Forde, as Commandant of the Mid-Limerick Brigade, repudiated the authority of the I.R.A. high command and attempted to occupy Limerick when it was evacuated by British troops. Open conflict between Forde's men and pro-Treaty troops who were ordered to take over the former British posts in Limerick was averted only by the intervention of Lynch and Traynor, who had not as yet moved against the Provisional Government. At the request of the Minister of Defence they went to Limerick on a peace mission, and were able to arrange a friendly settlement.

But the writing on the wall was becoming clear. The Republican element in the I.R.A. was prepared to accept no compromise over the Treaty, and was ready to resort to arms rather than give in. A crisis was reached on March 15, when the Dail Cabinet, which retained the nominal authority over the I.R.A. in spite of the establishment of the parallel Provisional Government, decided to cancel the arrangement for the Army Convention. The decision was taken, as explained in a Cabinet statement published a few days later, because "the Minister of Defence had to admit to the Cabinet that he could not guarantee that if this Convention was held there would not be set up a body regarding itself as a military government not responsible to the people".

Mulcahy's forebodings were soon to be fully justified, but before the dissident officers could take action the position was further inflamed by a speech made by de Valera at Thurles on March 17.

> "If [he said] they accepted the Treaty, and if the Volunteers of the future tried to complete the work the Volunteers of the last four years had been attempting, they would have to complete it, not over the bodies of foreign soldiers, but over the dead bodies of their own countrymen. They would have to wade through Irish blood, through the blood of the soldiers of the Irish Government, and through, perhaps, the blood of some members of the Government, in order to get Irish freedom."

It has been said in defence of this speech that it was not an incitement to civil war, but merely a far-sighted warning of the dangers which lay ahead if the Treaty were accepted. The difference between threat and warning seems rather a fine one, and in any case the speech was undoubtedly a condonation of civil war as an instrument of policy. It may be doubted, however, whether it had much influence on O'Connor's angry young men, who had small regard for politicians of any party.

By now the anti-Treaty section of the I.R.A. was openly breaking with both the Dail and the Provisional Government. The officers were not all of one mind: Lynch, as Commandant of the First Southern Division, was still willing to discuss proposals for a disciplined relationship between the I.R.A. and the new Government which would be appointed after the next general election, but O'Connor had thrown off all responsibility to any Governmental authority.

In defiance of the Cabinet's ban he arranged to hold the Army Convention, and he gave his reasons to a conference of Irish and American journalists summoned to the new Republican's Party's headquarters in Suffolk Street. The anti-Treaty officers, he declared, considered that the Government had done something which it had no moral right to do, and therefore they could not recognise it further; they repudiated the Dail, and there was no Government in Ireland to which they gave allegiance. To a journalist who asked: "Do we take it we are going to have a military dictatorship?" O'Connor replied: "You can take it that way if you like."

The prohibited Army Convention was held at the Dublin Mansion House on March 26. The Government did not try to prevent it, and the 211 delegates unanimously agreed to make the anti-Treaty part of the I.R.A. an autonomous body, claiming the title of Irish Republican Army and acknowledging no control except that of its own Executive. This was an elected body of 16 officers, among whom were Lynch, O'Connor, Mellows and O'Malley. Lynch was appointed Chief of Staff and set up his headquarters at Barry's Hotel in Gardiner Street.

Within three days the anti-Treaty I.R.A. Executive, whose forces soon became known as the Irregulars, began the campaign of violence which was to continue almost without interruption until the end of the Civil War in the following spring. *Freeman's Journal* was accused of having published a misleading article about the Convention; the Executive retaliated by sending men to raid the newspaper's office and destroy the printing machinery. A fortnight later they seized the Four Courts, the Masonic Hall, the Ballast Office, the Kildare Street Club and other Dublin buildings and made them military posts for anti-Treaty troops. The division between the pro-Treaty section of the I.R.A., from which the Government's new regular army was drawn, and the anti-Treaty section based on the Four Courts was now complete.

The Four Courts, where O'Connor and Mellows set up the Army Executive's headquarters, were a useful position because, though near to the centre of Dublin, they are sufficiently cut off from it to form a little world of their own. Moreover, the Executive hoped to disrupt the country's legal life by stopping the work of the Dublin Courts, which had now been functioning normally for many months, as the work of the Sinn Fein Courts had gradually slowed down in 1921. These hopes, however, were not fulfilled. Sir Thomas Moloney, the Lord Chief Justice, was not a man to be intimidated by a show of military force. He transferred the work of the Four Courts to the King's Inns, where justice continued to be administered, and Sir Thomas himself set an example of quiet dignity by arriving punctually every morning in spite of threats of assassination.

In the meantime the Irregulars had turned to organised theft and robbery to get funds for their maintenance. Post offices were raided in many parts of the country, and on May 1 they stole £250,000 from various branches of the Bank of Ireland. Their snipers, too, took up positions on Dublin roof-tops and fired at night on such buildings as Beggar's Bush barracks, the City Hall and the Provisional Government's departmental offices in Merrion Square. For most of the time the Ministers lived in these offices, and it was here that O'Higgins, who had gone on to the flat roof for a quiet smoke one warm evening, casually looked over the parapet and had his cigarette cut from his fingers by a sniper's bullet. The Army Executive's example of lawlessness was being followed, moreover, by thugs and ruffians who welcomed the chance of committing offences for which the Irregulars would almost certainly be blamed.

The drift towards open civil war was unmistakable. In a sense, indeed, that war had actually begun on March 28, when the Army Convention repudiated the Dail's authority, and in April the Irregulars drew first blood in their attacks on Government troops. Yet for a brief period it still seemed possible that the two sections of the old I.R.A. might forget their differences and unite in a shared offensive. The cause of this unexpected rapprochement was Ulster.

2

The Anglo-Irish Treaty had at least paid lip-service to Irish unity. It laid down that the Irish Free State, when legally established, should exercise in Northern Ireland all the powers reserved by the British Government under the Better Government of Ireland Act, *unless* within a month of the ratification both Houses of the Northern Ireland Parliament presented an address asking for the total exclusion of the six counties from the jurisdiction of the Free State. The time-limit was subsequently amended to become within a month after the actual constitution of the Free State, but this change did not in any way affect the absolute certainty that Ulster would "opt out" of a united Ireland.

The Treaty, therefore, provided for the partition of Ireland unless the hopes which Collins and Griffith had set on the projected Boundary Commission were justified, and English statesmen were relieved to think that the long wrangle over the north-eastern boundary line might at last be coming to an end. Churchill had spoken in the House of Commons of the vast changes which the First World War had brought to the world, and had drily commented: "But as the deluge subsides and the waters fall we see the dreary steeples of Fermanagh and Tyrone emerging once again. The integrity of their quarrel is one of the few institutions that have been unaltered in the cataclysm which has swept the world."

It was a quarrel, however, which vitally affected the Provisional Government, whose leaders still believed that it might be settled to southern Ireland's advantage. Griffith was still certain that the Treaty would not involve permanent partition; he was confident that the Free State would be given Fermanagh and Tyrone, and possibly South Armagh and South Down. Collins, too, remembered that Lloyd George had not contradicted him when he surmised that the Boundary Commission would reduce Northern Ireland to such small dimensions that it would be unable to exist separately. Neither of them knew that this interpretation of the Boundary Commission's functions (which seems to have been accepted by Lloyd George himself) was roundly denied by Birkenhead, who told Lord Balfour in a private letter, which was not published till 1924, that the Treaty would have been drawn up very differently if there had been any intention of taking away large slices of Northern Ireland. In Birkenhead's opinion Collins's hopes of large territorial gains for the Irish Free State had "no foundation whatever except in his own over-heated imagination".

In the early months of 1922 both Collins and Craig made considerable efforts to keep the peace between the six and the 26 counties. But the old Ulster feud between Catholics and Protestants was too strong for them. The I.R.A. had secret forces in the north-east, probably amounting to about 8,500 men; against them were set not only the British troops in Ulster garrisons and the section of the old R.I.C. now known as the Royal Ulster Constabulary, but also the special constabulary, which numbered 25,000 at the end of March and was later increased to 49,000. And behind these forces were the Protestant civilians who were easily aroused to retaliation by reports of Sinn Fein outrages or undercover activities.

The rioting of the previous summer had now begun again on an even larger scale. Cases of arson and brutal killing occurred almost every day, and in less than three weeks in February 138 casualties were reported—96 among Catholics, 42 among Protestants. In March the Northern Ireland Government introduced a drastic Special Powers Act, which set up new regulations regarding curfew, the possession of firearms or explosives, unlawful drilling, illegal uniforms, etc., and in particular made the possession of firearms punishable by flogging or death. At the same time Craig invited Sir Henry Wilson, who had retired from the post of Chief of the Imperial General Staff, to become Northern Ireland's military adviser, since the clash between Catholic and Protestant seemed likely to lead to open war between north and south. As the reign of violence continued thousands of Catholics were driven out of Northern Ireland, and terrible outrages were committed on both sides. In this month five members of a Catholic family, the MacMahons, were killed by uniformed men who entered their house during curfew hours; in a similar attack by Sinn Feiners on the house of an Orange family, the Donnellys, a baby was killed and the father and two small children horribly mutilated by a bomb, while the mother, who escaped the bomb, was shot by the raiders before they left.

It was at the end of March that Collins and Craig tried again to stop violence in Northern Ireland. After a meeting at the Colonial Office in London they signed an agreement beginning "Peace is today declared" and arranging for various measures of co-operation to restore peaceful conditions. Among these was a pledge by Collins that I.R.A. activity should cease in the six counties. The agreement was ineffective. Outrages continued to occur, and on April 27 Collins protested to Craig against "the abominations that have taken place in Belfast since the signing of our pact". The I.R.A. also resumed its attacks in Northern Ireland, since Collins apparently felt that he was no longer bound by his pledge to Craig.

This trouble in the north-east brought about a temporary alliance between the Provisional Government's forces and the Irregulars. Though the Irregulars' Army Executive had rejected proposals from Mulcahy for Army reunification, Collins and Lynch came together to work out plans for a combined I.R.A. offensive in the six counties. A prominent figure in these negotiations was Frank Aiken, commandant of the I.R.A.'s Fourth Northern Division, who had not yet broken with the Dail, though he was later to join the Irregulars against the Government. Experienced officers from the Southern Divisions were to be sent north to assist in making war on Crown forces, and for the moment it seemed as though the old brotherhood of the I.R.A. might be re-established. In June, indeed, the I.R.A. was again in conflict with British forces in Ulster, for its seizure of Belleek and Pettigo on the Northern Ireland border provoked a determined counter-attack by two battalions of British troops, supported by artillery, who cleared the area and restored it to the Northern Ireland Government. But the events of the next few weeks effectively dispelled any lingering hope of I.R.A. reunification.

The military cleavage was not the only one that worried the Provisional Government. There was also the political problem of coming to terms with de Valera and his new Republican Party, who had no connexion with, or authority over, the Army Executive at the Four Courts. In accordance with the terms of the Treaty, the Provisional Government was preparing a constitution for the Irish Free State, which was due to be submitted for approval at a general election to be held not later than June. The election seemed a good opportunity for restoring some sort of political harmony, and Collins and de Valera met to work out plans for a new deal. On May 20 it was announced that they had signed a pact governing the election and the appointment of the next Government.

The terms of this pact (which shocked and surprised the British Government, who felt that Collins and Griffith should have no dealings with the anti-Treaty party) were that a panel of Sinn Fein candidates, 66 nominated by the Provisional Government and 58 by the anti-Treaty Republicans, should be put up for the general election, though other parties would be free to nominate candidates if they wished. If, as seemed likely, most of those on the panel list were elected, it was then proposed to set up a coalition Government, consisting of a President, a Minister of Defence and nine other Ministers—five representing the pro-Treaty party and four the anti-Treaty, each party to choose its own nominees. It is difficult to see how such a divided

Cabinet could ever have hoped to govern the country effectively, and in fact no such Government was ever appointed; but the pact gave a political breathing-space, during which the Provisional Government pressed on with the preparation of the Free State constitution.

Griffith took the first draft constitution to London in May, when its extensive modifications of the Treaty's terms were at once rejected by the British Government. The draft was revised, and agreement was reached by the middle of June, but the revised constitution was not published in the newspapers till the morning of June 16, polling-day in the general election. The people of Ireland had little time to consider its terms before recording their votes.

It was a typical Irish election of those days. Each side rightly complained of intimidation by the other, and the dead, as usual, voted substantially. The election was held on an out-of-date register, yet it was not unusual for a 100 per cent. poll to be recorded, sometimes with all the first preferences cast for the same candidate. In a subsequent Dail debate it was ironically suggested that some of the new deputies should be classified as members for Glasnevin, and Ernest Blythe commented on one election return that it showed "the peculiar unanimity of the people in that district dead and alive". But though intimidation reduced the number of rival candidatures, nearly a quarter of the panel nominees were beaten. The new Dail consisted of 94 panel deputies (58 pro-Treaty and 36 anti-Treaty), 17 from the Labour Party, seven from the Farmers' Party, six Independents and four Unionists (representing Trinity College). Since all the non-panel deputies were pro-Treaty, the result could be interpreted as giving a popular vote of 92 to 36 in favour of the Treaty; but this interpretation was hotly denied by the anti-Treaty deputies, who claimed that the election had given an unmistakable popular mandate for a coalition Government to restore peace.

Such a Government, however, was made completely impracticable by the events which followed soon after the election. On June 22 Sir Henry Wilson was assassinated in London by two members of the London battalion of the I.R.A.—Commandant Reginald Dunne and Volunteer Joseph Sullivan, who were hanged without revealing on whose orders they had acted. O'Connor and de Valera both disowned responsibility, and though O'Connor was anxious to cause new friction between England and Ireland, so that English troops would resume the Irish war and the I.R.A. could unite to oppose them, it appears to be clearly established that neither he nor the Army Executive had anything to do with Wilson's death. The assassination has been blamed on Collins, and there is good evidence that at some much earlier time—possibly before the Truce—he had given Dunne orders to kill Wilson, and had never subsequently cancelled them; but in this month of June Collins was far from wishing to antagonise England, and it is quite incredible that he should then have ordered the assassination. Since the order is said to have been confirmed during the Treaty negotiations, it seems highly probable that the alleged confirmation came, not from Collins himself, but from one of his enemies in Dublin, who seized what appeared to be a golden opportunity of killing an enemy, infuriating England and making trouble for Collins. But this can be only a matter for speculation rather than for historical certainty.

The assassination certainly infuriated the British Government, which incorrectly supposed it to have been ordered by the anti-Treaty I.R.A. Lloyd George wrote to Collins insisting that he must take strong action against the Four Courts Republicans, and at the same time he sounded Macready, who had not yet left Ireland, about the possibility of capturing the Four Courts with the few British troops still in Dublin. Macready sagely pointed out that such action would only unite the I.R.A. against England again, and in the end Lloyd George agreed with him. It was clearly, he considered, the duty of the Irish themselves to clear out the Four Courts and suppress anarchy in Dublin, but the Provisional Government, though aware that it would have to act sooner or later, still hesitated to challenge the Irregulars.

While it waited O'Connor's men forced the issue. On the night of June 26 they raided a garage in Lower Baggot Street, but were surrounded by Government troops, who took one of their officers prisoner; and in reprisal for this officer's imprisonment the Irregulars kidnapped General O'Connell, the Government Army's Assistant Chief of Staff, and held him captive in the Four Courts.

That was the finishing touch. For months the Irregulars had been waging an unofficial civil war. It was now to become official. Collins borrowed two 18-pounder guns from Macready, and at midnight on June 27 Government troops surrounded the Four Courts and presented an ultimatum announcing that they would attack at 4 a.m. unless the garrison surrendered. O'Connor declined to surrender. A little after 4 a.m. the two guns, stationed on the other side of the Liffey, opened their rather ineffectual fire. The Civil War had begun in earnest.

3

The bombardment of the Four Courts was only the culminating incident in the tragic dissensions which had been going on all the year. Many clear-thinking Irishmen were shocked by the wrangling. George Russell sadly suggested to Lady Gregory that someone should write a play "about how the generations for 700 years fought for the liberation of beautiful Cathleen ni Houlihan, and when they set her free she walked out, a fierce vituperative old hag". All the gallant romantic talk about "dying for Cathleen" seemed very far away on that June morning when a friendly farmer said to de Valera as he came out of his house at Greystones: "I wouldn't go into Dublin if I were you, sir. The Free Staters are shelling the Four Courts."

De Valera had no hesitation in taking the side of the armed opponents of the Provisional Government. He issued a public statement describing the Four Courts garrison as "the best and bravest of our nation", and another statement was issued on behalf of the Army Executive by Liam Lynch, the Irregulars' Chief of Staff.

> "At the dictation of our hereditary enemy [he declared] our rightful cause is being treacherously assailed by recreant Irishmen. The crash of arms and the boom of artillery reverberate in this supreme test of the nation's destiny. . . . We therefore appeal to all citizens who have withstood unflinchingly the oppression of the enemy during the past six years to rally to the support of the Republic and to recognise that the resistance now offered is but the continuance of the struggle that was suspended by the Truce with the British."

In fact, of course, the Provisional Government was not acting "at the dictation" of Britain, since it had long realised that the intolerable situation created by O'Connor's seizure of the Four Courts could not be allowed to continue; but the suggestion that the attack was inspired by Britain was a good debating-point for the Irregulars. Their senior officers moved to their appointed posts. Lynch, Seumas Robinson and other officers of the Southern Division left Dublin by train for their own districts; O'Malley stayed in the city to direct from there the operations of his Northern and Eastern Command; Oscar Traynor took up the Dublin command and set up his brigade headquarters in a number of O'Connell Street hotels. Cathal Brugha reported for duty with the Irregulars and became a commandant; de Valera, Stack, Barton and Constance Markievicz were among others who hurried to Traynor's headquarters (though the story of a sniping duel lasting several hours between Constance Markievicz and a Government soldier in Henry Street is doubtless one of those fanciful legends which so often grew up around her).

The modest Government artillery took some time to subdue the Four Courts. Though the attack had begun on Wednesday morning, it was not until Friday that the building caught fire and the garrison was obliged to surrender.

As they left the Four Courts the Irregulars wantonly exploded a huge mine which blew up the law library and the priceless contents of the Public Record Office. More than 100 officers and men, including O'Connor and Mellows, were taken prisoner and sent to Mountjoy gaol, but six of them managed to escape on their way there. Among the escapers were O'Malley and Sean Lemass, who had served with the I.R.A. ever since he had fought in the G.P.O. as a boy in his teens.

The main Government attack was now directed against the Dublin Brigade's headquarters in the O'Connell Street hotels, and the Irregulars were driven from one building to another until the Hammam Hotel alone was left in their occupation. From here Traynor, Stack, de Valera and others escaped to hiding-places elsewhere in the city, while Brugha stayed behind with a small party to cover their retreat. On the following day—Tuesday, July 4—Traynor sent a message to Brugha telling him to surrender, since the hotel was on fire and further resistance could be of no use. But it was too much to expect a warrior like Brugha to surrender. The rest of the garrison came out under a white flag, but he was not with them. As the troops outside waited for the walls to collapse under the heat of the flames the small figure of Brugha was suddenly seen at the door, holding a revolver in each hand and firing till the end. A machine-gun was turned on him, and he fell to the ground with grave wounds, from which he died two days later.

Pearse's gospel of the blood sacrifice had found another believer. Even his enemies mourned their gallant and implacable comrade of earlier days, and Collins generously wrote of him: "When many of us are forgotten, Cathal Brugha will be remembered." Now the war between brothers was joined in earnest. Others were to see—and order—the deaths of old comrades in the months which lay ahead.

CHAPTER XXV

Birth of the Free State

I

ONCE AGAIN A week of fighting had left its mark on Dublin. Apart from the destruction at the Four Courts, much of the east side of O'Connell Street was burnt out, and Churchill spoke of the Provisional Government's courage in sacrificing millions of pounds worth of Irish property in order to stamp out armed resistance to the Treaty. But resistance was not stamped out. It was only transferred to other parts of the country.

The Civil War was not always a desperate business. Sometimes both sides were reluctant to take life, and the fighting on such occasions was not very serious. An example had been set in May, when the Irregulars occupied Kilkenny Castle and held it for a few days against Government troops attacking with rifles and revolvers. The scale of the fighting can be gauged from the fact that the Irregulars sent a message to one of their local girl-friends, asking her to bring out a bag of ammunition so that they could go on fighting for another day; but though the young woman duly brought the supplies, they soon surrendered after a siege in which there had been no casualties on either side. It was about this time, too, that the steward of a country estate wrote to the owner: "There was a terrible battle here today between the Staters and the Irregulars. They were shooting at one another all day, and it was a terrible battle. They stopped for a cup of tea and both sides admired your ladyship's antirrhinums." But as time went on such incidents became exceptional. The old war of ambush and secret attack was resumed more ruthlessly than ever, and raids, robberies and arson figured prominently in the Irregulars' campaign. Many of them were tolerably well armed, because the British troops and police, in evacuating their barracks, had been content to hand over their arms, ammunition, tenders and other equipment to any likely-looking body of men, and had not worried whether the recipients were Government troops or Irregulars.

"Nobody likes the Freak State," Constance Markievicz wrote in a letter to a friend, but not many people can have liked the Irregulars either, as they shot, bombed, robbed, raided, wrecked railway lines and bridges and made war on the whole social fabric of Ireland. The terror and counter-terror of Black and Tan days were back again on an even more savage scale. And all the time, as O'Higgins was to say later, the country was being administered by the Provisional Government, which was "simply eight young men in the City Hall, standing amidst the ruins of one administration, with the foundations of another not yet built, and with wild men screaming through the keyhole".

At first the Irregulars had a big advantage in numbers. Recruitment for the Government Army had begun slowly, and when Collins temporarily resigned the chairmanship of the Provisional Government to become Commander-in-Chief he had only 4,000 troops at his disposal. While a stronger Government Army was being built up the Irregulars, under Lynch's leadership, had many successes in the south, where they were able to seize and hold all the important positions in the counties of Waterford, Tipperary, Kerry and Cork. In the city of Cork, indeed, they not only raised funds by levying Customs duties and other taxes but they also took control of the *Cork Examiner* and insisted on its publishing every day a complete page of the Irregulars' own glowing accounts of their military successes. Yet they were not able to hold these positions long. In a few weeks, as the Government forces became more numerous and (with British assistance) better armed, the Irregulars had to evacuate every stronghold, and no part of Ireland remained under their control. So the war became once more an affair of Irregular flying columns being pursued by Government troops, and once again the rebels against established authority seized the advantage of wearing civilian clothes while their opponents were in uniform.

Since Government forces held all the ports and were thus able to obtain an uninterrupted supply of munitions, the war could end in only one way, but the Irregulars caused a great deal of material damage. In particular, they sought to interfere with Government supplies by attacks on the railways, and hundreds of cases of damage to bridges and permanent way and derailment of locomotives and other rolling stock were reported by the Great Southern and Western Railway. Their biggest achievement was the destruction of the railway viaduct over the Blackwater at Mallow—an operation which severed the rail link between Cork and the north.

August was a tragic month for the architects of the Irish Free State. Arthur Griffith, the great founder of Sinn Fein who had influenced every phase of Ireland's struggle for freedom, died on August 12. Strain, overwork and heartbreak over the disastrous split in the nation combined to cause his death from a cerebral haemorrhage when he was barely 50. Three days later Collins was ambushed and killed in his own county of Cork by Irregulars who had been waiting for a military convoy and did not know that they were shooting at Collins himself. As Commander-in-Chief Collins was unwise to expose himself to such danger, and Sean O'Casey, indeed, describes his last mission as "fooling about in the south"; but he was still a young man, and one who had never been afraid of living dangerously, and he may well have thought that he was taking no more risks in going to Cork than in staying in Dublin, where Irregular gunmen stalked him even as he walked the few hundred yards between the Government buildings and Oliver Gogarty's house in Merrion Square. Since the Blackwater viaduct had been blown up, his body was brought back by boat to Dublin, where he lay in state for days in the City Hall, while thousands of Dubliners filed past for a last glimpse of their greatest military leader. It was in this month, too, that Harry Boland, who had voted against the Treaty and had thrown in his lot with the Irregulars, was shot and killed in the Grand Hotel at Skerries by Government troops who had come to arrest him.

The vacant places of Griffith, as President of Dail Eireann, and Collins, as Finance Minister and chairman of the Provisional Government, were both filled by Cosgrave, who shared with O'Higgins, the Minister for Home Affairs, the main responsibility for the political conduct of the war; on the military side Mulcahy succeeded Collins as Commander-in-Chief. The new Dail had its first meeting at Leinster House on September 9, and three days later it passed a vote of confidence in Cosgrave's Government. Later in the month a Bill was passed to set up a Senate, of whom 30 members were to be nominated by the President and 30 elected by the Dail.

De Valera's Republican deputies did not, of course, attend the meetings of the Dail. Like their leader, they were now "on the run", though some were able to make secret visits to Dublin from time to time. De Valera, indeed, kept in touch with the Republican Party's office in Suffolk Street, and he was in regular communication with Lynch, the Irregulars' Commander-in-Chief. The result of these contacts was that the Irregulars' Army Executive at last agreed to ally itself with the political wing of the anti-Treaty movement. On October 28 it issued a proclamation saying that it had called on de Valera to form a Republican Government and promising to give this Government its wholehearted support and allegiance. The Republican deputies confirmed de Valera's appointment as President, and a

Cabinet was chosen to work under his leadership. Among the Ministers were P. J. Ruttledge (Home Affairs) and Sean Lemass (Defence).

So the dissident I.R.A. officers, who had begun the Civil War because they would not live under any other law except that of a Republic, now had their Republican Government at last. It was not destined for long life.

2

Throughout that autumn of 1922 the Provisional Government, which was still waiting for its official transformation into the Government of the Irish Free State, took increasingly drastic action to round up the Irregulars. It had the approval of the Roman Catholic Church, whose hierarchy had issued a joint pastoral from Maynooth on October 10, denouncing the Irregulars' "immoral methods" and declaring: "Our country that was but yesterday so glorious has become a byword among the nations—a section have wrecked Ireland from end to end. They have done more damage in three months than could be laid to the charge of British rule in three decades." But the Irregulars were not moved by the bishops' condemnation; they continued their campaign of destruction, and the Provisional Government decided that the ordinary processes of law were not powerful enough to deal with them. In Hugh Kennedy, who was assisted by John A. Costello, it had a most able law officer, but it felt obliged to set up Army courts with powers to try prisoners and to punish the unauthorised possession of arms or ammunition by fines, imprisonment, deportation or death. It was in virtue of these powers that Erskine Childers, who had gone "on the run" with the other Republican deputies and was still producing his small propaganda journal on a portable printing press, was tried and executed after his capture in November.

The execution of Childers was an indication of the severity with which the Provisional Government was now resolved to carry on the struggle. He had been tracked down by

Government troops to his cousin Robert Barton's house at Glendalough, and when he was taken prisoner he had in his hand a small revolver, which had been a present from Collins. That was enough to seal his fate. He was sentenced to death and executed a week after his trial, though an attempt was actually being made to secure a writ of habeas corpus on his behalf and the decision of the courts was still being awaited. After his execution Gavan Duffy acclaimed him in the Dail as "a great Irishman", and suggested that other matters, besides Childers's possession of a revolver, had influenced those who confirmed the sentence of death. Certainly O'Higgins was animated by a bitter hatred of Childers. He had described him as "the Englishman" who was "steadily, callously and ghoulishly striking at the heart of this nation", though in fact there was little if any evidence that Childers had much influence on the conduct of the Irregular leaders.

It was in December that the Irish Free State came officially into existence. The Dail had already passed the Free State Constitution Bill, including the clause which made the Oath of Allegiance (as given in the Treaty) obligatory on all its members; and the corresponding Bill in the British House of Commons received the Royal Assent on December 6. (It remained a matter of controversy whether the Dail or the House of Commons was the ultimate authority for the establishment of the Free State.) As had been expected, Northern Ireland at once exercised her right to "contract out" of the new Irish Government. In Dublin Tim Healy, the former Nationalist M.P., became the Free State's first Governor-General and took up his residence at Vice-Regal Lodge (which was soon ironically known as "Uncle Tim's Cabin"); and Cosgrave, now President of the Executive Council of the Irish Free State, issued his list of the 30 nominated members of the Senate. It included 16 Southern Unionists, and among many well-known names were those of Lord Glenavy, Dr. Oliver Gogarty, General Sir Bryan Mahon, Lord Mayo, Sir Horace Plunkett and

W. B. Yeats. The names of the 30 elected members, among whom were Mrs. Alice Stopford Green and Colonel Maurice Moore, were announced two days later.

But there was little joy in Dublin over the fulfilment of the promise of Irish freedom and the departure from Irish shores of the final remnants of the British garrison. Once more it was the end of the fighting, the terror and the executions that people were anxious to see, rather than the establishment of a new form of government; and within two days of its foundation the Free State Government gave new proof of its unflinching determination to stop the Civil War.

The Irregulars had openly threatened those deputies who had voted for the Bill setting up the Army Courts. On December 7 one of these deputies, Sean Hales, was shot dead in a Dublin street, and another deputy was wounded. The Government acted at once. At dawn on the following morning four of the Four Courts leaders who had been imprisoned in Mountjoy—O'Connor, Mellows, Joseph McKelvey and Dick Barrett—were taken out and shot in the prison yard. It was an act that could not be legally justified, but one that was intended, as Cosgrave said in the Dail, to show the Irregulars "that terror will be struck into them"; and it was one that called for a particular kind of courage from O'Higgins, who had been a close personal friend of O'Connor. Yeats described O'Higgins as

> A great man in his pride,
> Confronting murderous men.

Yet it was painful resolution, rather than pride, which he displayed in his speech in the Dail that day, when the memory of his dead friend made him break down in public for the only time in his life.

With the opening of 1923 it could be only a matter of time before the Irregulars were forced to surrender. Everywhere they were being captured in large numbers, and the Free State gaols and internment camps held about 12,000 military prisoners by the early spring. Among them were women whose names recalled famous chapters in Ireland's long struggle—Mary MacSwiney (Terence MacSwiney's sister), Grace Plunkett (who married Joseph Plunkett the night before his execution) and Nora Connolly O'Brien (James Connolly's daughter, whose husband, Seumas O'Brien, was also a prisoner). Hunger-strikes were again attempted, but broke down when the Free State Government, like the British of old, declared that those who chose to starve must take the consequences of their own actions.

Yet though the end was clearly in sight, the Irregulars continued their ambushes and attacks, most of which were now directed against private property. The homes of members of the new Senate were special targets for raiders. Among the Senators' country houses which were burnt to the ground, often involving the loss of valuable works of art, were those of John Bagwell, at Clonmel, county Tipperary, of Lord Mayo, at Palmerstown, county Kildare, of Sir Horace Plunkett, at Foxrock, county Dublin, of Maurice Moore, in county Mayo, of Sir Bryan Mahon, in county Kildare, of Sir John Keane, in county Waterford, of Lord Desart, in county Kilkenny, and of Oliver Gogarty, at Connemara. Both Bagwell and Gogarty were kidnapped by Irregulars, but managed to escape, Gogarty by jumping into the Liffey and swimming for a quarter of an hour to safety through its icy January waters.

But the war could not be won by burning country houses, and although Lynch still led the resistance in the south, a feeling that it was hopeless to go on with the struggle was beginning to grow among the Irregular commandants. De Valera, as head of the Republican Government, attended a meeting of the Army Executive held in the Nier Valley, in county Waterford, at the end of March, and suggested that a peace approach should be made to the Free State Government. He proposed to devise a formula which would recognise the Irish people's right to sovereign independence and would lay down that no test or oath should deprive people of their right to take a full share in the nation's political life.

Lynch was against any peace move at that moment, and de Valera's proposal was rejected by six votes to five; but on April 10 Lynch himself was shot and mortally wounded in an engagement with Free State troops near Newcastle in the Knockmealdown mountains. With his death the Irregulars lost their most brilliant and most irreconcilable military leader.

Frank Aiken succeeded him as Chief of Staff, and when the Army Executive met again in Tipperary on April 20 it was decided to send a deputation to confer with de Valera on proposals for peace. This time de Valera's plan was approved, and as a preliminary to negotiations with the Free State Government a proclamation suspending all offensive action was issued by de Valera and Aiken, giving April 30 as the date on which it would come into operation.

But the end was not yet. Some days had to pass in discussions between de Valera and two Senators, Andrew Jameson and James Douglas, who were appointed by Cosgrave to act as intermediaries; and de Valera's first proposals were promptly rejected by the Government. At last de Valera understood that the Government would not accept any proposal which sidetracked the Oath of Allegiance, and that his only course was to give way and call off the Civil War unconditionally. On May 24 he ordered the Irregulars to cease fire permanently and to conceal their arms in places where they were not likely to be found.

The Civil War was over. It had cost the Free State Government £17,000,000, and an army of 60,000 Free State soldiers had had to be enrolled to hunt down the Republicans. Now at last in May, 1923, the Government of the Irish Free State was definitely established as the supreme power in the 26 counties, and it could still cherish hopes (never to be fulfilled) that a boundary commission would transfer to the south at least two of the six north-eastern counties. The long day which had begun on that Easter Monday morning when Pearse and Connolly marched into the G.P.O. was ended at last. The tragedy for

Ireland was that the coming of freedom had brought division and bitterness that were to last for years.

3

There can be no concise epilogue to this story of the Irish fight for freedom, for it would take another book to follow the fortunes of those many leaders who survived the conflict (and still survive into the nineteen-sixties) and to trace the development of the Irish Free State into the present Republic of Ireland. That book would tell how the Free State's hopes of a readjustment of the Northern Ireland boundary were utterly frustrated, so that the lines of partition established in 1922 remained unchanged; how some of the irreconcilable Republicans maintained their active defiance of the Free State Government, which retaliated with measures of repression greater than any which Britain had ever imposed on Ireland; how O'Higgins was assassinated at the height of his powers by gunmen who were never discovered; how de Valera, who was arrested at Ennis in 1923 and kept in prison for a year, agreed in 1927 to bring his followers into the Dail under their new name of the Fianna Fail Party; how he became President of the Executive Council in 1932 and succeeded in abolishing the Parliamentary Oath a year later; and how his decision to withhold the land annuities payable to Great Britain led to the Anglo-Irish economic war of the nineteen-thirties.

It would tell, too, of the abolition of the office of Governor-General and the installation of Douglas Hyde as President of Ireland; of the emergence in southern Ireland of a rural middle class whose political and social preferences were reflected in the new Free State constitution of 1937; of the 1938 Anglo-Irish agreement for the transfer to the Free State Government of the Irish port facilities reserved for Britain under the Treaty, and of the difficulties this transfer caused for Britain when southern Ireland remained neutral during the Second World War; and as a constant accompaniment to the major political happenings there would be the story of the Irish Republican Army, heir to the Civil War Irregulars, repeatedly declared an unlawful association yet still maintaining its undercover activities and never ceasing for long to wage its individual war on partition by carrying out bombing affrays and raids for arms in Northern Ireland and sometimes in England.

The successful development in Northern Ireland of her new type of representative government, under which the provincial legislature divides responsibility with the Westminster Parliament, would have a distinguished place in this chronicle of events. It would reach a dramatic climax in 1948, when John A. Costello, who had held a minor legal post in the first Free State Government and had eventually succeeded to the leadership of Cosgrave's party, became Prime Minister and converted the Irish Free State into the Republic of Ireland, thus fulfilling the belief of Collins and Griffith that the Treaty signed in 1921 would be a stepping-stone to southern Ireland's complete independence.

But where would the story end? Not with the ending of partition, for that remains a dream which seems no nearer to coming true in the nineteen-sixties than it did in the nineteen-twenties. Yet one halting-place suggests itself. That other book, which would begin where the foregoing pages leave off, might well end on the day in 1959 when Eamon de Valera, one time commandant at Boland's Mills, took his final leave of Dail Eireann and succeeded his old comrade Sean T. O'Kelly as President of the Republic of Ireland.

THE END

BOOKS CONSULTED

References—not always agreeing with each other—for all statements of fact in the foregoing pages will be found in one or other of the following books, reports and periodicals:

American Commission on Conditions in Ireland: Interim Report (London, 1921)

ARTHUR, SIR GEORGE: *General Sir John Maxwell* (London, 1932)

BARRY, TOM: *Guerilla Days in Ireland* (Dublin, 1949)

BEASLAI, PIARAS: *Michael Collins and the Making of a New Ireland* (London, 1926)

BEASLAI, PIARAS (and others): *With the I.R.A. in the Fight for Freedom* (Tralee, n.d.)

BECKETT, J. C.: *A Short History of Ireland* (London, 1952)

BELL, G. K. A.: *Randall Davidson, Archbishop of Canterbury* (Oxford, 1935)

BENNETT, RICHARD: *The Black and Tans* (London, 1959)

BIRKENHEAD, 2ND EARL OF: *Frederick Edwin, Earl of Birkenhead* (London, 1935)

BIRRELL, AUGUSTINE: *Things Past Redress* (London, 1937)

BLAKE, ROBERT: *The Unknown Prime Minister* (London, 1955)

BOYLE, JOHN F.: *The Irish Rebellion of 1916* (London, 1916)

BREEN, DAN: *My Fight for Irish Freedom* (Dublin, 1926)

BRENNAN, ROBERT: *Allegiance* (Dublin, 1950)

BRIOLLAY, SYLVAIN: *Ireland in Rebellion* (Dublin, 1921)

BROMAGE, MARY C.: *De Valera and the March of a Nation* (London, 1956)

CALLWELL, MAJOR-GENERAL SIR C. E.: *Field-Marshal Sir Henry Wilson* (London, 1929)

CHESTERTON, G. K.: *Irish Impressions* (London, 1919)

CHURCHILL, WINSTON: *The World Crisis: The Aftermath* (London, 1929)

CLARKSON, J. DUNMORE: *Labour and Nationalism in Ireland* (New York, 1925)

COLUM, PADRAIC: *The Road Round Ireland* (New York, 1926)
CONNOLLY, NORA: *See* O'BRIEN, NORA CONNOLLY
COOPER, DUFF: *Old Men Forget* (London, 1953)
CRAWFORD, F. H.: *Guns for Ulster* (Belfast, 1947)
CROZIER, BRIGADIER-GENERAL F. P.: *Ireland for Ever* (London, 1932)
CURTIS, EDMUND: *A History of Ireland* (London, 1936 edition)
CURTIS, EDMUND and MCDOWELL, R. B.: *Irish Historical Documents, 1172–1922* (London, 1943)
CUSHENDUN, LORD: *See* MCNEILL, RONALD
DALTON, CHARLES: *With the Dublin Brigade, 1917–21* (London, 1929)
DIGBY, MARGARET: *Horace Plunkett* (Oxford, 1949)
DUFF, DOUGLAS V.: *The Way the Wind Blows* (London, 1948)
EGLINTON, JOHN: *A Memoir of AE* (London, 1937)
"ENGLISHMAN, AN": *See* GOLDRING, DOUGLAS
ERVINE, ST. JOHN: *Craigavon: Ulsterman* (London, 1949)
ERVINE, ST. JOHN: *Sir Edward Carson and the Ulster Movement* (Dublin and London, 1913)
EWART, WILFRID: *A Journey in Ireland, 1921* (London and New York, 1922)
FAY, GERARD: *The Abbey Theatre: Cradle of Genius* (London, 1958)
FIGGIS, DARRELL: *Recollections of the Irish War* (London, 1927)
FOX, R. M.: *James Connolly: The Forerunner* (Tralee, 1946)
FOX, R. M.: *Rebel Irishwomen* (Dublin and Cork, 1935)
FRENCH, HON. GERALD: *Life of Field-Marshal Sir John French* (London, 1931)
GALLAGHER, FRANK (under pseud. DAVID HOGAN): *The Four Glorious Years* (Dublin, 1953)
GALLAGHER, FRANK: *The Indivisible Island* (London, 1957)
GOGARTY, OLIVER ST. JOHN: *As I Was Going Down Sackville Street* (London, 1937)
GOGARTY, OLIVER ST. JOHN: *It Isn't This Time of Year at All!* (London, 1954)
GOLDRING, DOUGLAS (under pseud. "AN ENGLISHMAN"): *A Stranger in Ireland* (Dublin, 1918)
GOLDRING, DOUGLAS (under pseud. "AN ENGLISHMAN"): *Dublin Explorations and Reflections* (Dublin and London, 1917)
GOLDRING, DOUGLAS: *Odd Man Out* (London, 1935)
GWYNN, DENIS: *De Valera* (London, 1933)

GWYNN, DENIS: *Life and Death of Roger Casement* (London, 1930)
GWYNN, DENIS: *The History of Partition, 1912–1925* (Dublin, 1950)
GWYNN, DENIS: *The Irish Free State, 1922–27* (London, 1928)
GWYNN, DENIS: *The Life of John Redmond* (London, 1932)
GWYNN, STEPHEN: *John Redmond's Last Years* (London, 1919)
HAMMOND, J. L.: *C. P. Scott* (London, 1934)
HANCOCK, W. K.: *Survey of British Commonwealth Affairs: Problems of Nationality, 1918–36* (Oxford, 1937)
HARRISON, HENRY: *Parnell Vindicated* (London, 1931)
HEADLAM, MAURICE: *Irish Reminiscences* (London, 1947)
HEALY, T. M.: *Letters and Leaders of My Day* (London, 1928)
HENRY, R. M.: *The Evolution of Sinn Fein* (Dublin, 1920)
HISTORY OF "THE TIMES", VOL. IV (London, 1952)
HOGAN, DAVID: *See* GALLAGHER, FRANK
HONE, JOSEPH: *W. B. Yeats* (London, 1942)
HORGAN, J. J.: *Parnell to Pearse* (Dublin, 1948)
HOY, HUGH CLELAND: *40 O.B.* (London, 1932)
HYDE, H. MONTGOMERY: *Carson* (London, 1953)
INGLIS, BRIAN: *The Story of Ireland* (London, 1956)
"I.O.": *See* STREET, C. J. C.
IREMONGER, F. A.: *William Temple, Archbishop of Canterbury* (Oxford, 1948)
"IRISH LIFE": *Record of the Irish Rebellion of 1916* (Dublin, 1916)
"IRISH TIMES"
JONES, THOMAS: *Lloyd George* (Oxford, 1951)
KELLY, SEAMUS (pub. anonymously): *Pictorial Review of 1916* (Dublin, n.d.)
KETTLE, T. M.: *The Ways of War* (New York, 1918)
KNOTT, GEORGE H. (edited by): *Trial of Sir Roger Casement* (London, 1926)
LAVERY, SIR JOHN: *The Life of a Painter* (London, 1940)
LAZENBY, ELIZABETH: *Ireland—a Catspaw* (London, 1928)
LE ROUX, LOUIS N.: *Patrick H. Pearse* (Dublin, 1932)
LESLIE, SHANE (edited by): *Memoirs of Brigadier-General Gordon Shephard* (privately printed, 1924)
LESLIE, SHANE: *The Irish Tangle* (London, 1946)
LLOYD GEORGE, DAVID: *War Memoirs* (London, 1933–36)
LYNCH, DIARMUID: *The I.R.B. and the 1916 Insurrection* (Cork, 1957)

LYNCH-ROBINSON, SIR CHRISTOPHER: *The Last of the Irish R.M.s* (London, 1951)
LYONS, GEORGE A.: *Some Recollections of Griffith and his Times* (Dublin, 1923)
MACARDLE, DOROTHY: *The Irish Republic* (Dublin, 1951 edition)
MACCOLL, RENE: *Roger Casement* (London, 1956)
MACMANUS, M. J.: *Eamon de Valera* (Dublin, 1957 edition)
MACREADY, GENERAL SIR NEVIL: *Annals of an Active Life* (London, 1924)
MALONEY, WILLIAM J.: *The Forged Casement Diaries* (Dublin and Cork, 1936)
MANSERGH, NICHOLAS: *Ireland in the Age of Reform and Revolution* (London, 1940)
MARTIN, HUGH: *Ireland in Insurrection* (London, 1921)
MCCANN, JOHN: *War by the Irish* (Tralee, 1946)
MCCARTAN, PATRICK: *With de Valera in America* (Dublin, 1932)
MCCORMICK, DONALD: *The Mystery of Lord Kitchener's Death* (London, 1959)
MCCRACKEN, J. L.: *Representative Government in Ireland: Dail Eireann 1919–1948* (Oxford, 1958)
MCNEILL, RONALD (later LORD CUSHENDUN): *Ulster's Stand for Union* (London, 1922)
MIDLETON, EARL OF: *Ireland—Dupe or Heroine* (London, 1932)
MIDLETON, EARL OF: *Records and Reactions, 1856–1939* (London, 1939)
NEVINSON, H. W.: *Last Changes Last Chances* (London, 1928)
NICOLSON, HAROLD: *King George V* (London, 1952)
NOYES, ALFRED: *The Accusing Ghost or Justice for Casement* (London, 1957)
O'BRIEN, NORA CONNOLLY: *Portrait of a Rebel Father* (London and Dublin, 1935)
O'BRIEN, WILLIAM: *The Irish Revolution and How it Came About* (London, 1923)
O'CASEY, SEAN: *Drums Under the Windows* (London, 1945)
O'CASEY, SEAN: *Inishfallen Fare Thee Well* (London, 1949)
O'CONNOR, BATT: *With Michael Collins in the Fight for Irish Independence* (London, 1929)
O'CONNOR, SIR JAMES: *History of Ireland, 1798–1924* (London, 1925)
O'DONOGHUE, FLORENCE: *No Other Law* (Dublin, 1954)

O'Donoghue, Florence: *Tomas MacCurtain* (Tralee, 1958)
O'Faolain, Sean: *Constance Markievicz* (London, 1934)
O'Hegarty, P. S.: *A History of Ireland under the Union, 1801–1922* (London, 1952)
O'Hegarty, P. S.: *The Victory of Sinn Fein* (Dublin, 1924)
O'Malley, Ernie: *On Another Man's Wound* (London, 1936)
O'Sullivan, Donal: *The Irish Free State and its Senate* (London, 1940)
Owen, Frank: *Tempestuous Journey: Lloyd George, his Life and Times* (London, 1954)
Pakenham, Frank (now Lord): *Peace by Ordeal* (Cork, 1951 edition)
Pearse, Padraic H.: *Plays, Stories, Poems* (Dublin and London, 1918)
Pearse, Padraic H.: *Political Writings and Speeches* (Dublin and London, 1922)
Phillips, W. Alison: *The Revolution in Ireland, 1906–1923* (London, 1926 edition)
Pollard, Captain H. B. C.: *The Secret Societies of Ireland* (London, 1922)
Pound, Reginald and Harmsworth, Geoffrey: *Northcliffe* (London, 1959)
Repington, Lieutenant-Colonel C. à C.: *The First World War, 1914–1918* (London, 1920)
Report of the Labour Commission to Ireland (London, 1921)
Report of the Royal Commission on the Rebellion on Ireland: Cmd. 8311 (London, 1916)
Riddell, Lord: *Intimate Diary of the Peace Conference and After* (London, 1933)
Robinson, Sir Henry: *Memories Wise and Otherwise* (London, 1923)
Robinson, Lennox (edited by): *Lady Gregory's Journals, 1916–30* (London, 1946)
Roper, Esther (edited by): *Prison Letters of Countess Markievicz* (London, 1934)
Russell of Liverpool, Lord: *That Reminds Me* (London, 1959)
Ryan, A. P.: *Mutiny at the Curragh* (London, 1956)
Ryan, Desmond: *Remembering Sion* (London, 1934)
Ryan, Desmond: *Sean Treacy and the 3rd Tipperary Brigade* (London, 1945)

RYAN, DESMOND: *The Phoenix Flame* (London, 1937)
SALVIDGE, STANLEY: *Salvidge of Liverpool* (London, 1934)
SHAKESPEARE, SIR GEOFFREY: *Let Candles be Brought In* (London, 1949)
SHARPE, MAY CHURCHILL: *Chicago May: Her Story* (London, 1929)
SHEARMAN, HUGH: *Anglo–Irish Relations* (London, 1948)
SHEARMAN, HUGH: *Not an Inch* (London, 1942)
SHEEHAN, CAPTAIN D. D.: *Ireland Since Parnell* (London, 1921)
SMUTS, J. C.: *Jan Christian Smuts* (London, 1952)
SPENDER, J. A. and ASQUITH, CYRIL: *Life of Lord Oxford and Asquith* (London, 1932)
STEPHENS, JAMES: *The Insurrection in Dublin* (Dublin and London, 1916)
STREET, C. J. C.: *Ireland in 1921* (London, 1922)
STREET, C. J. C. (under pseud. "I.O."): *The Administration of Ireland, 1920* (London, 1921)
SULLIVAN, SERJEANT A. M.: *The Last Serjeant* (London, 1952)
TAYLOR, REX: *Michael Collins* (London, 1958)
"THE TIMES"
USSHER, ARNOLD: *The Face and Mind of Ireland* (London, 1949)
"WEEKLY IRISH TIMES": *Sinn Fein Rebellion Handbook* (Dublin, 1917 edition)
WELLES, WARRE B. and MARLOWE, N.: *A History of the Irish Rebellion of 1916* (Dublin and London, 1918 edition)
WHITE, CAPTAIN J. R.: *Misfit* (London, 1930)
WHITE, TERENCE DE VERE: *Kevin O'Higgins* (London, 1948)
WILLIAMS, BASIL: *Erskine Childers* (privately printed, 1926)
WILLIAMS, PROFESSOR DESMOND: *The Irish Civil War in Ireland.**
WILSON, THOMAS (edited by): *Ulster under Home Rule* (Oxford, 1955)
WINTER, SIR ORMONDE: *Winter's Tale* (London, 1955)
WRENCH, SIR EVELYN: *Geoffrey Dawson and Our Times* (London, 1955)

* The author is grateful for having been allowed to read this book in typescript before publication.

Index